D0146338

Brander Matthews

Brander Matthews,
Theodore Roosevelt,
and the Politics
of American Literature,
1880–1920

Lawrence J. Oliver

THE UNIVERSITY OF TENNESSEE PRESS / KNOXVILLE

BROOKLINE PUBLIC LIBRARY

Last MLN
10/04

815.4
O48b
copy 1

Copyright © 1992 by The University of Tennessee Press / Knoxville.
All Rights Reserved. Manufactured in the United States of America.
First Edition.

The paper in this book meets the minimum requirements of the
American National Standard for Permanence of Paper for Printed
Library Materials.   ∞   The binding materials have been chosen
for strength and durability.

Library of Congress Cataloging in Publication Data

Oliver, Lawrence J., 1949—
    Brander Matthews, Theodore Roosevelt, and the Politics
of American Literature, 1880-1920 / Lawrence J. Oliver.
        p.   cm.
    Includes bibliographical references and index.
    ISBN 0-87049-738-3 (cloth: alk. paper)
    1. Matthews, Brander, 1852-1929—Knowledge—Literature.
2. Roosevelt, Theodore, 1858-1919—Views on literature.
3. American Literature—20th century—History and criticism.
4. American Literature—19th century—History and criticism.
5. Literature—Political aspects—United States
6. Politics and literature—United States.   I. Title
PS2373.O43   1992
818'.409—dc20   91-24627
                                                    CIP

For my grandmother,
Marie Hathorne Saba

Contents

Acknowledgments

During the writing of this book, I incurred a debt of gratitude to many individuals. My greatest debt is to three colleagues at Texas A&M University: Harrison Meserole and Dennis Berthold read drafts of each chapter with painstaking care and offered many helpful comments and suggestions; Larry Reynolds read the final draft of the manuscript and gave me valuable advice. All three provided support and encouragement throughout the project. I benefited also from Bob Campbell's critique of a chapter draft, and from informal conversations with him and Kenneth Price, who shared books as well as ideas with me. As copyeditor, Stan Ivester executed his duties with scrupulous care.

Much of the information contained in the following pages is derived from unpublished materials in the Brander Matthews Papers, Rare Book and Manuscript Library, Columbia University. Kenneth Lohf, librarian for rare books, and his staff cordially responded to numerous queries and requests for documents during my two visits to Columbia; all quotations of Matthews's letters are by permission of Columbia University Libraries, the copyright holder. I would also like to thank Jean F. Preston, curator of manuscripts at Princeton University Library, and her staff for their gracious assistance during my research in the Laurence Hutton Correspondence, Paul E. More Papers, Charles Scribner's Sons Archives, and Julian Street Papers; permission to quote from letters in these collections was granted by Princeton University Library. My research trips to Columbia and Princeton were made possible by a National Endowment for the Humanities Travel to Collections grant and by two Texas A&M mini-grants.

I am grateful also to Nancy Johnson, archives librarian at the American Academy and Institute of Arts and Letters, for bringing to my attention a news clipping on and letter by Matthews, and to the following libraries for permission to quote from letters in the collections specified: Collection of American Literature, Beinecke Rare Book and Manuscript Library, Yale University; William Dean Howells Papers, Houghton Library, Harvard University; Mark Twain Papers, Bancroft Library, University of California, Berkeley; Stuart Sherman Papers, Record Series 15/7/21, University Archives, University of Illinois at Urbana.

Parts of chapters 3 and 4 are revised versions of my articles: "Brander Matthews and the Dean," *American Literary Realism 1870–1910* 21 (Spring 1989): 25–40, reprinted by permission of McFarland & Company, Inc., Publishers, Jefferson, N.C.; and "Theodore Roosevelt, Brander Matthews, and the Campaign for Literary Americanism," *American Quarterly* 41 (1989): 93–111, reprinted by permission of the American Studies Association. Revisions suggested by *American Quarterly*'s editor, Gary Kulik, not only improved the article on Matthews and Roosevelt but helped me sharpen the focus of the present book.

Finally, I am deeply grateful to my wife, Jane, and to my sons, Cory and Craig, for allowing me to spend all those Saturdays down at the office working on my book.

Introduction

Privately and unprofessionally, I think our authors take as vivid an interest in public affairs as any other class of our citizens.

—William Dean Howells,
"Politics of American Authors"

Professor of dramatic literature at Columbia University from 1892 to 1924, scholar, critic, essayist, playwright, and fiction writer, Brander Matthews (1852–1929) was one of the most prominent and influential American men of letters during the late nineteenth and early twentieth centuries. Author of such respected works as *French Dramatists of the 19th Century* (1881), *Molière, His Life and His Works* (1910), *The Development of the Drama* (1903), and *Shakspere As a Playwright* (1913), he was generally recognized during his day as America's foremost scholar of the drama. He was one of the literary realists' staunchest allies both during and after the "Realism War" of the late 1880s and early 1890s. At a time when few of his fellow academics viewed American literature as a subject worthy of serious study, he developed a course at Columbia on American writers; and his *An Introduction to the Study of American Literature* (1896) was among the first textbooks in the field, the quarter million copies it sold having a significant influence on the formation of the American canon during the opening decades of the twentieth century. His *The Philosophy of the Short-story* (1901) stands as the first extended study of the short story as a distinct literary genre.

Matthews's talents as a scholar, critic, and educator won him the respect and admiration of a remarkably large and diverse group of prominent figures: realist novelists like Mark Twain (who selected Matthews to write the introduction to the Uniform Edition of his own works) and William Dean Howells (who stated that Matthews's literary criticism was superior to that of any other critic of Matthews's generation); cultural nationalists like Henry Cabot Lodge and Theodore Roosevelt; British critics of American culture such as Rudyard Kipling and Andrew Lang; outspoken women writers such as Charlotte Perkins Gilman and Agnes Repplier; the archcapitalist Andrew Carnegie (whose Simplified Spelling Board was chaired by Matthews); the iconoclast James Gibbon Huneker (who, as a fellow member of the Friendly Sons of Saint Bacchus, drank, sang, and told jokes with the professor at a bohemian cafe); influential publishers such as Charles Scribner and George H. Putnam (who wanted Matthews rather than William P. Trent to be chief editor of the *Cambridge History of American Literature*); and the African-American poet and novelist James Weldon Johnson (whose writings were championed by Matthews a decade before the Harlem Renaissance caught the attention of white readers).

When he was not writing, editing, or teaching, Matthews was laboring to establish his beloved New York as the nation's literary capital by founding or cofounding such literary clubs as the Players, the Authors Club, and the Kinsmen, and by joining the fight for an international copyright act that would benefit American writers. He helped to organize and develop the National Institute of Arts and Letters and its offshoot, the American Academy of Arts and Letters, serving as president of the former (1912–14) and chancellor of the latter (1920–24). He was also an active member and president (1910–11) of the Modern Language Association. Through these and other achievements, Matthews succeeded in his quest to place himself at the center of literary power and authority.

In Matthews's day as in ours, one of the rituals by which one is officially recognized as being within the "center" is the testimonial dinner. The first of several testimonials to Matthews was held at the exclusive Sherry's restaurant in December 1893. The organizing committee itself signified the reputation that Matthews had by then achieved: Howells, Twain, Richard Watson Gilder, Henry Cabot Lodge, Charles Scribner, and other prominent men of letters. The highlight of the affair, which was presided over by Charles Dudley Warner, was Twain's affectionately humorous speech on Matthews's name: "B-r-r-RANder M-m-ATHews! You can curse a man's head off with that if you know how and where to put the emphasis. . . . When he got his name it was only good to curse with. Now it is good to conjure with."[1] Another playful tribute was offered, in poetic form, by H. C. Bunner:

> The way by which a man is known
> Is the company he keeps. That settles you.
> It's not my plan
> To say that you can write.

Such humor usually contains a grain of truth; the grain here is that Matthews did make a name for himself, largely on the basis of what he wrote, but also on the company he kept.

But, as the years of the new century proceeded, Matthews's center began to come apart. When the rebellious Young Intellectuals—whose ranks included two of Matthews's former students, Randolph Bourne and Ludwig Lewisohn—waged their revolt against the Genteel Tradition during the years surrounding World War I, the elderly Matthews was, like Howells and other members of the company he kept, a prime target of their verbal assaults. It was, of course, George Santayana who in 1911 coined the phrase "Genteel Tradition," in his famous essay, "The Genteel Tradition in American Philosophy." According to Santayana, the Genteel Tradition was the heir of Calvinism and Transcendentalism, but it had lost the passionate intensity of the former and the "calmly revolutionary" spirit of the latter; the result was a vapid idealism, which Santayana personified as a senile grandmother smiling serenely at a terrible world.[2] Santayana contended that the genteel mentality dominated academe, where most professors were happily engaged in "white-washing and adoring things as they are" (61). During the next three decades, Bourne, Lewisohn, H. L. Mencken, (the early) Van Wyck Brooks, Sinclair Lewis, Malcolm Cowley, and a host of other critics and writers who helped lay the foundations of the modernist movement in American literature added one negative attribute after another to the portrait limned by Santayana—sexual squeamishness, constrictive formalism, hypocritical moralism, provincialism, Anglophilism, vulgarity, sentimentalism, elitism—and invariably pointed the accusing finger at university English departments and at the literary clubs that Matthews had founded or presided over.[3]

Reading through the voluminous writings that Matthews produced between the publication of his first book in 1880 and his final one in 1926, one will frequently encounter passages (especially in the later works) that project some of the traits mentioned above; but one will just as frequently encounter passages that might have been written by Santayana, Brooks, or other disparagers of gentility. In attempting to fit Matthews into the genteel mold, his critics had to ignore such un-genteel behavior as his praise of Twain, Henry James, Ibsen, Zola, and other writers whom most of his contemporary critics slighted or damned; his repeated denunciations of provincialism and Anglophilism; his contention that women writers were more willing than male ones to explore the "animal nature" lurking within us all; his contempt for academic idealists; and his insistence that professors must come down from the Ivory Tower and confront their culture's pressing social and political problems. Moreover, though Matthews was a lifelong admirer of Matthew Arnold and in his later years allied himself with the New Humanists, he was in many ways, as John W. Rathbun and Harry H. Clark maintain, a "mediator and advocate of modernism."[4]

The Young Intellectuals succeeded so well in caricaturing Matthews as an effete genteel whose writings were unworthy of any serious attention that his name all but disappeared from American literary history during the decades following his death in 1929. In his study of the native grounds of American literature, Alfred Kazin, for example, mentions Matthews but once, and does so disparagingly; Henry May alludes to him in *The End of American Innocence* as "Columbia's specimen of the literary Grand Old Man"; Larzer Ziff's study of the American 1890s, which devotes space to numerous minor figures of the period, completely ignores him.[5] Despite Rathbun and Clark's positive reassessment more than a decade ago of Matthews's literary criticism, scholars today continue to overlook him. The list of several dozen "antimoderns" T. J. Jackson Lears appended to his weighty analysis of the transformation of American culture during the period 1880–1920 includes Matthews, but the text makes only a solitary reference to him. Matthews is altogether absent from Peter Conn's *The Divided Mind: Ideology and Imagination in America, 1898–1917*. Finally, though he was arguably the foremost American drama scholar of his age, Matthews receives only passing mention in Brenda Murphy's *American Realism and American Drama, 1880–1940*, the fullest account of that subject we have.[6]

The present book aims to restore Matthews to his rightful place in American literary and, more broadly, cultural history. I attempt to achieve that aim by situating Matthews's works in their historical and cultural context; in, that is, New York City during the period 1880–1920. These are the decades, of course, that bracket the Progressive Era. Nowhere was the impulse for progressive reform more vividly displayed than in New York, where the contest over who would wield cultural authority and power made the city, in Thomas Bender's words, an intellectual "battleground."[7] This was particularly true of Columbia University, whose faculty included such eminent progressivists as Felix Adler, Charles Beard, Franz Boas, John Dewey, Franklin H. Giddings, and Edwin R.

Seligman. Matthews was deeply influenced by the social and political theories circulating at Columbia, and these theories underpin much of his literary criticism. No colleague at Columbia, however, had a greater influence on Matthews's ideology than did the politician whose name is synonymous with progressivism, Theodore Roosevelt. As the following pages will document, Roosevelt's words are inscribed in virtually all the texts Matthews produced after the two became intimate friends in the late 1880s. Thus, while I am not about to substitute the label *progressive* for that of *genteel*, since all such labels are reductive and distorting in the final analysis, I explore in detail Matthews's connections with Roosevelt and the progressive "movement." The quotation marks around "movement" are necessary, for historians of progressivism agree that the politicians, academics, journalists, writers, and artists who banded together during the late nineteenth and early twentieth centuries to oppose the evils of political corruption, plutocracy, and anarchism were a heterogeneous group; they shared no political platform and were often at odds on particular issues. Most of them, however, embraced, at least in their rhetoric, the "manly" ethos embodied in the person of Roosevelt.[8]

Not only did progressive-minded reformers disagree with one another on social and political issues, they often seemed to be in conflict with themselves. As Conn argues in *The Divided Mind*, members of Matthews's generation were engaged in a profound internal dialectic. Taking his cue from Henry Adams's quip that he was a "Conservative Christian Anarchist" and Santayana's reference in "The Genteel Tradition" to the "two mentalities" of the American mind, Conn demonstrates that advocates of progressivism were pulled between the contradictory values of tradition and innovation, organization and individualism, order and liberation; they looked confidently to the future, while gazing nostalgically to the past. (Progressives, sneered Herbert Croly in *Progressive Democracy*, confronted the past and turned their back on the future.)[9] This split consciousness is reflected in Matthews's writings on realism, cosmopolitanism, imperialism, the "Negro Problem," the "Woman Question," and the many other literary, political, and social issues that preoccupied him. And like Roosevelt's, Matthews's "progressive" response to these issues usually projects an ideological conservatism; he acknowledged that American society had serious problems, but he believed that most could be solved by tinkering with rather than restructuring the status quo. Like Roosevelt, too, he had little patience with socialists or radical reformers of any sort.

In his *Criticism and Social Change* (1983), Frank Lentricchia claimed that scholars had not given due attention to literary intellectuals in their roles as "social and political actors."[10] That claim may have been true several years ago, but not today, as Bender's *New York Intellect*, to take a ready example, demonstrates. Yet, so wide is the scope of Bender's rich history of New York's civic, literary, and academic cultures that we catch only fleeting glimpses of many individuals who played key roles in that history, Matthews among them. Though in the following chapters I present a great deal of biographical material and discuss all of Matthews's major texts, I have not sought to provide a chronological and comprehensive account of his life and works. Rather, this book focuses on Matthews's role as a "political actor." To be more precise, it seeks to reveal the political subtexts of Matthews's ostensibly "disinterested" criticism and "realistic" fiction, and to examine the behind-the-scenes maneuvering in which he engaged as he sought to advance the "progressive" ideology within and beyond the literary-academic establishment.

1 From "Professional Millionaire" to "Literary Fellow"

James Brander Matthews (he dropped the first name when he became a professional author) was born in New Orleans in 1852. His father, Edward Matthews (1814–87), was a sixth-generation descendant of Cape Cod Puritans and Pilgrims (William Brewster was an ancestor). His mother, Virginia Brander (1827–1903), was a New Orleans belle of Scottish descent whose merchant father amassed a fortune during the decades between the War of 1812 and the Civil War. Thus, when they married in 1851, Edward and Virginia symbolized the union of North and South that their country was able to achieve only by means of a bloody war. Their son, who came of age during Reconstruction, when a political and cultural rather than military conflict raged between the victorious Yankees and defeated Confederates, would throughout his adult life trumpet the cause of national unity while at the same time maintaining a respect for regional differences.

There was, of course, a third region, the West; and during the second half of the nineteenth century it was the region on the rise, the region, in fact, that in the minds of many was virtually synonymous with "American." Though Matthews had no ancestral roots here, he lay claim to it by virtue of his father having headed West as a young man to become a speculator in cotton and provisions, the Mississippi River being his route of commerce. Edward Matthews, Brander writes in his autobiography, *These Many Years*, "was a true descendant of the merchant adventurers of Tudor England; and there was an Elizabethan spaciousness in his outlook upon opportunity."[1] And seize the opportunity he did: he became a millionaire. His trading and speculating proved especially profitable during the boom days of the Civil War.

According to Brander, Edward had to content himself with sending a substitute to the war (a common practice at the time, of course) because of ill health; yet at several points in his autobiography Brander emphasizes his father's hearty and energetic nature. In any case, whether unable or unwilling to enlist in the Union army, Edward remained in New York City during the conflict, where he had purchased a home for his family in 1859. While his substitute fought in the South, Edward did battle in the Wall Street arena. "He was," his son boasted, "as far-sighted and as courageous" in his real-estate purchases as he had earlier been in his Mississippi commercial ventures. Yet, despite his "manly" character, Edward was a connoisseur of art and exhibited an "almost feminine delicacy of taste" (*These Many Years*, 25, 28). By 1873 his Manhattan rental properties, which included the site on which the Empire State Building stands today, were alone bringing in more than a half million dollars of rent annually.

Brander's brief sketch of his mother in his autobiography is warm and admiring, but it reveals the extent to which his culture's patriarchal values shaped his perceptions of her: Virginia Matthews, he states, was the "ultimate embodiment of feminine refinement and of womanly delicacy," and consequently "a little too shrinking . . . a little too lacking in any forthputting energy, ever to seize a commanding position in society" (*These Many Years*, 33). Exactly what type of "commanding position" in Victorian-American society Virginia might have captured, had she been more energetic and aggressive, Brander does not say.

Edward spared no expense in attempting to groom his only son for the day when he would become a "professional millionaire." Brander began his formal education at a private boys' school in New York City. When it became apparent that he was, at age nine, wanting in self-discipline, he was enrolled in a New York military academy. One of the smallest boys in his class, he was often bullied and humiliated by his fellow cadets, who on one occasion nearly drowned him accidentally. After two miserable years at the institution, he "escaped" to his grandfather's; to his great pleasure, the academy director refused to permit him to return. Looking back at his school days, the mature Brander would claim that he never encountered a stimulating teacher at any of the private academies he attended.

The intellectual stimulation that eluded him in school was, however, amply supplied by his experiences outside the classroom. Edward often took his family with him on his business trips down south and abroad. The Matthewses enjoyed extended visits to Europe in 1857 and 1866–68. While living in Paris in 1867, Brander was thrilled by the Paris Exhibition and enthralled by performances at the Théâtre Français and Opéra-Comique; here began his lifelong love affair with French literature and culture. These and subsequent sojourns abroad developed in him the cosmopolitan perspective that marks much of his literary criticism.

Not all of Matthews's journeys were southward or eastward. During the summer of 1869 he experienced an easterner's *rite de passage* into the rugged western realm when he, a college friend, and a chaperone hired by his father toured the upper Mississippi region. The high point of the trip was a canoe excursion on the St. Louis River, during which he and his companions employed two Chippewas as guides and camped at the Chippewa reservation for several days. Reflecting on the experience, Matthews wrote: "It was the first time I had ever entered the forest primeval; the first time I had ever come into personal relations with the red man, whom I knew then not from Cooper and Parkman, but only from Edward S. Ellis's stories in the yellow-back Beadle's Dime Novels" (*These Many Years*, 115). Though he would later embrace the "western" ideology of Theodore Roosevelt and champion the "manly" novels of Owen Wister and Hamlin Garland, this brief adventure was apparently his only experience at roughing it.

Young Brander, however, did not have to travel beyond his living room to encounter famous personages, for visitors to his father's fashionable Fifth Avenue residence included such prominent figures as Governor Hamilton Fish (whose two sons had roomed with Brander at the military academy); Townsend Harris, America's first consul to Japan; John Hay, private secretary to President Lincoln (and, later, secretary of state to Theodore Roosevelt); Richard Grant White, who, after training as a physician and lawyer, became a prominent Shakespearean scholar; and John R. Thompson, Poe's successor as editor of the *Southern Literary Messenger*. Commission merchant Isaac Brownell was also a frequent guest; his son William Crary, with whom Brander developed a lasting friendship, would become a respected literary critic and act as literary advisor to Charles Scribner's Sons for forty years (1888–1928). One suspects that the discussions these and other of Edward's guests engaged in during their visits stimulated Brander's curiosity in literary, political, and social issues he would later address in his writings. Perhaps more important, many of these men—Hay most especially—were living models of the Victorian conviction that literary intellectuals should be as interested in political and social problems as in aesthetic ones.

In 1868, sixteen-year-old Brander enrolled (as a sophomore) in Columbia College, at that time a small and unimpressive institution. He found its curriculum and teachers no more challenging or inspiring than those of the private academies he had attended. Typical of American colleges of the day, Columbia offered no courses in American literature and only one in English literature, and in it, students did not actually read any literature, the entire course being a series of lectures on the lives and works of the authors covered. He studied no philosophy and had little practice in composition. Writing practice he would gain aplenty in later years, but the few references to philosophy and philosophers in his voluminous published works suggest that he never developed a serious interest in the subject. Somewhere along the way, however, he read enough of Aristotle and Plato to state that "Aristotle is my man" and to declare Platonic idealism "dangerous."[2]

Matthews's curriculum at Columbia did include Greek and Latin, but most of the classes were devoted to boring rote exercises, with little attention given to literature. Though the professor of Greek, Henry Drisler, was an erudite scholar, he failed, according to Matthews, to focus on the dramatic and poetic aspects of the works studied; for Drisler, a Greek play was merely a text for translation, affording "endless opportunities for a strictly grammatical inquisition into the darker interstices of our linguistic half-knowledge" (*These Many Years*, 111). Once again, the most valuable part of Matthews's education occurred outside the classroom. At Edward Matthews's request, Professor Drisler selected a number of books from his personal library that he believed would broaden Brander's education. Among the group of works he lent his student were the first series of Matthew Arnold's *Essays in Criticism*, James Russell Lowell's *Among My Books*, and August Wilhelm Schlegel's *Lectures on Dramatic Literature*. Matthews credits Schlegel with opening his eyes to the range and power of the drama, but he objected to the German's hostility toward French writers and in later years came to look at the stage through the lens provided by the French critic Francisque Sarcey (*These Many Years*, 205). The ideas of Arnold and Lowell, however, had an enduring influence on Matthews's literary theory and praxis.

Arnold's influence was at its peak in the United States during the 1880s and 1890s; Matthews continued to idolize the eminent Victorian, however, long after his reputation had waned. We find Matthews, for example, extolling Arnold in a 1916 essay as the critic who "opened our eyes to the value of culture, to the purpose of criticism and to the duty of 'seeing the thing as it is.'"[3] Matthews goes on to say that his generation (in its twilight years, by this time) "felt an increasing stimulus as we came to know Arnold's writings more intimately, as we absorbed them, as we made their ideas our own, as we sought to apply their principles and to borrow their methods." In addition to Arnold's doctrines regarding the high seriousness of criticism, the duty of the critic to view literary works with objectivity, and the value of culture as a bulwark against anarchy, Matthews also seems to have absorbed, or at least found welcome support for his own views in, the Englishman's insistence that the critic be tolerant, avoid didacticism, and take a historical point of view.

In describing his contributions to American literary criticism of his era, Matthews (who was awarded the French Legion of Honor in 1907 for his service to French literature) pointed proudly to, among other things, his "advocacy of a cosmopolitan outlook or the turning to France and to Greece rather than to England."[4] Ever the opponent of provincialism, Arnold, who was largely unimpressed by his contemporary British writers, turned also to France and Greece, arguing, for example, in "The Literary Influence of Academies" (which appeared in the first series of *Essays in Criticism*, read by Matthews in college) that the French and Athenian spirit exhibits an "openness of mind and flexibility of intelligence" absent in the Anglo.[5] Such a cosmopolitan or urbane taste in literature, Arnold contends, could be fostered by the establishment in England of literary academies analogous to the venerable French Academy. (He calls for academies rather than an English Academy because independent-minded Britons would resist a "sovereign organ" of literary judgment such as the French Academy.) The academies would serve as literary "centres," imparting the "correct information, correct judgment, correct taste" that would check the "eruptive" and

Brander Matthews

"aggressive" spirit of provinciality—a spirit most evident in the vulgar newspaper journalism of the day.

Matthews seems to have been greatly inspired by Arnold's plea for literary academies; no American devoted more time and energy to the creation and development of literary clubs and organizations than he did. In 1882, for example, he helped establish the Authors Club, the first distinctively literary club in New York, according to Matthews (*These Many Years*, 220). (Even the "shy and elusive Herman Melville" graced its doors on occasion.) The club's first honorary member was none other than Arnold, to whom Matthews was personally introduced in 1883. In that same year, Arnold proposed Matthews for membership in England's most prestigious literary club, the Athenaeum, though it took some eighteen years for the American to rise to the top of the lengthy waiting list of applicants (*These Many Years*, 306–7). In 1885 Matthews joined with several others who were interested in promoting the publication of books on American drama to found the Dunlap Society. Matthews also was one of the original organizers of the National Institute of Arts and Letters, and one of the earliest members of the academy that developed from it; he served as president of the institute from 1912 to 1914, and as chancellor of the academy from 1920 to 1924. He was an influential member of several other organizations as well, including the Modern Language Association, which elected him its president in 1910.

Matthews's writings, early and late, are as replete with references to the author of *Among My Books* as to that of *Essays in Criticism*. Though antagonistic to many of Arnold's views, especially as regarded the deficiencies of American culture, Lowell shared Arnold's conviction that works of literature must ever be judged according to universal rather than transitory standards. Thus, though he was keenly interested in furthering the development of American literature, Lowell remained committed to the cosmopolitan ideal and rejected the literary jingoism that swept up so many of his contemporaries. Though he was not, as we shall see, entirely impervious to the jingo influence, Matthews nonetheless remained a student of Arnold and Lowell in insisting that every culture must measure its own "local favorites by the cosmopolitan and eternal standards," lest a "local gosling" be hailed as a "Swan of Avon."[6] The idea that factors of race, class, gender, and ethnicity might play a significant if not determining role in critics' attempts to separate the goslings from the swans troubled Matthews no more than it did Lowell, Arnold, or other Victorian defenders of the Great Tradition.

Lowell also shared Arnold's belief that the United States stood in need of an intellectual center to counteract the dominating spirit of provincialism. "The situation of American literature," he wrote in 1857, "is anomalous. It has no centre, or, if it have, it is like that of the sphere of Hermes. It is divided into many systems, each revolving round its several suns."[7] As editor of the *Atlantic Monthly* and coeditor of the *North American Review*, Harvard professor, and organizing member of the Saturday and Dante clubs, Lowell worked assiduously to establish Boston-Cambridge as the cultural sun around which the provincial satellites would revolve, setting an example that Matthews could later follow as he strove to make New York the nation's literary capital.

Given the interest in French literature and culture Matthews developed as a child, it is not surprising that his theory and practice of criticism were greatly influenced by French currents of thought. As already noted, Sarcey replaced Schlegel as the major influence on Matthews's understanding of the drama. He also greatly admired the critical writings of Jules Lemaître and Sainte-Beuve. However, among the many French writers whom Matthews read, none produced a more lasting imprint on his mind than the historian Hippolyte Taine (1828–94).

To call Taine a historian, however, is something of a misnomer, for this energetic thinker ranged freely through, and sought to syncretize knowledge gained from, the study not only of history but of literature, psychology, philosophy, and science. As one critic has aptly remarked, Taine was a "philosophical historian who sought the psychological factors behind people and events."[8] Taine's claim to originality lies not in developing a theory of history but rather of applying the Positivist historiography to the study of literary history. This he did most fully in his massive *History of English Literature* (1864), the opening line of which announces that "History has been revolutionized."[9]

Taine's system, like that of virtually every major "new historicist" of the nineteenth century, was totalistic, seeking, as Michel Foucault would say, to draw all data "around a single centre."[10] For Taine, the organizing center was his theory of "race, environment, and epoch." He presents this theory most clearly in the introduction to his *History of English Literature*. Reading it, Matthews would have been instructed that a work of art is never, as Romantic historians and critics claimed, the production of a solitary imagination but rather a "transcript of contemporary manners, a type of a certain kind of mind" (1). He would also have been advised that the literary critic's task is to "study the document only in order to know the [essence of the] man," which can only be accomplished if the critic strives to situate the writer and the work in their historical-cultural context, paying due attention to racial differences. Taine was a racialist, not a racist.[11] As he employed the term, "race" was associated with *Volkgeist* or national character. Each race, he believed, had its peculiar genius, and none could lay scientific claim to being the master race. According to Taine, though there is great variety within the races, each individual exhibits the "general disposition of mind and soul" that characterizes the race, and every work of art, in turn, is imprinted with the "seal" of race traits (9). Such ideas about race were, of course, hardly revolutionary; they can be traced back at least to the Renaissance. The other two determinants—environment (which would include political and social systems as well as geography and climate) and epoch (the evolution or momentum of ideas concerning the nature of man)—exert pressures that alter but never completely erase the "primordial" racial characteristics.

In good Positivisitic fashion, Taine contended that, by calculating the "magnitude and direction" of the three elementary forces as an engineer would a mechanical problem, the literary archaeologist could account for the brilliant triumphs in the cultural life of a people and, furthermore, predict those to come. Literary artifacts form the most valuable fragment of the historical record because "when the work is rich, and one knows how to interpret it, we find there the psychology of a soul, frequently of an age, now and then of a race." Thus, in the attempt to reconstruct the moral history of a people and detect the psychological springs of that people's actions, the great work of art is more instructive than a "heap of historians with their histories" (25).

In subsequent chapters of his *History of English Literature*, Taine attempts to reveal how the climate and geography of England instilled certain traits in the Anglo-Saxon race and how those traits in turn form the essence of English literature from *Beowulf* to the poetry of Tennyson. In every country, Taine argues, "the body of man is rooted deep into the soil of nature" (32), and the cold, moist, and marshy soil of Saxon England produced a breed of people who were violent, gloomy, and severe; yet beneath the harsh and often brutal surface lay more positive traits—a grand sense of duty, a yearning for moral beauty, an inclination for the poetic. As the centuries proceeded, changes in environment and epoch (the invasion of Roman, Norman, and, finally, Christian world views) modified but did not completely erase the primordial Saxon traits: "The modern Englishman [and, correlatively, modern English literature] existed entire in this Saxon" (39).

From the present perspective, Taine's notion that the scientific-minded historian can, by "knowing how to interpret the evidence," uncover individual and racial "essence" and illuminate the universal laws governing historical development seems naive at best, pernicious at worst. But, in the age of Darwin, Marx, and Spencer, few thinkers rejected the aims or methodology of the Frenchman's study of history, even when they disagreed with its conclusions. As Taine's countryman Ferdinand Brunetière expressed it, no one since Hegel had "put into circulation more new and profound ideas about the history of literature and art, perhaps true, perhaps false, but at any rate *suggestive* and *provocative*" (emphasis Brunetière's).[12]

And, Brunetière might have added, *ideological*, because, as Hayden White argues, theories of history project ideological implications.[13] Taine's social and political views were in fact conservative: he favored, for example, the aristocratic over the democratic form of government and was opposed to universal suffrage.[14] Taine's mechanistic and ideologically conservative vision of life should have, one would assume, received a chilly reception in post–Civil War America, where the prevailing ideology was that of republican humanism. Yet, though there were a few skeptics and detractors (including Lowell, who grumbled that Taine's literary analysis too often seemed to "shape the character of the literature to the race rather than to illustrate race through literature"), the Frenchman's writings were immensely popular, winning the admiration of such diverse figures as Emerson; Whitman; Henry James, Jr. (whose study of Nathaniel

Hawthorne employs Tainean principles); Hamlin Garland; Edward Eggleston; Edward Bellamy; Fred Lewis Pattee; and William Dean Howells.[15] But to admire Taine's *History of English Literature* was not necessarily to accept its deterministic outlook. In his 1872 review of Taine's *History*, Howells probably spoke for most of his fellow American men of letters when he stated that Taine's method of demonstrating the shaping influences of daily life on a work of art was "admirably brilliant and effective," but then went on to reject the argument that a work of art can be deduced from its sociohistorical context: "M. Taine's method," Howells asserts, "does not take into sufficient account the element of individuality in the artist. Rigorously applied, it would make us expect to find all the artists of a given people at a given time cast in one mould." Taine's theory of race, environment, and epoch, Howells suggests, needs a fourth factor—that of the individual author's personal circumstances.[16] Adding that fourth factor made it possible for critics like Matthews to embrace Taine's general theory while maintaining their ideology of democratic humanism.

Taine's writings did not begin to attract the attention of American readers until about 1870, when Matthews was a student at Columbia.[17] But Matthews, whose fluency in French would have allowed him to read Taine's works before they were translated into English, may have encountered them even earlier, for he remarks in his autobiography that the Frenchman was one of his father's favorite authors (*These Many Years*, 25). In any case, Brander thoroughly absorbed Taine's racial, literary, and psychological principles during the 1870s, and they came to form the dominant theoretical framework for his later criticism.

After completing his undergraduate studies in 1871, Matthews left the literature for the law classroom. He enrolled in Columbia's law school, not because he had any interest in jurisprudence but because his father believed that a knowledge of the law would prove useful to his son when he took control of the family fortunes and entered, as Edward hoped Brander would, the field of politics. Finding the studies in this "trade school for lawyers" exceedingly dry, Matthews devoted more time to literary matters, especially to the drama, than to Blackstone's *Commentaries* (*These Many Years*, 135). Though he took his law degree in 1873, he made little use of it thereafter. But if his two years as a law student failed to arouse a desire to enter the legal profession, they did, it seems, incite his interest in the political reform movement that was then gaining momentum in New York City. Here again, an extracurricular activity proved to be a formative experience for him. During Matthews's first year in law school, the Tweed Ring was exposed. A group of Columbia law students organized the Young Men's Reform Association for the purpose of aiding Big Bill Tilden in his fight to eliminate plural or repeat voting (*These Many Years*, 138). As a member of the association, Matthews canvassed a local precinct verifying voter eligibility, one of his visits bringing him inadvertently into an illegal gambling house that was protected by Tammany Hall. Though he claimed that politics never engaged his interests the way the theater did, Matthews carried the spirit of the Young Men's Reform Association into his career as a man of letters, a career that was from start to finish marked by political activism.

Eighteen seventy-three was Matthews's watershed year. After graduating from law school, he married the London actress Ada Smith (who, interestingly, receives hardly a comment in his autobiography) and prepared to embark on his adventures as a "professional millionaire." But the Panic of 1873 abruptly terminated those plans. Edward Matthews was apparently more courageous than farsighted in his business investments, especially that in a North Carolina rail line. To purchase it, he had to heavily mortgage his real estate holdings. The line failed to make a profit, and when the panic occurred, Edward lost many of his income-producing Manhattan properties; in 1876 a fire took most of what remained in his possession. By the end of the decade, he was virtually bankrupt and in failing health. Since Brander's mother had a modest inheritance, the family was not plunged into poverty, but they were forced to sell their Fifth Avenue home and move into an apartment owned by the sister of Bret Harte. The carefree days of Brander's privileged youth were over. Yet, Brander would claim, retrospectively, that the bankruptcy that ruined his father was for him a fortunate fall: *unearned* wealth, he believed, might have corrupted him as it had so many members of the upper class. With the doors to the leisure-class life closed to him in 1873, twenty-one-year-old Brander had to find his own way, and that way led first to the theater. Down this road he began, guided by the lights of Arnold, Lowell, and Taine, and buoyed by the "incurable cheerfulness . . . tolerant good humor . . . and indurated optimism" that his aristocratic upbringing had instilled in him (*These Many Years*, 10).

Drawn to the "enchanted realm of the theatre" almost from the moment that his family moved to New York, Matthews became a steady playgoer for the rest of his life (*These Many Years*, 49). Even before his father's financial ruin, Brander was writing drama reviews and composing his own scripts, the first being an adaptation of a French farce that played (for one night) at the Indianapolis Academy of Music in 1871. Another Americanized adaptation of a French play, *Frank Wylde*, was published in 1873; though never staged professionally, it became a favorite of the Comedy Club of New York and was often performed by amateur actors (*These Many Years*, 148–49). Five other plays followed. Two that Matthews coauthored with George H. Jessop—*A Gold Mine* (1887) and *On Probation* (1889)—were performed around the country, but none was the hit that

Matthews hoped for. Out of print and never staged today, *A Gold Mine* nonetheless continues to live on, but in a way that Matthews would not have appreciated: it is the play, one might recall, that charms Dreiser's Carrie and engenders her "great awakening" that she must pursue a career on the stage. Dreiser was less charmed than Carrie: "The play," he sarcastically remarks, "was one of those drawing-room concoctions in which charmingly overdressed ladies and gentlemen suffer the pangs of love and jealousy amid gilded surroundings. Such bon-mots are ever enticing to those who have all their days longed for such material surroundings and have never had them gratified."[18]

Matthews's failure to achieve distinction as a playwright did not, however, dampen his enthusiasm for the theater. During the 1870s he attended virtually every play that opened in New York, continued his self-education in classical and modern drama, and produced a steady output of reviews and articles that appeared in such periodicals as *Appleton's Journal, Harper's Monthly, Lippincott's Magazine, Puck, Scribner's Monthly*, the *Atlantic* (then edited by Howells), and the *Nation*. The 1870s and 1880s were of course the golden age of the magazine in America, and by publishing regularly in the most prestigious periodicals Matthews not only established his reputation as an expert on the drama but gained the acquaintance of many of the Gilded Age's most influential writers, editors, and publishers. His association with the *Nation* was particularly important in this regard.

When the *Nation* was established in 1865, its founders, most of whom had participated in the Abolitionist movement, conceived of the new magazine as the successor to the *Liberator*. Where William Lloyd Garrison's paper had crusaded for emancipation of the slaves, the *Nation* would in the post–Civil War years champion the "enlightenment, elevation, and enfranchisement of the Negro race."[19] Because of dissension among the financial backers, however, the joint-stock company was dissolved in 1866, and E. L. Godkin, the magazine's editor and part-owner, assumed full control of the periodical. A firm believer in Anglo-Saxon racial superiority and a supporter of white rule in the defeated South, Godkin was the champion not of the black freedmen but of Anglo culture; and the model upon which he constructed his magazine, as Matthews remarks in his autobiography, was not the *Liberator* but the London *Spectator* (*These Many Years*, 172). In the first issue, Godkin announced that one of the *Nation*'s principal objectives was to "promote and develop a higher standard of criticism," a goal that any follower of Matthew Arnold (who would come to consider the magazine the best in the United States and possibly in the world) and James Russell Lowell was bound to admire.[20] To achieve that goal, Godkin solicited reviews from the most distinguished writers and critics of the day, including Lowell; Charles Eliot Norton (who in the first number contributed a review of a book on Shakespeare by Edward Matthews's friend Richard Grant White); Henry James, Sr., as well as Henry, Jr., and William; Yale professor and Fenimore Cooper biographer Thomas R. Lounsbury; the historian Francis Parkman; Thomas Wentworth Higginson; Howells; Matthews's boyhood friend, William C. Brownell; and Matthews himself. From 1875 to 1895, Matthews was the *Nation*'s chief reviewer of books directly or indirectly concerned with the theater, and he wrote on a potpourri of other topics, including politics, as well. (He was also a stockholder in the magazine from 1877 to 1881, when it was absorbed by the *New York Evening Post*; Matthews and other investors lost money on the sale.) Looking back at his long association with the *Nation*, Matthews expressed pride at being "permitted to stand by the side of my seniors, and to be enrolled in their goodly company" (*These Many Years*, 171–75).

In 1880 Matthews collected a group of his previously published essays into his first book, *The Theatres of Paris*. Since the book is little more than a tour guide to the Parisian theater world (individual chapters introduce readers to such subjects as the Comédie-Française, Théâtre Française, and French actors and actresses), it need not occupy us here. The work he published the following year, *French Dramatists of the 19th Century*, however, gained him international recognition as a critic and scholar of French drama. This study reveals not only Matthews's impressive knowledge of his subject but the extent to which his racial and political views contaminated his efforts to practice an Arnoldian "disinterested" criticism.

French Dramatists is a history of French drama from 1830 to 1880 (second and third editions added chapters on the 1880s and 1890s). The first chapter focuses on the "literary wars" that raged in France between the Classicists and Romanticists during the first quarter century; subsequent chapters assess the achievements of individual playwrights, beginning with Victor Hugo and concluding (in the first edition) with Émile Zola. In the preface, Matthews states that the central question his study seeks to answer is why French drama during the five decades that followed the production of Hugo's *Hernani* was "conspicuously and incomparably superior" to that of any other nation's during the same period.[21] Though Taine's name never appears in the book, it is clear from the outset that Matthews examines his subject through the Tainean lens of race, environment, and epoch. The French, Matthews asserts in the preface, have excelled in the drama primarily because that form is "best suited for the expression of certain qualities in which the French excel the men of other races." These traits include lively wit, cleverness (or love of effect for its own sake), and a passion for order and symmetry—all of which are reflected in the works of such great French playwrights as Corneille,

Molière, Racine, and Voltaire. If such racial characteristics were a sufficient cause for brilliant drama, then French plays would be equally excellent in every age. But this is clearly not the case; indeed, during the first quarter of the nineteenth century, the French stage was "chill and lifeless" (1).

Matthews attempts to account for this decline by applying the remaining two factors of Taine's trinity, moment and milieu: the sorry state of early nineteenth-century French drama, he postulates, can be attributed to the political situation that existed in France during the period. Under the imperial rule of Napoleon, Parisian theaters were under the control of the government, which dictated what style of play (opéra-comique, vaudeville, melodrama, etc.) each could produce. This "lack of liberty brought about the usual result of restriction,—a dearth of novelty and a desolating monotony" (2). The lack of liberty also resulted in a decline of dramatic realism. As I shall discuss in chapter 3, Matthews became a staunch ally of Howells and the realists when the "Realism War" broke out in America during the mid-1880s, but his analysis here reveals that he had in fact begun crusading for literary realism several years earlier. Instead of drawing their inspiration from the rich materials provided by everyday life, he argues, French playwrights became imitative and timid, their rule-restricted creations marked by a "literary" rather than a "lifelike" quality. Tragedy, whose life depends on language "plucked from the roots of humanity, and racy of the soil," especially suffered; laced in a tight corset of "rules," it nearly expired. It is easy to see why Howells, who disdained the French "well-made play," would find Matthews's dramatic criticism so appealing.

Matthews proceeds to explain, in language laden with war imagery, that the fall of Napoleon in 1815 changed the moment but not the environment that was detrimental to the development of drama, because the Bourbon milieu was preoccupied with dignity and correctness. But then "a new generation, born in the thick of the Napoleonic combats and conquests," grew to maturity; restless and militant, these "impatient romanticists" revolted against the old guard. Their leader was Hugo, an able "chief" who was "void of fear" (11). In recounting Hugo's role in the theater wars that followed, Matthews implicitly engaged in dialogue with the venerable Arnold, who had two years earlier attacked Hugo in "The French Play in London."[22] Arnold argued that Hugo's devotion to the French Alexandrine, which Arnold believed an inadequate form for tragedy, prevented the author of *Hernani* from producing truly great drama. Arnold rather peevishly chastised the "confident young generation" of Englishmen for claiming that Hugo was "of the race and lineage of Shakespeare" and for attempting to transplant the French theater of the *homme sensuel moyen* to the more severe soil of Protestant England.

Though Matthews's chapter on Hugo in *French Dramatists* does not mention Arnold, he clearly had him in mind, for he echoes the Englishman's claim that Hugo was not a "great dramatic poet of the race and lineage of Shakspere." But Matthews rejects Arnold's thesis that the damning defect of Hugo's plays is their Alexandrine verse. Hugo, argues Matthews, needed the restraint of the Alexandrine and was in fact at his best when exploiting that form. His plays failed to reach the heights of tragedy not because of his defects as a poet but because of his strengths as one; that is, he was a poet who tried to write drama, rather than (as in Shakespeare's case) a dramatist who wrote poetic plays. Lacking the two chief qualities of the great dramatist—the ability to create characters who are true to nature and the capacity to attain elevation of thought—Hugo could write clever melodramas but not great drama (41–42). Here Matthews applies a central tenet of his theater criticism—that drama be judged according to its own special demands and not by those of any other genre.

Although he could agree with Arnold that Hugo was no Shakespeare, Matthews nonetheless offers a favorable assessment of the French writer overall, and in doing so reveals that, at this point in his life (age twenty-nine), he was ideologically closer to the romantic admirers of Hugo than to the conservative Arnold, who would, during his 1883–84 tour of the United States, infuriate Lowell, Howells, Twain, and a host of democratic-minded American writers with his insistence that Americans wanted "distinction."[23] For Matthews, Hugo's virtues as a man dwarfed his deficiencies as a dramatist or a poet: literature, he asserts, was too small to contain Hugo's gigantic heart, so the "best part of him has got out of literature into life" (44). After praising Hugo's political and philanthropic activities during the "darkest and dirtiest days of the Second Empire," Matthews—in a passage that is anything but "genteel"—eulogizes the Frenchman as the "poet of the proletarian and of the people; he is the poet of the poor and the weak and the suffering; he is the poet of the over-worked woman and of the little child; he is the friend of the down-trodden and the outcast" (44).

Ranged in "battle-array" against Hugo and his hearty band of guerillas were the "serried ranks of the [French] Classicists," men "full of years and honors, and all so carefully forgotten now of the public that their names can be recalled only with an effort, even by the professed student of the stage of that time" (12). (These words must have seemed painfully ironic to Matthews thirty years later, when the Young Intellectuals dismissed him in similar terms.) Employing an analogy from the realm of politics, Matthews disdainfully states that this "die-in-the-ditch party" brooked no compromise with the Romantics and always "voted the straight ticket" (13). Yet, though he clearly takes sides with the Hugo-led "reformers" against the defenders of the status quo, Matthews ultimately rejects the young rebels because their revolt was entirely negative and prone to anarchy; when they had swept away the "rubbish of Classicism" (266), they had little more than melodrama and sensationalism to offer in its place. Matthews now turns his attention to a third camp, a tiny band of men who stood "halting between the old and the new," but nearer the Romantic rebels. Casimir Delavigne and the other "mitigated Classicists," as he calls them, were more amiable than members of the other two camps. Seeking the "safety of the middle path," they "confessed some of the failings and abuses of the existing state of things, but believed in 'reform within the party'" (13). Matthews, whose favorite philosopher, we recall, was the formulator of the Golden Mean, views these middle-wayers sympathetically, but he is forced to admit that, during the fierce battle between the two larger factions, the amiable compromisers were ineffectual; thus the revolt of the Hugo-led romanticists was, despite its anarchistic character, necessary.

There were clear parallels between the French "theater war" of the early nineteenth century and the factional political warfare raging in the United States at the time Matthews wrote *French Dramatists*, and it seems that his response to the latter influenced his critique of the former. That is to say, by 1881 Matthews, like so many other intellectuals exasperated by rampant political corruption during the 1870s, had come to believe that "reform within the party" was futile; only by revolting against the two-party system could the "rubbish" of the past be cleaned away. One such revolt had occurred in 1872, when Republican mavericks unsuccessfully attempted to establish the Liberal Republican party.[24] A more successful insurgency took place three years after Matthews published *French Dramatists*. In the election of 1884, the Mugwumps, outraged by the Republican party's nomination of James G. Blaine for president, threw their support to Grover Cleveland, tilting the election in his favor. Though Blaine was not the scoundrel and Cleveland not the righteous reformer that the Mugwumps portrayed each to be, the Mugwumps interpreted Cleveland's election as a resounding victory for their reform movement.[25]

By remaining loyal to the Republican party, Theodore Roosevelt and Henry Cabot Lodge—who represented the pragmatic, though certainly not the amiable, temperament of the "mitigated Classicists"—incurred the wrath of Godkin and other Mugwumps. Matthews admired Roosevelt and Lodge, and he developed close friendships with both. However, though he apparently respected the two men's decision to stay with their party, he sided with the Mugwumps in 1884, as an essay he published that year in the London *Saturday Review* makes clear.[26]

The announced purpose of the piece is to clarify the term "Mugwump" for a British audience, but in reality the essay is a polemic in support of the Mugwump revolt. Matthews begins by condemning the disgraceful conduct exhibited by both Democrats and Republicans in the 1884 presidential campaign, and he cites Blaine's attempt to secure votes by inviting clergymen to meet with him ("as though to say that he was a candidate specially blessed by the Church") as being particularly noxious. While admitting that Americans had good reason to feel ashamed of the two major political parties, he portrays the scandal as a sort of gracious affliction. The causes for despondency, he argues, "are all on the surface. Those who care to look more closely into the matter will discover at once and without difficulty signs of the most healthy awakening of American political life. The foulness of this campaign is the scum which has risen to the surface while the waters below were purifying themselves." The purification agent is the Mugwump, a term which, he observes, has its roots in the Algonquin word *mugquomp*, or "great man." Prior to the 1884 campaign, the Republican party enjoyed the support of the politically active "literary class," but, angered by the unseemly

Brander Matthews

practices of both parties, a large portion of this class broke its party allegiance and joined the Independent party, the "party of the centre," in Henry Adams's words.[27] Moreover, where the "better class" of easterners had previously displayed a remarkable indifference to political affairs, young men of "social prominence" (lawyers, journalists, businessmen) were taking a greater interest in political issues, many of them even going so far as to enter the political arena. Thus Matthews portrays the Mugwumps as the vanguard of "great men" who will purify—not radically restructure—the existing political order. Matthews's *Saturday Review* piece does not list the names of the most prominent Mugwumps, but such a list would have included many of New York City's most powerful editors and publishers: Godkin; George W. Curtis, editor of *Harper's Monthly*; Richard Watson Gilder, editor of the *Century* (formerly *Scribner's Monthly*), and his successor to that position, Robert Underwood Johnson; Charles Scribner; J. Henry Harper; George Haven Putnam; Henry Holt. Matthews developed friendships with all these "mugquomps." In so doing he helped place himself at the center of the nation's literary center; as he himself boasted in 1886, since half the established publishing houses, the majority of the foremost monthly magazines, and a large corps of prominent writers were located in New York, that city had become—as he had always hoped it would—the nation's literary capital.[28] If there was any doubt about the legitimacy of that claim, Howells's move from Boston to New York in 1890 settled the matter.

As Gerald McFarland discovered when he investigated socioeconomic data on nearly four hundred members of the New York Mugwump movement of 1884, the reformers were a remarkably homogeneous group. The typical New York Mugwump belonged to the upper middle class, possessed a college degree (and often a law degree as well), had New England roots, held membership in the Century Association and other exclusive clubs, was devoted to the development of professional organizations, and had inherited from his parents a strong sense of civic responsibility.[29] Though Godkin, Curtis, and other leaders of the movement had been born early in the century, most Mugwumps in 1884 were of the generation that came to maturity after the Civil War. Matthews's background matches this profile point for point.

Grounded in laissez-faire economic and social theory, the classical liberalism to which Matthews and his fellow Mugwumps subscribed was, of course, a far cry from liberalism as we know it today. The major planks of classical liberalism were free trade, hard money, home rule, and the merit system. These principles were championed by Godkin's *Nation* and Curtis's *Harper's Weekly*, the two foremost Mugwump organs. The "party of the centre" had no doubts about the righteousness of its cause. Curtis asserted that the independents' revolt was the first battle of a new Revolutionary War, the enemy being the party system. Lowell looked to the Civil War for his analogy, suggesting that where the antislavery forces had emancipated the Negro, the Mugwumps and their allies would "emancipate the respectable white man" from the shackles of a corrupt political system.[30]

In 1894, New York City Mugwumps scored a major success for the "respectable white man" and against Tammany Hall by helping to elect reform candidate William L. Strong to the mayor's office, an event that Godkin celebrated as the "Triumph of Reform."[31] Ironically, in order to gain that triumph, the Mugwumps were forced to seek the support of Republican boss Tom Platt. As Godkin well knew, the Mugwump moral crusade, which had peaked in the late eighties, had, for a variety of reasons, largely run out of steam by the time of Strong's election, and by the end of the decade it had expired.

"O, you Mugwumps!" Civil Service Commissioner Theodore Roosevelt wrote Matthews in 1889, "The way you go and arrogate all virtue to yourselves is enough to exasperate an humble party man like myself."[32] Roosevelt's remark was meant to be facetious, but, as Matthews's *Saturday Review* essay illustrates, Mugwump rhetoric often had a self-righteous tone to it. More important, though they might have sincerely agreed with Curtis's and Lowell's claims that the moral crusade against Gilded Age corruption bore comparison with the heroic struggles against British tyranny and Southern slavery, most Mugwumps held elitist views and had little concern for the economic and social problems plaguing the lower classes. The liberals' commitment to the doctrine of laissez-faire and their conviction that most economic, social, and political problems would be eliminated if only the "best men" could wrest power from the corrupt and ignorant led them to oppose virtually every significant reform of the 1890s.[33]

Many of the leading Mugwumps were, in fact, deeply suspicious of, in some cases hostile to, the democratic ideal. Godkin is a case in point. Though born in Ireland, he was a lifelong Anglophile (he emigrated to England in 1901, the year before his death) who defended hereditary monarchy and opposed universal manhood suffrage. He dismissed agrarian and labor reformers as cranks, and was contemptuous of ethnic immigrants who "choose to herd like pigs in the slums." To his mind, the creation of culture took precedence over the protection of personal liberty. The shortage of capable servants, he informed the *Nation*'s readers, was a most serious national problem.[34]

Matthews's sketch of Godkin in *These Many Years* reveals that, though he may have been proud to be a member of the *Nation*'s "goodly company" in the 1870s and 1880s, he was by no means an uncritical admirer of Godkin. Matthews describes Godkin as an able editor who never pressured contributors to alter their opinions, and he expresses his admiration for the "unflagging energy and unfailing felicity" with which the testy Irishman expounded the principles of hard money, free trade, home rule, and the merit system—principles that, in Matthews's view, spoke to the country's social and economic problems during the years following the Civil War. Significantly, Matthews makes no mention of the racism and snobbery so amply documented in William Armstrong's biography of Godkin. But Matthews does state that Godkin had a closed mind and that he was never an original political thinker; all his ideas derived from the education in Manchester political economy he had received at Queen's College in England. It was this ideological rigidity and lack of imagination, Matthews stresses, that led to the decline of Godkin's influence in the 1890s: the *Nation's* editor, he writes, was "impervious to every new idea in sociology or in statecraft; when he died he was limited to the beliefs he had held when he immigrated to America." Godkin's damning flaw, however, was that he turned cynical: "His faith in the future failed him; he sank into a praiser of past times and a disparager of the present. He came to feel that a people that would no longer listen to his advice must be on the road to ruin; and his main regret was—as he once expressed it to an associate—that he would not live to see the fulfillment of his prophecies of evil" (*These Many Years*, 173–74).

Godkin, in other words, refused to become a progressivist. Many of the leading figures of the progressive movement were, like Matthews, reform-minded independents attracted to the new liberalism that was emerging during the nineties in opposition to the laissez-faire ideology embraced by Godkin and the fading Mugwump coalition. The universities were centers of progressivist thinking, none more so than Columbia, where Matthews was elected to the faculty as professor of literature in 1892 (after spending one year as an instructor there).

Many of the new ideas in sociology and statecraft which Godkin and the old guard resisted were propounded by Matthews's colleagues in the social science departments at Columbia—men like Edwin R. Seligman, Charles Beard, Franz Boas, Felix Adler, and John Dewey. One of his age's most eminent economists (he would serve on the League of Nations committee on economics and finance during 1922–23), Seligman was deeply committed to the social-reform movement; he helped found the NAACP and served as president of the Society for Ethical Culture. He also edited for many years the influential journal *Political Science Quarterly*, housed at Columbia. Seligman had joined the college's Economics Department in 1885, the same year in which the American Economic Association was founded. In drawing up the association's statement of purpose, the organization's founder, Richard Ely (whom Godkin assailed in the *Nation*), spoke for Seligman and other proponents of the new liberalism when he asserted that laissez-faire economics was "unsafe in politics and unsound in morals."[35] Where laissez-faire economists like Yale's William Graham Sumner had faith in the individual will and Spencerian social evolution, Seligman emphasized the power of material conditions to mold individual and national destinies. His *The Economic Interpretation of History* (1902) inspired, among others, the Columbia graduate student who would one day produce the landmark work *An Economic Interpretation of the Constitution of the United States* (1913). Beard joined Columbia's political science faculty upon receiving his Ph.D. there in 1904. Boas, the father of American anthropology, arrived at Columbia in 1896. Adler was appointed professor of social and political ethics at Columbia in 1902. As founder and director of the Society for Ethical Culture, he was at the forefront of New York's social reform movement. Dewey's relocation from Chicago to Morningside Heights in 1904 further enhanced Columbia's already considerable reputation as a progressivist think tank.

However "progressive," Columbia was plagued by inter- and intradepartmental conflicts and faculty squabbling, and the combative Matthews, characteristically, was seldom far from the center of the action. As Lionel Trilling notes in a brief—and predominantly negative—verbal portrait of Matthews, the drama professor engaged in a long and bitter feud with colleague George Woodberry, a feud that finally resulted in Woodberry's resignation.[36] Despite his hostile relations with Woodberry, Harry Thurston Peck (whom Matthews denounced as an "abscess"), and other members of his department, Matthews greatly enjoyed and was intellectually stimulated by his association with scholars, particularly those sharing his progressivist world view.[37]

Matthews's most explicit statement on the duties and responsibilities of the literary-academic community to which he belonged is to be found in "'Those Literary Fellows,'" a 1909 essay in which he attempted to refute the charge (not unheard-of today) that literary intellectuals have no business dabbling in politics.[38] In the Emersonian vein, Matthews argues that the scholar must be actively engaged with life outside the Ivory Tower, especially in an age of increasing specialization. In characteristic fashion, he seeks to locate the Aristotelian mean between the extremes. In this case, the extremes are the romantic idealists (such as Hugo and Rousseau) who have no grasp of political realities, and the "practical" politicians who are adept at achieving political ends but are not guided by high ideals. Midway between these polar opposites stands the "practical idealist": the truly great men, Matthews maintains, "have been idealists who had a sustaining grasp on the realities of life" (314). Not surprisingly, Matthews cites Theodore Roosevelt, the man of letters who became president, as one such great man.

But, Matthews continues, academic humanists need not enter, as Roosevelt did, the political arena to engage the world; they can do so from within the academy, applying the fruits of their "disinterested" pursuit of knowledge to solving society's problems. Indeed, he insists that the best professors are more than excellent scholars and teachers: they are good citizens who are "seriously interested in the teeming life about them and [take] a manly part in the movement for social uplift." "They profit," continues the professor who had been raised to be a professional millionaire, "by their academic detachment from the business of making money to attain a wider perspective." This wider vision gives them the advantage over the merely practical politicians, who employ "makeshift devices" to treat the "symptoms of a distemper in the body politic without regard to the real cause of the disease." Finally, the university humanist exemplifies the democratic spirit, never disdaining (as Godkin and certain other Mugwumps did) the "plain people" (324–25).

Feminist readers of Matthews's essay would be quick to add a trait that Matthews never explicitly states but implies throughout: the literary "fellows" are all men; women are completely excluded from the discussion. Yet, at the time he was writing, roughly 20 percent of American professors were women. If Matthews was not aware of that fact, he certainly knew that Columbia's sister institution, Barnard College, had a substantial number of women on its faculty.[39]

Interestingly, Matthews's conception of the ideal "literary fellow" is similar in many respects to the figure of the "literary intellectual" that the Marxist-oriented Frank Lentricchia constructs in the opening essay of *Criticism and Social Change*.[40] Expressing respect for Matthews's colleague John Dewey and the pragmatic tradition, Lentricchia echoes Matthews in asserting that the "literary act is a social act," and that the ultimate goal of every university humanist must be a more just and democratic society. And Matthews would certainly have concurred with Lentricchia's contention, rooted in the progressive tradition, that the educational system should function as a catalyst for social change. But where Lentricchia, who identifies with his working-class roots and takes the perspective of an "outsider," believes that our society is "mainly unreasonable" and therefore requires radical *transformation*, Matthews—an "insider"—believed the capitalist-industrialist structure to be mainly reasonable. In his view of things, the world was "not so bad, after all"; moreover, it was, Herbert Spencer had convinced him, getting inevitably better.[41] His group of literary fellows, therefore, had no more room for Marxists than for women.

However, while he was inimical to the Socialist movement, which he considered a form of romantic idealism—fine in theory but impractical in reality—Matthews did not wholly dismiss Marxian historical determinism. As he did with most other modern ideas that challenged the mainstream ideology of his America, he attempted to accommodate Marxist theory to his existing values and beliefs. Matthews never discusses Marx in his writings; the little he knew about Marx's ideas he probably learned from his colleague Seligman. When Matthews delivered his paper "The Economic Interpretation of Literary History" as the presidential address to the 1910 convention of the Modern Language Association, he profited not only from having read Seligman's *The Economic Interpretation of History* but from having received the economist's critique of an early draft of the essay.[42] If members of the audience missed the title's implicit reference to Seligman's seminal book, they were immediately instructed, for Matthews began by praising Seligman's "acute and brilliant" demonstration that economic factors govern social change.[43] Where he had earlier embraced the Romantic "great men" theory of history, as his Mugwump piece of 1884 testifies, he had by 1910 come to accept the Marxist claims that economics is the engine that drives history and that class conflict underlies all social and political change. Following Seligman rather than Marx,

Matthews went on to say that material conditions cannot account entirely for artistic productions (Taine's deterministic theory, we recall, had been similarly diluted by his American advocates). But economic factors can be powerful enhancers or constrainers of literary development.[44] As evidence for his position, Matthews cited the deleterious effect that the Puritan closing of London theaters had had on English drama of the late seventeenth century. Choosing a less obvious example, he suggested that the remarkable productivity of French dramatists in the nineteenth century could be attributed to the secure position they enjoyed as members of the Society of Dramatic Authors (a trade union) and to the support they received from the Théâtre Française. Thus, he asserted, the economic paradigm—the examination of the "economic and political and legal conditions" that shape a work of art—offered a much more fruitful approach to the writing of literary history than did the more established one, which too often yielded nothing more than a "chronological collection of biographical criticisms" (39). Such remarks must have disquieted conservative-minded listeners in attendance.

As my summary thus far of the address suggests, much of what Matthews said to his fellow MLA members in 1910 would find a receptive audience at an MLA convention today. Yet, though portions of "The Economic Interpretation of Literary History" have a New Historicist ring to them, the essay closes on a decidedly Victorian note:

> He who possesses the potentiality of becoming one of the great men of literature may be born out of time or he may be born out of place. For the full expansion of his genius he needs [as Taine maintained] the right moment and the right environment; and without the one or the other he may be crusht [sic] and maimed. And yet if he has the ample largeness of true genius,

he is likely to have also the shrewd common sense of the man of affairs. He will have the gift of making the best of things as they chance to be, without whining and without revolt. He will rise superior to circumstances, either because he is supple enough to adapt himself to them, or because he is strong enough to conquer them, turning into a stepping-stone the obstacle which weaker creatures would find only a stumbling-block. (56)

This is precisely the kind of "strenuous" rhetoric that one would expect to find in a speech by the rough-writing Roosevelt. In fact, the passage was probably meant to be a thinly disguised tribute to the literary-minded politician whom Matthews viewed as the epitome of "manly" progressivism. Roosevelt's name has surfaced several times in this chapter; it is now time to examine his relationship with Matthews in detail.

**"They Are Not as We Are":
Theodore Roosevelt and the
Progressive View of "Others"**

For Theodore Roosevelt—who once exclaimed, "Why, I owe
everything to the West! It made me!"—the American West
symbolized the rugged and independent American spirit that
he believed was being emasculated by the "overcivilized, over-
sensitive, over-refined" eastern establishment.[1] And though he
could admire the poetry of such easterners as E. A. Robinson
and George Cabot Lodge (son of Henry Cabot Lodge),
Roosevelt was most attracted to those writers who celebrated
the "strenuous life" of the frontier.[2] Foremost among such authors was Owen Wister, who dedicated *The Virginian* to the
former Rough Rider upon its first publication in 1902 and again
when it was reprinted in 1911, asserting then that Roosevelt
was the "greatest benefactor we people have known since Lincoln." The object of that compliment, needless to say, loved the
"manly" novel. But the New York critics, Wister emphasizes
in his biography of Roosevelt, "heartily damned" the tale. The
hostile reaction of the genteel easterners came as no surprise to
Wister, who, borrowing an expression from Kipling, quipped
that in the United States "East is East and West is West, and
never the twain shall meet."[3]

Yet, as Wister well knew, the conflicting ideologies represented by the terms "easterner" and "westerner" did in
fact meet in uneasy tension in many Americans: in Wister
himself (who was born in Philadelphia and educated at
Harvard), and, most notably, in the Harvard-educated author of *The Winning of the West*. As several of Roosevelt's
commentators have stressed, though he emphasized his association with cowboys and Rough Riders (many of whom
were fellow Ivy Leaguers), the "eastern" connection was as

important as the "western" one in shaping his character and career.[4] And one of the central links in that connection was a certain club-loving Columbia professor whose father had raised him to be a professional millionaire.

Though scholars have given due attention to Roosevelt's accomplishments as a man of letters, they have all but ignored his relationship with Matthews.[5] Yet for over three decades the professor was not only one of the Rough Rider's most intimate friends but his literary mentor. Matthews encouraged Roosevelt's literary efforts, critiqued drafts of his writings, and published numerous essays extolling his literary and political talents.[6] Indeed, Matthews may have been the single most important influence on Roosevelt's determined attempt to succeed as a "literary feller," as he once described himself to Matthews.[7] Their relationship, however, was not one-sided; Roosevelt exerted an immense influence on the development of Matthews's progressivist ideology, and therefore on the texts in which that ideology is embedded. A good many of Matthews's and Roosevelt's works explicitly or implicitly draw the boundary between the progressivist and all those "Others"—immigrants, blacks, "effeminate" anti-imperialists, New Women—who threatened the cultural hegemony that the two men sought. As Peter Conn and others have argued, the progressivist response to the "problem" posed by those of different races, classes, ideologies, and gender was profoundly dialectical; in their attempt to come to terms with the Other, both Matthews and Roosevelt exemplify Conn's "divided mind" thesis.[8]

Exactly when and where Matthews and Roosevelt first made each other's acquaintance is not known. They might have been introduced to each other at one of the New York City social clubs that Roosevelt (despite his many public denunciations of the eastern genteel lifestyle) and Matthews frequented. Or perhaps they met during Roosevelt's unsuccessful campaign for mayor of New York in 1886.[9] In any case, they had become personal friends as early as 1887, for in the 1889 letter in which he facetiously taunts Matthews for being a Mugwump (see chap. 1, note 32), Roosevelt refers to a discussion that he and Matthews had had two years earlier regarding a story Matthews was writing. Titled "Memories," the tale appeared in the August 1889 *Scribner's Magazine*. Matthews published several novels and numerous short stories, but "Memories" is his only western; the rest of his fictions explore life in metropolitan New York or in fashionable East Coast resorts where he summered. "Memories" occupies our attention here because it stands as the first of many public tributes Matthews would pay Roosevelt during their more than thirty years of friendship.

That Matthews had Roosevelt in mind when he composed the tale is suggested by the setting—a fictional Fort Roosevelt in the Northwest Territory. Here army troopers must battle not only hostile Indians but fierce winter weather. As he sits by the fireside during a blizzard, Robert Douglas, the protagonist, reflects on his days in an eastern military academy, where the older boys made life painful for him. But not nearly as painful as the broken heart he suffered when the beautiful young woman he loved married an Italian nobleman and died of illness in Rome shortly thereafter. Douglas's mournful reveries are broken, however, when he is informed that two children have wandered into the storm. Immediately he and nine other volunteers set out in search of the children, the men connected by a rope. "There was no use repining;" proclaims the narrative voice, "a strong man does not die of a broken heart. Work there is in plenty in the world for a man to do, if he is but willing."[10]

Upon reading "Memories," Roosevelt wrote to Matthews: "I was electrified when I struck the name of the fort. It may be prejudice on my part, but I really think it is one of the best of your stories, and I am very glad to have my name connected with it in no matter how small a way."[11] Roosevelt had reasons other than the name of the fort to be favorably prejudiced toward the piece. Five years before the story was published, he had lost his beloved wife Alice (and, almost simultaneously, his mother); like Douglas, he did not wallow in self-pity. After sampling cowboy life in the rugged Dakota territory, he returned east and plunged back into politics. "Memories" is thus not only a celebration of the "strenuous life" but a thinly veiled tribute to Roosevelt for overcoming personal anguish and taking up the banner of progressive reform.

No issue loomed larger to Matthews and Roosevelt and to most of their fellow progressivists than that of race. During the years in which the two men received their formal educations and embarked upon their professional careers, racial theorizing was approaching its zenith in the United States, and virtually every facet of American life felt its influence. We have already seen how Taine's theory that works of art reveal "race traits" influenced Matthews's practice of literary criticism, but Taine was only one of a host of racial theorists who succeeded in giving "scientific" credence to the notion of innate racial differences. Some of the most pernicious racial theorizing emanated from the nation's prestigious universities, including Harvard and Columbia. During his years at Harvard (1876–80), Roosevelt came under the tutelage of Nathan Southgate Shaler, a geologist and historian who enthusiastically preached the doctrine of white supremacy and Negro inferiority and who feared that the swarms of "new immigrants" threatened to destroy the "purity" of the "American race."[12] After graduating from Harvard in 1880, Roosevelt studied law for a year at Columbia, where his racial biases were further solidified under the instruction of John Burgess, a professor of political science and one of America's most prominent Teutonists.

Matthews's letters reveal that he shared Roosevelt 's preoccupation with the idea of race, and that Matthews made a practice of informing his friend of new books and articles on the subject. This was especially true during the years that Roosevelt was president; Matthews sent a steady stream of reading matter to the White House, much of it authored by members of Columbia's social-science faculty.

In 1903, for example, Matthews urged Roosevelt to read Franklin H. Giddings's "American People."[13] Professor of sociology at Columbia, Giddings was very active in the social reform movement, and he served for a time as director of New York's Settlement House. He was also a firm believer in Anglo-Saxon supremacy and a vocal supporter of United States imperialism. His *Democracy and Empire* (1900) opens with the assertion that western imperialism "must continue until all the semi-civilized, barbaric, and savage communities of the world are brought under the protection of the larger civilized nations," preferably the English-speaking ones.[14] In "American People," Giddings addressed the topic that would virtually obsess Roosevelt in his later years—the supposed decline of the Anglo-Teutonic race due to the influx of immigrants of Celtic, Latin, and Slavic stock. Though the essay, which is saturated with demographic data, makes claims to being "scientific," its major arguments are rooted in racial ideology rather than empirical evidence. Giddings speaks glibly, for example, about such distinctive "race traits" as American mental quickness and Italian hot-bloodedness, and the notion that Americans are a chosen people runs as a subtext throughout. The central thesis is that the Melting Pot would remain "essentially English" in its language and its ideals, its ability to "convert the most unpromising foreign born citizen" as strong as ever.[15] Put simply, Giddings told those who feared race decadence not to worry.

A year later Matthews received Roosevelt's permission to send him a copy of Burgess's "Germany, Great Britain, and the United States."[16] Matthews might have felt it necessary to seek Roosevelt's approval before mailing him Burgess's piece because Roosevelt's imperialist actions during the Spanish-

American War had soured the two men's friendship. (Burgess was sensitive to Germany's fear that the annexation of the Philippines was motivated by America's desire to achieve world domination.) In recommending Burgess's essay to Roosevelt, Matthews may have been attempting to mediate their differences. If so, he apparently succeeded. By 1908 Burgess and Roosevelt had reconciled, Burgess extolling his former pupil as one of the two great statesmen of the world, Kaiser Wilhelm being the other.[17]

When he sent Burgess's article to Roosevelt, Matthews remarked that it expressed ideas he had previously only vaguely felt.[18] Thus the essay deserves close attention here because it sheds light on Matthews's racial ideology at the time.

Burgess opens by paying tribute to Theodor Mommsen, the German professor under whose tutelage Burgess developed his knowledge of the Teutonic heritage and his appreciation of the "ethical and political consensus" that unites the three great Teutonic nations—Germany, Great Britain, and the United States. The social and political ideals that these countries have inherited from their Teutonic ancestors are in sharp contrast to those of the "inferior" Romanic, Celtic, and Slavic races. Foremost among these Teutonic ideals is a strong sense of individual worth and rights, out of which have grown respect for individual liberty, freedom of conscience, sacredness of the home and family, security of private property, respect for individual liberty, and, curiously, female chastity. Teutonic nations are also united by their devotion to democracy and hostility to authoritarianism, their sense of national purpose, and the "high moral tone" of their literature and art. The "Teutonic genius and the Teutonic conscience," Burgess concludes, are in general the "two greatest forces in modern civilization and culture." This being the case, Germany, Great Britain, and the United States bear a moral obligation to extend Teutonic culture into the "dark places of the earth for the enlightenment and advancement of the inhabitants of these dark places."

Acknowledging that recent historical events such as the Boer War and the American invasion of the Philippines have produced tensions among the three countries, Burgess pleads with them to put aside their differences and recognize their common interests. Issuing a caveat that was to become a staple of American political rhetoric in the twentieth century, he warns that if the United States "has a natural enemy in political principle in the world, that enemy is Russia." In a passage Roosevelt would have taken special note of, Burgess urges the United States to seize the initiative in forming an alliance of the Teutonic nations, adding that the "leadership in directing such a combination of reason, righteousness and power for the civilization of the world would be a divine appointment." Though he announced in the opening of the essay that he would speak in a calm and reasonable tone about issues that have engendered an abundance of inflammatory rhetoric, Burgess closes on a feverish pitch: "Barbarism has thrown, and probably will again throw, obstacles in the way of a [Teutonic] advance; but it has been and will be good for barbarism, whether primitive or luxuriously effete, to be brought under their sway."[19] Such, then, were the ideas that Matthews had long felt but never articulated.

It would be inaccurate, however, to label Matthews a Teutonist, for though he was attracted to Burgess's racial ideology, he shared his generation's tendency to be vague and inconsistent in his use of the term "race." His writings, like Roosevelt's, are punctuated with references not only to the Teutonic, Anglo-Saxon, and Latin races but to white, black, red, brown, French-speaking, Spanish-speaking, and English-speaking ones. Thus any nation, culture, or people sharing a common language could be designated as a "race."

Matthews and Roosevelt believed that the American

"race" was a unique branch of the English-speaking race and that American literature was a unique branch of English-language literature. Americans carried in their blood the Teutonic/Anglo-Saxon character traits—positive ones such as courage, energy, individualism, love of adventure; negative ones such as a tendency toward violent aggression and a lack of respect for other people's rights.[20] (In his autobiography, Matthews, we recall, emphasizes his father's lineal descent from the Elizabethan maritime adventurers.) But those traits had been modified by the unique environment of the New World. Like Taine, Roosevelt and Matthews broadly defined environment to include economic, political, and social conditions. While Americans had much in common with other members of the English-speaking "race," their special conditions—most notably their democratic form of government and (alleged) absence of class distinctions—differentiated them from their British cousins, whom Roosevelt and Matthews viewed with a mixture of admiration and disdain. In short, Roosevelt and Matthews concurred with Crèvecoeur's assertion that the New World "melting pot" had produced a "new man," the American; but however mixed the blood of the American Adam, he was in essence an Anglo-Saxon. Matthews gave explicit expression to this view in his congratulatory letter to Roosevelt after the election of 1904: "You are chief of a people . . . compounded now (as ever) from all the other peoples of the world—and yet remaining (or acquiring) the old Anglo-Saxon respect for character and courage and straightforwardness."[21]

As readers of Crèvecoeur's *Letters from an American Farmer* are aware, the optimistic vision projected in the letter (III) in which he describes the New Man is undercut by the encounter (Letter IX) with the Negro slave starving to death in a cage hanging from a tree. The Civil War would abolish slavery, but not the "Negro problem," and that problem, which included the horror of lynching, hovered specter-like before Roosevelt and Matthews as it had before Crèvecoeur. On no other issue were the minds of these two sons of Yankee fathers and Southern mothers more divided.[22]

Roosevelt said as much in a 1913 letter to Matthews. "Ugh!" he wrote. "There is not any more puzzling problem in this country than the problem of color. It is not as urgent, or as menacing, as other problems but it seems more utterly insoluble. The trouble is that the conflict in many of its phases is not between right and wrong, but between two rights."[23] Considering that lynchings and other forms of violence against blacks reached an all-time high during the Roosevelt administration,[24] Roosevelt's suggestion here that other problems were more important than the problems of Others reveals a remarkable insensitivity to the victims of white racism. Though he condemned lynching as an indefensible wrong and insisted that blacks, as he wrote Matthews from the White House in 1903, be given a "square deal,"[25] he does not seem to have felt the rage that, for example, prompted Mark Twain to write (in 1901, the year Roosevelt assumed the presidency) his scathing essay "The United States of Lyncherdom." Moreover, in such writings as "The Negro Problem" (1905), "The Education of the Negro" (1905), and "The Progressives and the Colored Man" (1912), Roosevelt's sense of racial superiority and sympathy for the white segregationist point of view are clearly evident.

In "The Negro Problem," an address delivered to the Republican Club of New York City in 1905, Roosevelt, for example, insists that blacks be afforded equal opportunity and legal and social justice, and reminds his audience (as Matthews implicitly did in "Memories" when Douglas and his troopers linked themselves by a rope) that all Americans, white and black, are "knit together . . . and shall go up or down together." Yet, the image of being united is undercut by his announcement that "reflecting men of both races" concur that "race purity must be maintained" (*Works* 16: 348–

49). "The problem," he says in the essay's key, albeit awkwardly expressed, statement, "is so to adjust the relations between two races of different ethnic type that the rights of neither be abridged nor jeoparded." The "backward race," he goes on to say, must be trained to handle freedom, while the "forward race" must ensure that the "high civilization wrought out by its forefathers" be preserved. Since the working out of this problem must necessarily be slow, blacks must be patient; and as they are biding their time, they must devote their energies to "moral and industrial uplifting." While whites were lynching blacks with virtual impunity—oftentimes for offenses the victims did not commit—Roosevelt was insisting that blacks not only obey the law themselves but that they aid the police in capturing fellow members of their race accused of crimes. In a statement that must have seemed incredible to most blacks and even some whites (certainly to Twain), Roosevelt warned that laziness and shiftlessness were "evils more potent for harm to the black race than all the acts of oppression of white men put together" (*Works* 16: 346). When he delivered his address "The Education of the Negro" at Booker T. Washington's Tuskegee Institute a few months later, Roosevelt tempered his language and avoided the phrase "backward race," but the message was essentially the same (*Works* 16: 351–55).

Roosevelt did not believe that *all* blacks were inferior to whites. Accepting the Lamarckian idea that positive traits developed by individuals in their lifetime can be passed on to their offspring, he admitted that the American environment had produced some blacks, such as Booker T. Washington, who were the intellectual and moral equals of whites.[26] Unfortunately, he never abandoned his conviction that Africans were a "backward race," whose march up the evolutionary ladder would take considerable time. Indeed, he became more convinced as the years went by that African Americans were simply incapable of participating in a democratic system of government, and when he ran for president on the Bull Moose ticket in 1912, he sought to exclude them from an active role in the party. Blacks, he argued in "The Progressives and the Colored Man" (1912), could best serve their own interests by handing over what little political power they had to "the wisest and justest white men of the South." These wise bearers of the White Man's Burden would in turn see that political rights were extended—gradually—to all those blacks who, in the eyes of their white custodians, demonstrated intelligence, integrity, and self-respect (*Works* 17: 305). Apparently Roosevelt was not troubled by the fact that these virtues were not always evident in white voters and politicians.

But, if Roosevelt spoke for most progressivists, there were a few who questioned the whole notion of superior and inferior races. Chief among these was Matthews's colleague at Columbia, Franz Boas. Though he had begun in the 1890s to challenge the dominant racial ideology as professed by Burgess and other academic racialists, Boas did not address specific social issues until 1904.[27] In May 1906, one year after President Roosevelt had spoken at Tuskegee, Boas gave (at the invitation of W. E. B. Du Bois) the commencement address at Atlanta University. Titled "The Outlook for the American Negro," Boas's speech in many respects concurs with the perspective offered by Roosevelt in his Tuskegee address. Negroes, Boas stated, must recognize that it was not within their power to rapidly alter racist feelings in whites; thus they had to be patient but persistent in their quest for equal rights. Paralleling the advice Roosevelt gave his black audience, Boas suggested that the best way for Negroes to undermine white racism was to become more clean, healthy, energetic, and, above all, moral. An immoral act committed by a black, especially an educated one, he cautioned, will be all too readily interpreted by some whites as a "relapse into the old ways of an inferior race."[28] Certainly Roosevelt would have so interpreted, but Boas did not; for if he in general accepted Roosevelt's outlook for African Americans as being realistic, given the deeply entrenched prejudice against them, he completely rejected Roosevelt's notion that the African race was still at the savage stage of evolution. Pointing to such historical facts as the African invention of the iron-smelting process and the sophisticated military and governmental organizations of the Zulus, the eminent anthropologist informed his audience that the historical record indicates "an early and energetic development of African culture." If, therefore, Boas went on to say in a passage that must have stirred his audience, "it is claimed that your race is doomed to economic inferiority, you may confidently look to the home of your ancestors and say, that you have set out to recover for the colored people the strength that was their own before they set foot on the shores of this continent."[29]

In the same year that he published "The Outlook for the American Negro," Boas appealed to Andrew Carnegie for funds to establish an anthropological institute that would conduct a dispassionate investigation into the conditions of the Negro in America while also disseminating knowledge of the achievements of African cultures. "All that we can say at the present time," Boas informed Carnegie, "is that it seems unfair to judge the Negro by what he has come to be in America, and that the evidence of cultural achievement of the Negro in Africa suggests that his inventiveness, power of political organization, and steadiness of purpose, equal or even excel those of other races of similar stages of culture."[30] Such unbiased scientific research, he argued three years later in "Race Problems in America," would not only explode the myth of Negro inferiority but would help counter the fear that the great migration of "new immigrants" was transforming the United States into a "mongrel" nation. Reminding his audience that the populations of England and of Europe were products of racial intermixture, Boas forcefully

Brander Matthews

attempted to deconstruct the theory of racial purity. The whole question of race, he concluded, had not received sufficient scientific study and was therefore *completely* unsolved.[31]

Unfortunately, Boas's arguments were either ignored or rejected by most proponents of the prevailing racial theories. Certainly they had no demonstrable effect on Roosevelt's thinking on the subject. In his well-known "Race Decadence" (1911), for example, the former president warned that the declining birthrate of "old stock" Americans in conjunction with the rising tide of immigration would lead inevitably to "racial decay" (*Works* 12: 184–96). As he put it to fellow racialist Wister, "If all our nice friends in Beacon Street, and Newport, and Fifth Avenue, and Philadelphia have one child, or no child at all, while the Finnegans, Hooligans, Antonios, Mandelbaums and Rabinskis have eight, or nine, or ten—it's simply a question of the multiplication table."[32]

In the most thorough investigation of Roosevelt's racial ideology, Thomas Dyer remarks that Roosevelt, despite his wide reading in racial theory, was apparently unaware of Boas's work. But Roosevelt was in fact introduced to Boas's seminal book, *The Mind of Primitive Man* (published in 1911, the same year as Roosevelt's "Race Decadence"), in 1915 by one of the anthropologist's admiring fellow professors— Matthews. Responding to the letter in which Matthews recommended Boas's book, Roosevelt promised that he would read it, and then asked: "What is he—a German or a Jew or what?"[33] Matthews's answer to that question reveals a mind somewhat more committed to the ideal of the Melting Pot than the one that asked it: "Boas," he wrote back, "*was* a German; but he *is* an American" (emphasis Matthews's). As Matthews would have known, Boas was also a Jew; he might have consciously withheld that fact for fear that, if so informed, Roosevelt would have read Boas's anthropological studies with biased eyes. In the same letter, Matthews expresses his high regard for Boas as a teacher, remarking that his anthropology courses were extremely popular with Columbia undergraduates.[34]

Since Roosevelt nowhere else, to my knowledge, mentions Boas or *The Mind of Primitive Man*, he either did not keep his promise to Matthews or else he dismissed the book after reading it. He need only have glanced at the first chapter, titled "Racial Prejudices," to discover that Boas was intent on dismantling, plank by plank, the entire structure of the theory of Anglo-Teutonic racial supremacy that formed the framework of essays like Burgess's "Germany, Great Britain, and the United States" as well as of Roosevelt's own "Race Decadence." Summarizing the major arguments of the chapter, Boas writes:

> We have found that the unproved assumption of cultural achievement and of mental ability is founded on an error of judgment; that the variations in cultural development can as well be explained by a consideration of the general course of historical events [i.e., historical accident] without recourse to the theory of material differences of mental faculty in different races. We have found, furthermore, that a similar error underlies the common assumption that the white race represents physically the highest type of man, but that anatomical and physiological considerations do not support these views.[35]

Elsewhere in the work Boas speaks harshly of the growth of modern nationalism engendered by an "exaggerated self-admiration of the Teutonic race" (174), rejects the notion of universal stages of cultural evolution, and contends that there is no close relationship between race and culture. The final chapter is a reprint of Boas's earlier essay "Race Problems in America" with the following eloquent passage added as a closing:

Brander Matthews

I hope that the discussions contained in these pages have shown that the data of anthropology teach us a greater tolerance of forms of civilization different from our own, and that we should learn to look upon foreign races with greater sympathy, and with the conviction, that, as all races have contributed in the past to cultural progress in one way or another, so they will be capable of advancing the interests of mankind, if we are only willing to give them a fair opportunity. (278)

It seems certain that, in recommending this book to Roosevelt, Matthews sought to offer his friend a more "progressive" theoretical perspective from which to approach the problem of race. Yet, though *The Mind of Primitive Man* seems to have led Matthews to reject Burgess's theory of Anglo-Teutonic supremacy on intellectual grounds, it did not resolve his internal dialectic over the Negro Question. Like Roosevelt, Matthews continued throughout his life to include blacks and other minorities in the English-speaking "race" while simultaneously excluding them as Others. This is dramatically illustrated by his relationship with the African-American writer James Weldon Johnson.

Novelist, poet, songwriter, journalist, lawyer, civil rights activist, and diplomat, James Weldon Johnson (1871–1938) was truly a renaissance man. His novel *The Autobiography of an Ex-Coloured Man* (1912) stands as a landmark in African-American literary history, with writers such as Richard Wright, Ralph Ellison, and James Baldwin owing a debt to its example.[36] In his own day, he exerted an incalculable influence on young black writers, and he has justly been called the elder statesman of the Harlem Renaissance. Several studies of Johnson call attention to his friendship with Matthews, but none examines it in any detail. Yet, for over twenty years Matthews acted as Johnson's trusted advisor, and unpublished letters indicate that no other member of the white literary establishment worked more assiduously to promote his career. Before exploring the two men's fascinating relationship, it will be profitable to recall Johnson's remarkable career.

Rather well-to-do and conservative, Johnson's parents inculcated in him the values of the white middle class, and they provided him and his younger brother Rosamond with many of the advantages that Brander Matthews had enjoyed; two of these—music lessons and frequent visits to the theater—would be especially important to the two boys in their adult years. As a student at Atlanta University from 1890 to 1894, Johnson met Booker T. Washington and Paul Laurence Dunbar, and he heard Frederick Douglass speak at the Chicago Exposition in 1893. The words of these and other black leaders helped stimulate Johnson's lifelong commitment to the campaign for racial justice. After graduation, he served as a school principal in his native Jacksonville, Florida; operated a newspaper for a time; and earned a law degree, his admission to the bar protested by white segregationists. It was as a composer of songs and musicals, however, that Johnson would first gain fame. In 1900 he and Rosamond collaborated on "Lift Every Voice and Sing," the song that would later become known as the "Negro National Anthem." They scored an even bigger hit with "Under the Bamboo Tree," which sold over 400,000 copies and earned them substantial royalties. After several years of traveling back and forth between Jacksonville and New York City to work with Rosamond (who was enjoying some success as a Broadway vaudeville performer), Johnson moved permanently to New York. With their partner Rob Cole, the Johnson brothers continued to build their reputations as talented composers of lyrics and musicals. The high point of their stage career was a six-weeks' engagement at London's Palace Theatre in 1905.

A year earlier, the black politician Charles W. Anderson

had recruited Johnson as an officer in the "Colored Republican Club," whose chief activity at the time was campaigning for the election of Roosevelt. Johnson and his brother became staunch supporters of the president who outraged white racists by inviting ("accidentally," as he later claimed) Booker T. Washington to the White House for lunch. With Rosamond and Cole, Johnson coauthored a campaign song titled "You're All Right, Teddy," which Roosevelt proclaimed a "bully good song."[37] In 1906 Johnson was rewarded for his support of Roosevelt and the Republicans by being appointed consul at Puerto Cabello, Venezuela. As Roosevelt was leaving office in 1909, Johnson hoped to be transferred to a more appealing post in Nice, France, but was transferred (at a higher grade) to Corinto, Nicaragua, where the living conditions and job duties dismayed him.

While still stationed at Corinto, Johnson anonymously published his only novel, *The Autobiography of an Ex-Coloured Man*, which many readers and reviewers believed to be a factual autobiography. Product of the illicit union between a southern "gentleman" and his mulatto mistress, the central character (who remains unnamed) is raised as a "little aristocrat" by his mother. Because he wants his illegitimate son to receive the best education possible, the father sends the narrator and his mother to Connecticut, where the boy develops into a skilled pianist. As light-skinned as most of his white schoolmates, the narrator does not discover that he is a "nigger" until a grade-school teacher callously makes him aware of his "difference." When his mother dies and his father (who has married a member of his own race) breaks off contact, the narrator begins an episodic journey through the North, the South, and Europe. During this symbolic exploration of the "Negro question," Johnson provides glimpses of a cross-section of African-American culture. The divergent perspectives of whites on the racial issue are brought into sharp focus in the scene in which the narrator (who is passing for white) overhears several white men in a Pullman car debating the "Negro problem." One of the men, a Texan, vigorously defends southern segregation and the theory of Anglo-Saxon supremacy that underpins it. The opposing position is espoused with equal vigor by a northern liberal, who demolishes the theory of white superiority with arguments that he might have read in Boas's essays. The Yankee scores his most crippling verbal hit when he informs the Texan that most of the great achievements and discoveries of world civilization were made not by Anglo-Saxons but by the allegedly inferior dark races.[38] Such facts, however, fail to alter the Texan's views. The impotence of rational argument as a weapon against virulent racism is more dramatically demonstrated in a later scene when the narrator witnesses the horror of lynching. Ashamed that blacks could allow themselves to be treated so inhumanely, he abandons the civil rights cause and pursues the "white man's success"— money. He falls in love with and eventually marries a white woman (to whom he revealed his secret racial identity), has two children (who will never know that Negro blood runs in their veins) by her, and prospers financially. The novel, however, closes on a note of despair: not only does the narrator lose his wife to illness, but he feels small and selfish when he compares his life to those of Booker T. Washington and other blacks fighting for racial justice, and he cannot escape the thought that he has "sold his birthright for a mess of pottage" (211).

By the time the novel was published, the Democrats had gained control of Washington, thereby extinguishing the Republican Johnson's hope of being transferred to Nice. Disheartened, he resigned from the foreign service in 1913 and returned to New York, where he became a contributing editor to the black weekly, *The New York Age*. In 1916 he was appointed field secretary for the NAACP (which had been established in 1909); his duties included the unpleasant and sometimes dangerous task of investigating cases of lynching and racial violence.

Johnson's nomination as NAACP field secretary was supported by W. E. B. Du Bois, who in 1905 had split the ranks of black activists by launching the militant Niagara movement. Johnson and Du Bois had been on friendly terms since their initial meeting in 1904; Johnson greatly admired *The Souls of Black Folk* (1903), and Du Bois would feel similarly about *The Autobiography of an Ex-Coloured Man*. But, as his praise of Booker T. Washington at the end of *The Autobiography* suggests, Johnson did not join the Niagara movement. During the years of feuding between the Niagara and Tuskegee factions, Johnson tried to take the middle path, maintaining cordial relationships with both Du Bois and Washington. By the time Johnson joined the staff of the NAACP, whose office was across the hall from that of Du Bois and *The Crisis* staff, Booker T. was dead, and Johnson was ready to take a more aggressive posture in the struggle for racial equality.[39]

When the United States entered World War I, Johnson, who had urged blacks to do their patriotic duty, decried racist treatment of Negro servicemen and workers in arms factories. In 1918, in the wake of the horrible lynchings in St. Louis, Houston, and other cities, he appealed in vain to ex-President Roosevelt to speak out publicly against racial injustice in the military.[40] Johnson had, as noted, been a political supporter of Roosevelt since at least 1904, and it is clear that from that time on he desired to gain Roosevelt's attention. He did not begin corresponding with him, however, until 1917. By then, Johnson's name and several of his writings had become well known to Roosevelt, largely through the efforts of Brander Matthews.

Johnson's friendship with Matthews began shortly after he moved to New York in 1902. Seeking to alleviate the boredom and loneliness he felt when Rosamond and Cole were performing on the road, Johnson decided to take courses at Columbia. Since he was particularly interested in studying theater, he sought out Matthews, whose writings on the drama had attracted his attention. Johnson's recollections of the meeting, recorded in his autobiography *Along This Way*, leave no doubt that Matthews had a profound and enduring influence on his literary views and career. Johnson was impressed by Matthews's cordiality and flattered that the eminent professor was familiar with his work in musical comedy, an aspect of the theater that Matthews followed closely. The meeting, Johnson explains,

> was the beginning of a warm and lasting friendship between Brander Matthews and me. He talked to me a great deal about the musical comedy stage and the important people connected with it. In his lectures he frequently set me in an enviable light before the class. When we reached the classic drama of Spain, he often called on my knowledge of the language in dealing with the plays in the original. When we came to the contemporary American stage he cited me a good many times as a journeyman in the theatre. I was fascinated with my work under him. I was especially impressed with his catholicity, freedom from pedantry, and his common sense in talking about the theatre. I believe that he shocked most of us in his class when he declared that the best plays of Weber and Fields were the same sort of thing as the theatre of Aristophanes; that, except for the fact that no Weber and Fields playwright ever attempted to imitate the occasional lofty lyrical flights of the Greek comedian, the two theaters were comparable.[41]

Three years later, as he was preparing to leave for Puerto Cabello to begin his foreign-service career, Johnson showed Matthews a draft of the first two chapters of *The*

Autobiography of an Ex-Coloured Man as well as some of his poetry. Impressed by what he read, Matthews encouraged Johnson to complete the novel (and to keep the title, which Johnson, at Rosamond's suggestion, considered changing to *The Chameleon*), and he also gave the fledgling writer a letter of introduction to Harry Thurston Peck, a colleague of Matthews at Columbia and then editor of the (American) *Bookman*. Peck liked the poems and published two of them in his magazine.[42]

What Johnson does not say in *Along This Way* is that he sent Matthews a draft of the *entire* novel when he completed it in 1908, as an unpublished letter he sent from Puerto Cabello to the professor evidences. Contrary to Robert Fleming's recent assertion that Johnson constructed the fictional autobiography with apparent ease,[43] the letter indicates that he experienced a great deal of anxiety and frustration as he struggled to complete the work. Speaking in a plaintive tone throughout, Johnson informed Matthews that finishing the book had been a fearful task; that he felt he had lost the spirit of the story; and that the ending of the book was weak because he was unable to write convincingly of love.[44] Though he believed that he had the power to write better than ever, the difficulties confronting him in his present position (which included threat of plague and violent revolution) sapped his incentive to write. If he was not soon transferred from Puerto Cabello to a better post, he would resign his position and return to New York. (Johnson may have emphasized his displeasure with his situation in Venezuela in hopes that Matthews would exert influence on Roosevelt, who, as noted, did transfer Johnson the following year, though not to the post in Nice the latter had hoped for.)

We do not have Matthews's response to Johnson's letter, but we do know that Johnson made several substantive revisions in the manuscript before it was printed—including the replacement of the original ending with a new one. In the manuscript version, the narrative concludes on an upbeat note: the narrator's wife is alive, and they are relatively happy. One can only speculate whether Matthews recommended the more somber closing.

There is little doubt, however, that Matthews directly or indirectly influenced the section in chapter 9 contrasting the Parisian to the London spirit and chastising the British for accusing Americans of degrading the English language, since these paragraphs echo passages in Matthews's writings. For example, Johnson's defense of American slang and criticism of the British for claiming ownership of the English language closely parallel Matthews's arguments in "Americanisms and Briticisms" and other of his polemical attacks on British superciliousness.[45] Johnson made no such disparaging remarks about the British in his accounts of his own visit to England in 1905.[46]

As is well known, *The Autobiography of an Ex-Coloured Man* was virtually ignored until 1927, when, in response to the increasing interest in black literature created by the Harlem Renaissance, it was reissued with an introduction by Carl Van Vechten, author of the popular *Nigger Heaven*. Van Vechten, who extolled Johnson's novel as an "invaluable sourcebook for the study of Negro psychology," is usually credited as being the first white critic to promote the work among the literary establishment.[47] But, fourteen years before Van Vechten wrote his introduction, Matthews had praised the work in very much the same terms in "American Character in American Fiction," in which he reviewed the anonymously published *Autobiography* alongside Howells's *New Leaf Mills* and Robert Herrick's *One Woman's Life*.[48]

Matthews begins by announcing one of his major critical tenets: that in fiction, character rather than plot is paramount, for whereas cleverly constructed plots may entertain, complexly drawn and lifelike characters provide insights into human nature. Feigning ignorance of knowing who wrote *The*

Autobiography of an Ex-Coloured Man and that it was a novel, not an autobiography, Matthews claims that the "indisputable veracity" of the story convinces him that the author is indeed a Negro, and if the events are fictional rather than factual, they present "what is higher than actual fact, the essential truth." Revealing Taine's continuing influence on his critical views, Matthews asserts that Johnson's book "has significance for all of us who want to understand our fellow citizens of darker hue" (i.e., their "race traits"). The work, he adds, is written calmly, clearly, simply; it is composed in full accord with the principle enunciated by Taine in one of his letters: "that a writer should be a psychologist, not a painter or a musician; that he should be a transmitter of ideas and of feelings, not of sensations."

Matthews's correspondence with Johnson indicates that, in addition to the published review, he worked behind the scenes to promote the book. At Johnson's request, he sent a copy of it to his colleague Felix Adler, whom Johnson may have met while studying at Columbia. He also sent copies to two of the age's most prominent racialists—Roosevelt and Rudyard Kipling.[49] Matthews's friendship with Kipling was as warm and as deep as that with Roosevelt; indeed, it was largely on account of Matthews's influence that Roosevelt (whose initial impressions of Kipling were anything but positive) and the British writer became close friends. Kipling's response to the work, if he read it, is unknown, but it apparently did not change his Anglo-Saxon prejudice. In a later letter to Matthews, he warned that non-Anglo writers were degrading American literature.[50]

Roosevelt, however, did read the novel, though it seems to have taken some prodding from Matthews to get him to do so. Matthews sent a copy of the book to Roosevelt in 1912, when Roosevelt was, as Matthews quipped, in the "throes of Progressivism."[51] For whatever reason, Roosevelt let a year go by without giving Matthews his reaction to the novel. At

Johnson's request, Matthews wrote Roosevelt in January 1913, asking if he had read the fictionalized autobiography by the "colored man of letters": "It is not exactly fact," Matthews stated, "but it is the truth! And it lets the light into some dark and curious places."[52] When Matthews received Roosevelt's reply a few days later, he immediately sent a letter off to Johnson, quoting Roosevelt's remark that he was "much impressed" by the novel.[53]

Johnson must have been very pleased to hear that, for his letters to Matthews and to Roosevelt reveal that he keenly desired to impress the ex-president not only with his literary abilities but with the seriousness of the nation's race problems. As we have seen, in essays such as "The Negro Problem" and "The Progressives and the Colored Man" (the latter published in the same year as Johnson's novel), Roosevelt insisted that blacks must above all obey the law and assist the police in apprehending members of the "backward race" who broke it. If Johnson did not actually read Roosevelt's essays, he would almost certainly have received summaries of them through press reports, or from Booker T. Washington, Charles W. Anderson, and other close friends who served in Roosevelt's unofficial "Black Cabinet."[54] In any case, Johnson's novel, particularly the lynching episode, may be read as a dramatic refutation of the progressivist solution to the "Negro problem." Indeed, he may have had his sights on Roosevelt when he had his narrator say, in reflecting upon the torture-murder of the lynched black, that "I could understand why Negroes are led to sympathize with even their worst criminals and to protect them when possible. By all the impulses of normal human nature they can and should do nothing less. . . . Whenever I hear protests from the South that it should be left alone to deal with the Negro question, my thoughts go back to that scene of brutality and savagery" (188).

Unfortunately, the novel's images of white savagery

failed to alter Roosevelt's schizophrenic attitude toward the "Negro problem"; the letter in which he claimed to be "much impressed" by *The Autobiography* was the very one in which he made his aforementioned remark that racial conflict was not "between right and wrong, but between two rights."[55] Any satisfaction Johnson may have derived from Roosevelt's praise of the novel would certainly have been offset by those words, which Matthews chose not to transmit to Johnson.

Matthews worked equally hard, and somewhat more efficaciously, to promote Johnson's poetry. Shortly after *The Autobiography of an Ex-Coloured Man* was published, Johnson wrote "Fifty Years," a poem commemorating the fiftieth anniversary of the signing of the Emancipation Proclamation. Celebrating African Americans' strength of character and emphasizing their contributions to the building of the nation, the poem is Johnson's proclamation that the sons and daughters of slaves are entirely *American*, and proud to be so:

> This land is ours by right of birth,
> This land is ours by right of toil;
> We helped to turn its virgin earth,
> Our sweat is in its fruitful soil.
> . . . .
> And never yet—O haughty Land,
> Let us, at least, for this be praised—
> Has one black, treason-guided hand
> Ever against [the] flag been raised.

The poem also reveals Johnson's conviction—which he would later come to question—that western civilization was superior to African:

> Far, far the way that we have trod,
> From heathen kraals and jungle dens,

To freedmen, freemen, sons of God,
Americans and Citizens.[56]

Johnson urges his fellow blacks to "stand erect and without fear" in the face of their foes and to face the future with courage. Demonstrating that Nativist rhetoric was not the exclusive property of whites, he asserts that the sons and daughters of slaves have a more legitimate claim to the American heritage than "new-come foreign hordes."

Upon completing the patriotic poem, Johnson sent it to Matthews, who then submitted it for him to the *New York Times*, where it appeared (by design) on January 1, 1913, exactly fifty years after Lincoln signed the Emancipation Proclamation. On the following day the *Times* printed an editorial lauding the poem as a work of genius.[57] Matthews, furthermore, included "Fifty Years" in the copies of Johnson's novel that he sent Kipling and Roosevelt, the latter declaring the poem a "striking thing"; he also mailed the poem to his good friend Senator Elihu Root, who praised the verse for its rhythm and dignity.[58]

Several months later, Johnson sent Matthews a selection of his poems that he hoped to publish as a volume, with "Fifty Years" as the lead piece. Matthews was impressed by the poems, but he advised Johnson to rearrange their order by placing at the beginning the half-dozen verses "in which you speak for your race."[59] He also volunteered to offer the collection to his own publisher, Scribner's, where he had connections, and to write an introduction to the book if it was accepted. Despite Matthews's efforts, Scribner's declined, and the manuscript was not published until 1917 by the Boston publisher Cornhill, under the title *Fifty Years and Other Poems*. As Matthews had advised, "O Black and Unknown Bards," "The Black Mammy," and the several other poems focusing on the African-American experience form the opening section of the book.

While he was trying to find a publisher for *Fifty Years*, Johnson was back in New York speaking for his race not as a poet but as contributing editor of the *New York Age*, a position he held from 1914 to 1923. Though most readers of the *Age* were black intellectuals, it is clear that Johnson hoped to influence the opinions of white ones as well, of Brander Matthews in particular. In 1916, he sent a group of his editorials to his former drama professor, who found them "excellent"—especially in their "temper."[60] The "temper of the Afro-American mind wherever it comes to its consciousness," Howells had observed in his admiring review of Booker T. Washington's *Up from Slavery*, is "conservative."[61] If that statement implicitly denied consciousness to W. E. B. Du Bois and other black militants, it was nonetheless accurate in respect to Johnson at this point in his life, as well as to the *Age*'s publisher Fred Moore. An ally of Washington and the Tuskegee circle, Moore had informed Johnson before hiring him that he expected the new contributing editor to take a "conservative and constructive" position when addressing racial topics, and Johnson, in general, did.[62] Staunchly opposed to political radicalism of any sort, Matthews—who, like Roosevelt and Howells, supported Washington while ignoring Du Bois and the Niagarans—would have concurred wholeheartedly with Moore's editorial policy.[63]

Matthews's support of Johnson's literary endeavors, and for the conservative-but-constructive "temper" that engendered them, continued into the 1920s. When *Fifty Years and Other Poems* finally found a publisher, Matthews fulfilled his promise to write an introduction to it. The essay commends Johnson's craftsmanship and pays special tribute to the "superb and soaring" stanzas of "Fifty Years."[64] Once again Matthews acted as Johnson's conduit to Roosevelt, sending—at Johnson's urging—a copy of *Fifty Years* to him; when Roosevelt wrote to express his high opinion of the poems, Matthews shared the letter with Johnson.[65] In 1922,

Matthews included "Fifty Years" in the revised edition of his anthology *Poems of American Patriotism* (originally published in 1892) and assured Johnson that the poem would "shine out as one of the finest things in the book."[66] Though he declined Johnson's requests that he review *The Book of American Negro Poetry* (1922) and *The Book of American Negro Spirituals* (1925) because he did not feel sufficiently knowledgeable of their subject matter to do so competently, Matthews attempted to have each of the books reviewed to advantage by fellow critics.[67]

Considering that Anglo-American literary critics at the time offered little or no aid and encouragement to minority writers, Matthews's efforts on Johnson's behalf are commendable. Yet, ironically, even as he sought to include Johnson in the literary "center," Matthews marginalized him as Other. Boas's challenge to the predominant racial ideology might have moderated Matthews's sense of Anglo-Saxon superiority, but it did not dislodge his belief in inherited "race traits." From Matthews's perspective, Johnson's writings were 100 percent American—Us; but their spiritual "essence" was Negro—Them. Thus Johnson and his fellow blacks were simultaneously included in and excluded from the American melting pot. This contradiction comes across very clearly in Matthews's introduction to *Fifty Years and Other Poems*. After emphasizing a fact that Roosevelt, Giddings, and most Anglo celebrators of American consensus tended to ignore—that the nation's ten million blacks were descended not from people who came to America in search of freedom but from those whom the freedom-loving adventurers enslaved—Matthews suggests that African Americans have been completely assimilated: they have the rights and duties of all other Americans, and they know "no language, no literature and no law other than those of their fellow citizens of Anglo-Saxon ancestry." (The idea that they had no knowledge of any language or literature other than

English would have come as a surprise to many blacks, including the Spanish-speaking Johnson.) Yet, immediately after sounding the *e pluribus unum* theme, Matthews represents African Americans as *aliens*: "They," he asserts, "are not as we are," the "we" here clearly referring to Anglo Americans. Negroes, he proceeds to explain, "stand apart, more or less; they have their own distinct characteristics"; thus it behooves "us" to gain a better understanding of "what manner of people they are." Implicitly invoking Taine's theory, Matthews claims that, since the differentiating "racial characteristics" and "abiding traits" of Negroes can most easily be discovered in their art, Johnson's poems—especially those embodying the "voice of his race"—ought to be of great interest to Anglo readers.[68] In his *A Book about the Theater* (1916), published a year earlier, Matthews had voiced essentially the same argument in urging that students of American drama acquaint themselves with the history of Negro minstrelsy. This special form of theatrical art, he maintained, was worthy of serious attention not only because it was—as Johnson had argued—the only one indigenous to the United States, but also because—as Johnson would never have argued—it embodied the "special comicality of the darky." Elsewhere in the same volume, he praised the "coonful melody" of Cole's and Johnson's "Under the Bamboo Tree."[69]

There is no evidence to indicate that Johnson objected to Matthews's racialist remarks; indeed, Johnson, we recall, speaks in *Along This Way* with unqualified admiration for the professor. Like most blacks of his day, Johnson rejected the theory of white supremacy but believed in racial differences. However, though he never became a political radical, he did take a more aggressive stance against racism after becoming field secretary of the NAACP in 1916, by which time it had become evident that the "conservative and constructive" strategy practiced by Moore and other followers of

Booker T. Washington had failed not only to advance the cause of racial equality but even to stem the tide of lynchings. Obviously, Johnson's change in temper owed much to the influence of Du Bois and other militant blacks, but there was at least one white intellectual who urged Johnson to speak out more boldly against racism—H. L. Mencken. In *Along This Way*, Johnson states that Mencken's writings had made a sharper impression on him than had those of any other author (Richard Wright would later make a similar statement in his autobiography).[70] As I will detail in chapter 6, Mencken debunked Matthews, Roosevelt, and the ideology of Anglo-Saxon supremacy they represented. Suffice it to say here that when in 1915 Johnson visited the office of the *Smart Set* to introduce himself to the nation's foremost iconoclast, he entered what was to Matthews's mind the den of the enemy. (It would be interesting to know Matthews's reaction to Johnson's visit, if he was informed of it.) As his letters and diary make painfully clear, Mencken was no more free of racial prejudice than was Roosevelt. But this unpleasant truth does not negate his championing of Johnson and other African-American writers; according to Johnson, Mencken declared during their meeting that black writers "made a mistake when they indulged in pleas for justice and mercy, when they prayed indulgence for shortcomings, when they based their protests against unjust treatment on the Christian or moral or ethical code, when they argued to prove that they were as good as anybody else." Mencken instead urged Johnson and his fellow blacks to be more assertive, and to emphasize those qualities and talents in which they *outshone* the Anglo-Saxon. Johnson left Mencken's office feeling "buoyed up, exhilarated," as if he had taken a "mental cocktail."[71] Johnson never received such mental "cocktails" from Matthews, who, though a trusted friend and ally, believed that Johnson and all Others should strive to be conservative-tempered "Afro-Saxons."

As earlier mentioned, Matthews faulted Godkin for re-fusing to embrace the new "statecraft" that drove American foreign policy at the turn of the century. The imperialist ide-ology underpinning this statecraft was inextricably linked to the theory of white racial superiority, especially in Roosevelt's mind.[72] Nowhere is this more disturbingly apparent than in one of Roosevelt's letters to the English imperialist Cecil Arthur Spring-Rice. Writing in 1899 as the United States was using military force to quash the Filipino rebellion and as England was attempting to suppress revolts against its colo-nial rule, Roosevelt (governor of New York at the time) ex-pressed his hope that the two countries would work together to ensure the world supremacy of the "English-speaking race." "If only you can send enough settlers to Africa," the hero of San Juan (Kettle) Hill added, "and let some men like Kitchener deal in his own way with the Boers, if it is absolutely neces-sary, I think that the future of the African continent will lie in your hands and be under your direction. And what a splendid work this will be! It is enough to establish a race for all time" (*Letters* 2: 1052).

In general, Matthews avoided the violent rhetoric of im-perialism that Roosevelt reveled in, and he seems to have had reservations about his country's annexation of the Phil-ippines. But his published essays and private letters written during and after the Spanish-American War leave no doubt that he was at heart a territorial expansionist and that he viewed the dark-skinned victims of American imperialism as Others who, like the American Indians earlier, had to be subdued in order for the "English-speaking race" to achieve its manifest destiny.

Roosevelt summed up his "western" view of the red man with his infamous statement: "I don't go so far as to think that the only good Indians are the dead Indians, but I believe nine out of every ten are, and I shouldn't inquire too closely into the case of the tenth."[73] While he never explicitly defended the white man's slaughter of the continent's native inhabitants, Matthews shared Roosevelt's contempt for them (though his attitude toward them may have softened after reading Boas's *The Mind of Primitive Man* in 1915). In his *An Introduction to the Study of American Literature* (1896), for example, he reproves James Fenimore Cooper for failing to sufficiently dramatize the red man's "ugliest traits," especially the "ingrained barbarity and cruelty which was perhaps the chief characteristic of the Indian warrior."[74]

In his chapter on James Russell Lowell in the same book, Matthews reveals his attitude toward the Mexican War when he offers a rather curious "defense" of the Brahmin's vigorous opposition to the conflict: "Although," writes Matthews, "it is easy enough now to see that we needed the new lands we were to gain by force of arms, and that without them the proper expansion of the United States was not possible, it was hard to foresee this then" (198–99). What was obvious at the time, and what Lowell was correct in denouncing, were the base motives of the jingoes who sought to profit from the war. Matthews seems to imply here that the use of arms to ensure the "proper expansion" of the United States is morally acceptable so long as mercenary motives do not come into play.

The contradictions in Matthews's attitude toward American imperialism of the late 1890s are clearly evident in his "Americanism" (1897), an essay that drew the praise of Roosevelt.[75] Attempting to distinguish between a healthy sense of patriotism and a pernicious jingoism, Matthews emphasizes (as we earlier saw him do in a letter to James Weldon Johnson) the importance of controlling one's temper. The jingoes, he maintains at one point, may love their country, but their expressions of patriotism tend to be "too frothy, too hysteric, too unintelligent, to inspire confidence." Jingoes are also wrong, he argues, for suggesting that the United States is a perfect country, superior in every respect to all European ones, including, of course, his beloved France.

Such sentiments more closely reflected the perspective of Howells than of Roosevelt. And here we need to say a word about Matthews's relationship with the Dean of American Realism. If Roosevelt was Matthews's political idol, Howells was his literary one; in fact, Howells fulfilled the role, as I shall later demonstrate, of Matthews's literary father. Howells and Roosevelt had been on good terms during the early 1890s, but their ideological differences strained and, by the end of the decade, ruptured their friendship.[76] In an 1897 letter to Curtis Guild, Jr., Roosevelt gave his assurances that Matthews was a "trump" (a term that he reserved for his most dependable allies), but qualified his word of praise by remarking that the professor was influenced by unnamed "false gods" who did not have a proper respect for patriotism (*Letters* 1: 710).

Howells was probably one of the "gods" in question, for on no issue did he and Roosevelt disagree more strongly than on that of "true Americanism." Roosevelt, of course, approached the matter from the "western" perspective, which demanded that true patriots demonstrate what Howells contemptuously termed "muscular ideals" and support the nation's use of military force to carry out its mandate of "civilizing" the darker races. Though he hailed from the Midwest, Howells, who was an advocate of Christian socialism and pacifism, represented (in Roosevelt's eyes, at least) the "eastern" perspective, as clearly projected in his essay "The Modern American Mood." Published in July 1897, shortly before Matthews's "Americanism" appeared, Howells's essay condemned jingoism and, implicitly rebuking Rooseveltian "strenuous rhetoric," advocated the "quiet" sense of patriotism that is the sign of self-assurance. Significantly, in attempting to clarify his conception of true patriots, he reached for a religious analogy: true patriots, he explained, are like people "whose religion has become their life; it is no longer an enthusiasm, and it is certainly not a ceremonial. They do not seek for a sign; the light is in them."[77]

Upon reading "The Modern American Mood," Matthews wrote Howells to express his admiration for the piece. In his letter thanking Matthews for the complimentary remarks, Howells stated that he looked forward to reading the professor's forthcoming essay on the topic.[78] If the Dean did read "Americanism," he would undoubtedly have been pleased by its criticism of the jingoistic temper. But he would also have been repelled by other passages that reverberate with Rooseveltian "strenuous" rhetoric. Displaying the same sort of "frothy" temper that he denounces, Matthews declares that true Americanism projects a "confidence in [the country's] destiny, a buoyant hopefulness that right will surely prevail." That this cheery outlook derives from a belief in Spencerian evolution and Anglo-American racial superiority is made manifest when Matthews asserts that reforms are inevitable in the long run and that, in the struggle for existence, weak races will be "crushed" by races of "stronger fibre and of sterner stock." The essay ends by quoting Lowell's assertion that the United States is a "good country to live for, and a good country to die for" (873–74). Thus Matthews, intentionally or unintentionally, merged the Howellsian and Rooseveltian, or eastern and western, points of view on his topic, the result being an essay that is at odds with itself.

When the sinking of the *Maine* provided the sterner race with its opportunity to crush the weaker, thereby furthering the "proper expansion" of the United States into not only Cuba but the Philippines as well, Matthews continued to demonstrate his jingoistic impulses even as he condemned the jingoes. Writing his friend William P. Trent, a critic of United States imperialism, Matthews agreed that the war cry

"Remember the *Maine*" was "rubbish" and assured Trent that no one at Columbia University was "really in favor" of the conflict. But if Matthews was not for the war, neither was he against it. Like Roosevelt, who once remarked that a "just war is in the long run far better for a man's soul than a prosperous peace," Matthews saw war as an instrument for steeling the national character and for promoting cultural hegemony.[79] In a "wealth-seeking" country like the United States, he informed Trent, "it is well that the warlike virtues have a chance to show themselves now and again," adding that the conflict with Spain would have a "welding effect" on the country.[80]

Matthews's mind was similarly split on the question of what to do with the territories wrested from Spain. He claimed to be against the annexation of the Philippines, but his opposition was based more on pragmatic than on moral grounds: fearing that governing the islands would greatly increase the White (American) Man's Burden, he believed that the United States would be "better off without them."[81] "And yet—and yet—," he confided to Trent, "I am glad the decision does not lie with me." If it were his decision, he went on to say, he would "vote against any colonial expansion"—but he would do so plagued by the thought that he would live to regret his action.[82]

Not only Trent but many other of Matthews's close friends did not have such split minds on the subject: Howells, Richard Watson Gilder, and Hamlin Garland, for example, were firmly opposed to American imperialism. Yet, though they were outraged by United States aggression, especially in the Philippines, these men were restrained in their public protests at the time. Twain, who by his own admission was a "red-hot imperialist" when the war began, did not speak out publicly against American imperialism until 1901, in his powerful "To the Person Sitting in Darkness."[83] Of the academics who opposed the war with Spain and the annexation of the Philippines, none did so with more courage than Harvard's Charles Eliot Norton. One of the founders of and a frequent contributor to *The Nation*, Norton had been a committed Mugwump in earlier years, and he remained throughout his life an intimate friend of Godkin (who once told him: "You are the *Nation*").[84] Like Godkin, Norton was an Anglophile who often disparaged American culture, or rather the lack of it. Nonetheless, he remained convinced during the decades preceding the Spanish-American War that the United States would in the future fulfill its destiny as the shining city on a hill. A moral and literary idealist, he reacted with revulsion against the jingoistic clamor of the 1890s; when the shooting began in 1898, he urged his Harvard students not to volunteer for service in the "criminal war," and he publicly condemned his country's "bastard imperialism." Implicitly disputing the definition of "true Americanism" offered by those like Matthews who believed that the United States was a good country to die for, Norton insisted in "True Patriotism" (1898) that the truest patriots were those who stood against the war effort.[85]

When Roosevelt assumed the presidency in 1901, Norton hoped that the nation's new leader would terminate McKinley's "detestable policy and proceedings in the Philippines," since he believed that the Harvard alumnus was not as hard-hearted as his Rough Rider image suggested.[86] He soon changed that opinion. Deeply disappointed by Roosevelt's foreign policy and his autocratic style of governing, Norton was forced to confess that he had overestimated both Roosevelt and the American people: "The substitution of Roosevelt as an ideal in place of Washington and Lincoln," he plaintively remarked in 1904, "is not encouraging."[87] And when in the following year Harvard made plans to honor the hero of San Juan Hill, Norton refused to attend the "semicivilized festival to celebrate the good cowboy become President."[88]

Norton's opposition to the Spanish-American War and United States imperialism brought a storm of rebuke upon him, including threats of physical violence. He was psychologically crushed by the accusations that he was, as the *Los Angeles Times* put it, an "un-American ass," and his idealism turned to pessimism.[89] His detractors included not only the yellow press and war-fevered jingoes but certain academic progressivists, Brander Matthews among them.

As a former Mugwump and member of *The Nation's* "goodly company," Matthews in the 1880s had shared many of Norton's values, but the Harvard professor's Anglophilia and his revolt against the new statecraft established an inseparable gulf between the two men during the nineties. Though he refrained from publicly assaulting Norton's character, Matthews in 1896 privately charged that Norton had become an "evil influence" at Harvard; and when Norton later spoke out against the Spanish-American War, Matthews sneered that his Harvard colleague was behaving like a "hysteric old maid."[90] In 1905, after both Norton and Roosevelt had been elected to the National Academy of Arts and Letters, Matthews sent a letter to the White House offering his congratulations to Roosevelt and expressing his disgust over the president's having to share the honor with "that literary parasite" from Harvard.[91]

Whatever doubts Matthews had about American imperialism during the Spanish-American War seem to have evaporated once Roosevelt took possession of the White House. In a series of essays and addresses written during the early years of the new century and later collected under the title *The American of the Future* (1909), Matthews, who sent copies of the individual pieces to Roosevelt as they were published in the magazines, set out to defend the Square Deal President and his "bully" vision of America against the criticism of Norton, Godkin, and all others who were opposed to—or excluded from—that vision. Here again, Matthews's arguments are firmly rooted in his "progressive" theory of racial difference.

The volume's lead and title essay immediately invokes the specter of the threatening Other, for its point of departure is Thomas Bailey Aldrich's "Unguarded Gates" (1892).[92] Like Roosevelt's essay "Race Decadence," Aldrich's poem warns that the immigration gates must be closed against the swarms of "unassimilable" aliens who were pouring into and, in Aldrich's view, forever polluting the melting pot:

> Wide and unguarded stand our gates,
> And thru them presses a wild motley throng—
> Men from Volga and the Tartar steppes,
> Featureless figures of the Hoang-Ho,
>
> . . . .
>
> O Liberty, white Goddess! is it well
> To leave the gates unguarded?

The response Matthews develops to that question brings into sharp focus the tensions resulting from his and other progressivists' endorsement of two conflicting propositions: that the United States should remain the "melting pot" refuge for the world's oppressed and downtrodden, and that immigration must be restricted so as to ensure that the Goddess of Liberty would remain "white."

Matthews devotes most of his attention in "The American of the Future" to combatting the arguments of the radical Nativists, who urged that the immigration gates should be sealed not only to Asians and Africans but also to the Italians, Hebrews, and other "new immigrants." America, Matthews reminds these xenophobes, has never been racially pure; as evidence for that assertion he quotes a passage from Roosevelt's history of New York, adding that the president himself was of Dutch, Huguenot, and Scotch-Irish rather than of Anglo descent (7–8). To those who charged that the ghettos were being filled with the "scum of Europe," Matthews cites the "shrewd observer of social conditions," Jane Addams, who contended that "undeveloped" immigrants generally found it easier than their more highly specialized counterparts to form the "acquired characteristics which the new environment demands" (11). Moreover, though the census data might seem to indicate that New York was being "de-Americanized" by the swelling population of aliens, the fact is that the masses of immigrant children quickly learn the English language, salute the flag, and amuse themselves with the "traditional games of Anglo-Saxon youth" (12). Thus the evidence clearly suggests that the "fire still glows beneath the crucible and the process of fusing is as rapid and as complete to-day as ever it has been in the past" (9).

And yet—and yet—Matthews does not completely reject Aldrich's xenophobic position on immigration; he insists that Chinese (whom Roosevelt despised as a race) must be kept from contaminating the crucible. In a passage that vividly displays the racist core of his thinking on immigration, he explains that

> the "featureless figures of Hoang-Ho" are denied admission [by the Chinese Exclusion Act]; and the wisdom of this exclusion is evident, however harsh we may sometimes seem in its application. These orientals have a civilization, older than ours, hostile to ours, exclusive and repellent. They do not come here to throw their lot with us. They abhor assimilation and they have no desire to be absorbed. They mean to remain aliens; they insist upon being taken back when they are dead,—and we do well to keep them out while they are alive. (5)

In the cold tone of Social Darwinism, he goes on to argue

that the United States must also shut the doors against "the wastrel and the broken driftwood of humanity," some of whom are insane and diseased but most of whom are "mere weaklings likely soon to become dependent" (5–6). Summing up his view on the issue, he states: "We are glad still to provide a refuge for the opprest, but only when those who demand hospitality are fit to be incorporated in our body politic and only when they are willing to accept loyally the laws under which they seek shelter" (6).

Having thus defined and categorized the Others who will be excluded from the melting pot, Matthews attempts in subsequent chapters of the volume to limn the American of the future. Not surprisingly, emphasis throughout is on the "race traits" that Americans have either inherited (if they are WASPs) or acquired (if they are assimilated ethnics) from their sturdy Anglo-Saxon forebears—courage, aggressiveness, love of justice, and so on. Not surprising also, given that the essays were written with Roosevelt in mind, is their strenuous, rough-riding tone. Matthews, for example, speaks proudly of the "warlike temper, the aggressiveness, the imperialistic sentiment" that is "in our blood" (29). Though Matthews, it bears repeating, never wore a soldier's uniform (nor even, it seems, engaged in the "manly" sport of hunting), he proclaims unhesitatingly that, when the youth of America are ready to "shrink from combat, then the end will be near, and society will stagnate into a morass of moral malaria" (263). Those who are so unfortunate as to miss the opportunity of fighting in a war may nonetheless temper their souls and find an outlet for their Anglo-Saxon aggressiveness in the Darwinian environment of the capitalist marketplace. Seeking to counter the charge that commercialism was weakening the American character, Matthews declares that the man of business is less materialistic than is commonly supposed: "It is the process he enjoys, rather than the result; it is the tough tussle in the open market which gives him the keenest pleasure. . . . He girds himself for battle and fights for his own hand; he is the son and the grandson of the stalwart adventurers who came from the Old World to face the chances of the new" (31).

In "The Scream of the Spread-Eagle," an essay in which, ironically, Matthews labels as "immature" the very kind of nationalistic boasting that he engages in elsewhere in *The American of the Future*, he suggests that, if representatives of the "superior" civilizations joined together to draw up a list of the ten most desirable race traits, their opinions would probably differ on all but one—physical courage, since it is "most obviously indispensable to independent national existence" (129). Without it, he goes on to say in a passage that might have disturbed Franz Boas or James Weldon Johnson, a people would "sink swiftly to the sad condition of the lowly dwellers in the Valley of the Nile, downtrodden tillers of the scanty soil . . . ever ruled by aggressive aliens of more stalwart stocks" (134).

Matthews, however, is not about to celebrate "predatory aggression" toward the "inferior" races, since to do so would violate the high ideals upon which the United States—and the progressivist movement—was founded. As regards the recent war between the United States and Spain, he emphatically denies that his country acted dishonorably. Conveniently ignoring what the stalwart descendants of the Anglo-Saxons did to the downtrodden Filipinos, he defends the war: "We said that we were going to war for the sake of the ill-used people in the suffering island close to our shores; we said that we would not annex Cuba; we did the fighting that was needful; and then we kept our word. It is hard to see how even the most bitter of critics can discover in this anything selfish" (47).

The bitter critics of the Roosevelt administration and, more generally, of American culture are the target of another essay in *The American of the Future*, "Reform and Reformers," which Roosevelt praised as the "very best thing of the kind I have ever yet seen done."[93] Roosevelt's enthusiasm was to be expected, for Matthews, as he acknowledged in a letter to him, wrote his critique of reformers with "the memory of many things you have said" and with the "[Saturday] Evening Post crowd in plain view."[94] That newspaper was, of course, one of the leading outlets for such "muckrakers" as David Graham Phillips, whose novels, Roosevelt complained to the paper's editor George Horace Lorimer, "contain so much more falsehood than truth that they give no accurate guide for those who are really anxious to war against corruption" (Letters 5: 269). Published in the North American Review several months after Roosevelt delivered his famous "The Man with the Muck-Rake" speech, "Reform and Reformers" seeks to draw the distinction between the corruption-fighting progressivist and other types of reformers, to the advantage of the former.[95]

Asking why it is that a long and distinguished line of American writers (e.g., Lowell, Hawthorne, Emerson, Thoreau) have expressed scorn for the reformer, Matthews focuses, as he was apt to do, on the matter of temper. Zealous reformers, he contends, are often guilty of violent speech and "vulgar outbreaks of temper" (289). That accusation, of course, might be—and was—leveled against the Rough Rider whom Matthews idolized. But Roosevelt at least had a sense of humor, a trait Matthews found wanting in zealous reformers. Another fault of such reformers, argues Matthews (who, we recall, admired Aristotle and disdained Plato) is that they tend toward an airy idealism, losing touch with the hard facts. Matthews cites William Lloyd Garrison as an example. But Progressive-Era America, he suggests, has its own cranky Garrisons among the anti-imperialists and other dissident groups. Though he does not name names, he surely had in mind not only the Saturday Evening Post crowd but Norton (that "hysteric old maid") and Godkin (the Mugwump who "came to feel that a people that

Brander Matthews

would no longer listen to his advice must be on the road to ruin") when he wrote such passages as: "In time, opposition enrages [these agitated reformers]; and they begin to feel that it can be due only to the malign influence of a personal devil. They are firmly assured that he who is not with them is against them; and they are no longer in doubt that he who is against them is an enemy of mankind" (288). And when he speaks scornfully of the "self-seeking" reformer who was forever holding high the "banner of the Ideal," Matthews echoes a contemptuous remark he once made about his colleague (and Norton's former student) George Woodberry: "The idealism [he] preached is sickening to anyone who knows—as I do—how petty are his own standards of conduct, how mean he is, how self-seeking."[96]

In contrast to the "mob" of ill-tempered, impractical, and hypocritical reformers stand the "better class of politicians" and "public-spirited" citizens who go about their business with a "stalwart disinterestedness." Though they are guided by high ideals, they act pragmatically to achieve their objectives. They exemplify, in short, the "practical idealism" that was the hallmark of Rooseveltian progressivism. From the present perspective, they also exemplify the ideological conservatism that underpinned the progressive movement: Matthews's practical idealists put more faith in Spencerian evolution than in revolution, and while they recognize that American society is not perfect, they satisfy Emerson's admiration for the "'strong and worthy persons who support the social order without hesitation or misgiving'" (292–93).

Aware, perhaps, that his analysis thus far in the essay has fallen somewhat short of the ideal of Arnoldean disinterestedness, Matthews makes an effort in the closing paragraphs to say something positive about the reformers he has verbally lashed, but even here his remarks are condescending: eccentrics and cranks, he suggests, often are sincere in heart; and though their actions may be misguided, the zeal and energy with which they promote their particular causes help to keep the public's attention focused on social problems that might otherwise be ignored. Thus do the "long-haired men and the short-haired women" do their part in keeping the "clock of progress" ticking (305).

Intentionally or unintentionally, Matthews alluded to *The Bostonians* (1886) when he referred to "long-haired men and short-haired women"; James employs that very phrase in his satire of reformers, particularly of the feminist variety.[97] Matthews no doubt found much to admire in the "manly" character of Basil Ransom and in the novel's patriarchal response to the Woman Question. On that question, Matthews's perspective was, as usual, in essential agreement with Roosevelt's.

Roosevelt was as deeply interested in the Woman Question as in the Negro one. His undergraduate thesis at Harvard was titled "Practicability of Equalizing Men and Women Before the Law" (1880), and he later wrote several essays on the rights and responsibilities of women.[98] Roosevelt's response to the woman "problem" was inextricably linked in his mind to that of "race decadence" because he feared that the decline in the birth rate among women of Anglo-Saxon stock would inevitably lead to the numerical superiority of the "inferior" races. Though he often declared, as he did in "Women's Rights; and the Duties of Both Men and Women" (1912), that he emphatically supported "woman's full equality with man," he was much more energetic about informing women of their duties than of their rights, and he never abandoned his conviction that a woman's place was in the home. The following passage, from "Women in Science" (1910), capsules Roosevelt's "progressive" reaction to the women's movement:

Advocates [of women's rights] who demand that woman shall cease doing her primary duty as wife and mother, as the bearer and rearer of children, are not only foolish but wicked. They stand on an exact level with the criminal demagogue who in the name of democracy and of the rights of labor preaches murder and demands for mankind freedom from the stern law which insists that the race can rise only through the individuals who do not shirk hard work or slip back from the laws of morality. (*Works* 12: 209)

The professor who chastised the anti-imperialists and other reformers for their "vulgar outbreaks of temper" never assailed the opposite sex with this kind of verbal violence. Moreover, while many of his contemporary Victorian men of letters either ignored or slighted fiction by women, Matthews celebrated the achievement of women writers in his "Of Women's Novels" (1892). The essay's central thesis is that women novelists of the late nineteenth century were, as their sisters in the fields of music and acting had already done, putting themselves on equal footing with their male counterparts. Matthews supports this argument not only by citing the achievements of such major English and American women novelists as Jane Austen, Charlotte Brontë, George Eliot, and Harriet Beecher Stowe (who was considered a major talent by many of Matthews's fellow men of letters) but by urging that critics (re)discover the merits of such talented but ignored women writers as Margaret Oliphant, Margaret Deland, Mrs. Burton Harrison, Susanna Rowson, Catharine Maria Sedgwick, and Rose Terry Cooke. Referring to Henry James's remark (in an essay on George Sand) that the English novel was almost totally devoid of passion, Matthews suggests that, if the American novel is ever to explore candidly the sexual passions, women rather than men will be the pioneers: "Women are more willing than men to suggest the animal nature that sheathes our immortal souls; they are bolder in the use of the stronger emotions; they are more willing to suggest the possibilities of passion lurking all unsuspected beneath the placidity of modern fine-lady existence."[99] That passage demonstrates, perhaps more vividly than any other, why Matthews cannot be pigeonholed as a priggish genteel.

"Of Women's Novels" may have convinced none other than Charlotte Perkins Gilman that Matthews was an ally of the women's movement. Shortly after the essay appeared, America's leading feminist sent a nine-page letter to Matthews, in which she accused Ambrose Bierce of making "unmanly" and slanderous verbal attacks on defenseless women writers and sought Matthews's assistance in bringing the "scurrilous" Bierce before a tribunal of his peers for trial and punishment. Though Gilman's letter did not allude to "Of Women's Novels," it is clear that she was familiar with and respected Matthews's literary criticism, and that she believed she was appealing to one who would be sympathetic to her complaint.[100]

Though he closes "Of Women's Novels" by predicting that women will one day take their rightful place alongside men in the mastery of all the arts, Matthews had doubts about the capacity of women to equal men in producing powerful drama. More than two decades after celebrating the achievements of women novelists, he addressed, in "Women Dramatists" (1915), the question of why the field of drama had been, and still was, dominated by male playwrights. Since women novelists and actors had demonstrated that they could overcome any barriers that male prejudice placed in their way, sex discrimination was not to him a plausible explanation. There were, he argued, two reasons why the nineteenth century had failed to produce any female playwrights who could rival the novelistic achievements of a Jane Austen or George Eliot: ignorance of life experience and deficiency "in the faculty of construction." Their life experience restricted almost entirely to that of the domestic sphere—the setting of most women's novels—women lacked the wide and deep knowledge of life that is reflected in the great works by the Greek tragedians, Shakespeare, and Molière. This handicap, however, will be removed once "the feminist movement shall achieve its ultimate victory." The second deficiency, however, Matthews attributes to gender difference. He argues that, whereas a novel may succeed in spite of its sprawling plot structure (as works such as *Tristram Shandy*, *The Pickwick Papers*, and *Huckleberry Finn* exemplify), a loosely constructed play is doomed to fail because the drama, like its "sister art of architecture," depends upon a tight, well-proportioned plot line. And women, he goes on to say, seem to be the inferiors of men in this constructive skill; at least, they have "not yet revealed themselves as architects, altho they have won a warm welcome as decorators—a subordinate art for which they are fitted by their superior delicacy and by their keener interest in details."[101]

That sexist remark aside, Matthews in this essay as in "Of Women's Novels" projects the image of the open-minded supporter of the feminist movement. His behind-the-scenes actions, however, tell another story, one that would have greatly disappointed Gilman. Matthews in fact vigorously resisted the efforts of women to gain not only their ultimate victory but even to achieve such modest ones as equal access to Columbia literature courses and equal opportunity to be elected to the patriarchal halls of the National Institute/Academy of Arts and Letters.

Though Columbia's English Department voted in 1903 to open all its course offerings to women, Matthews refused to allow members of the "delicate" sex into his classrooms until 1906, and only then because he was forced to do so by mandate of the Faculty of Philosophy. Matthews sought exemption from the faculty's policy on the grounds that the presence of women in his classes would inhibit men from engaging in frank discussion about such topics as sexual ethics. (Women students would also, one imagines, inhibit the professor from engaging in such antics as referring to *Godey's Lady's Book* as *"Ugly Ladies" Book*, as he did in a letter to Roosevelt.)[102] As a compromise measure, Matthews asked permission to offer a series of lectures on the principles of the drama, for women only. When that proposal was rejected, he won approval to divide his drama course into two sections—one for men and one for women.[103] Discussion of sexual ethics was, one assumes, out of bounds in the women's class.

As we saw in the previous chapter, Matthews was an active member of the National Institute of Arts and Letters and its offshoot, the Academy of Arts and Letters, both of which, he believed, were essential instruments for establishing New York as the nation's literary "center." They could also, Matthews recognized, serve *political* purposes by privileging certain writers and artists over others: in response to a query from the White House regarding President Roosevelt's membership in the institute, Matthews remarked that in the future the organization might be able to "wield an influence on the right side."[104]

The institute and academy were indeed ideologically to the right: the early roster of members was composed almost entirely of elderly eastern WASPs who threw themselves into the task of defending the gates of "culture" against all Others.[105] Through its closed system of nomination and election (and veto), the institute/academy could ensure that its membership would remain exclusive. Among the many prominent figures Matthews nominated or supported for membership were Hamlin Garland, whose western fiction was much admired by Roosevelt; Harvard professor Irving Babbitt, chief of the New Humanists and defender of the Great Tradition literary canon; and Franklin H. Giddings, who was, as noted earlier, a firm believer in Anglo-Saxon supremacy and in American imperialism.[106] Yet Matthews apparently never recommended James Weldon Johnson for membership, despite his high regard for Johnson's musical and literary achievements. (No black, in fact, was admitted to the institute/academy until 1944, when Du Bois was elected.) Nor did he ever, it seems, nominate or support the nomination of a woman; in fact, as we shall see in chapter 6, during his presidency of the institute, Matthews sided with the "literary fellows" who wanted to bar women from entering the organization.

Thus, though Matthews embraced in theory the twin ideals of Arnoldean disinterestedness and progressive democracy, in practice he was ever ready to engage in literary politics on behalf of the "right," or Rooseveltian, side. While he deserves credit for his championing of James Weldon Johnson and his praise of women novelists, Matthews's behind-the-scenes maneuverings generally aimed to exclude women and other Others from the academic and literary "center," thereby reinforcing the hegemonic grip of white, well-to-do, "progressive-minded" males like himself.

3   "Fighting in the Open" for Howells, Twain, and Literary Realism

Embracing the cause of literary realism, writes Warner Berthoff in *The Ferment of Realism*, "was much like joining an insurgent campaign in American politics."[1] The political analogy is apt, for literary realism was closely associated with the insurgent campaigns of the Mugwumps and other progressive-minded reformers who belonged to the "party of the centre" during the latter decades of the nineteenth century. If social and political progress was to occur, the public had to have its eyes opened to the corruption emanating from Tammany Hall, the squalid conditions in which tenement dwellers lived, the chicanery of Wall Street tycoons, and so on. Like Jacob Riis, Lincoln Steffens, and other progressivist journalists, many of the foremost American novelists of the Age of Realism—Howells, Twain, Garland, Harold Frederic (who once described himself as the "original mugwump")—were united not by any coherent political program but rather by the desire to expose the unpleasant facts obscured by the glitter of the Gilded Age.[2] Thus it is not surprising that Matthews stood with the realists during the "Realism War" that raged in the United States during the 1880s and 1890s. Yet, on the issue of literary realism as on those of the "Negro Problem" and "Woman Question," Matthews's mind was in conflict with itself. On the one hand, he subscribed to the realist-progressivist credo that unvarnished portraits of life could spur social progress by illuminating "how the other half lives"; on the other, he remained an adherent of the Victorian conviction that works of literature must project a "wholesome" vision of life overall, must "cheer" as well as enlighten.[3] The tension arising from these contradictory views marks virtually all of Matthews's discourses on literary realism.

Matthews's affinity with the realist movement is evident

as early as 1880. In the concluding chapter of *Theatres of Paris*, for example, he defends French drama against the charge that it is "decadent." Quoting Alexandre Dumas's remark that he knew no immoral plays, only ill-made ones, Matthews contends that French drama draws its power from its frank and "virile" treatment of contemporary life. A French drama, he asserts, "may discuss a deep social problem; it is not spoon-meat for babes, and a French theater is no place for young ladies' boarding-schools."[4] In *French Dramatists of the 19th Century*, Matthews devotes an entire chapter (11) to assessing the realist movement in French drama. By mid-century, he states, there was in France a sharp reaction against the "violence of the melodramatists" and against the "childishness of the machine-made plays": "Fact began to take the place of fantasy. Dramatists invented less, and observed more. A photograph of modern life was offered in place of a pretentious historical painting, the maker of which had relied on his fancy for all the details." In short, "Romanticism was followed by Realism," with dramatists seeking to "give an exact transcript of life as [they] saw it around [them], to do for the stage what Balzac was doing in prose fiction." The realist revolt was, Matthews contends, all for the good; but by the end of the third quarter it had spent itself. The "coming power," he correctly predicts, would be Naturalism, with M. Zola as its "prophet."[5]

As Matthews emphasizes, Zola had an "unsavory reputation" in the United States during (and beyond) the 1880s; and no one despised him or the literary movement he represented more than did Roosevelt. Though he is usually associated with the neoromantic revolt against the realist novel in the 1890s, Roosevelt in fact considered himself a realist in literature as well as in politics. In his essay "Dante and the Bowery" (1911), for example, he praises Dante for being "quite simply a realist" because he drew on the everyday life around him, low as well as high, in constructing the *Divine*

Comedy. In the same essay he chides American poets for not following the lead of Walt Whitman (a poet whose art "is not equal to his power") in giving poetic expression to the teeming life of the Bowery, one of the "great highways of humanity."[6] This endorsement, however reserved, of Whitman's poetry is remarkable, considering that the American poet's reputation was at the time hardly more savory to his countrymen than was Zola's.

"Dante and the Bowery" may have been influenced by Frank Norris's well-known essay "A Plea for Romantic Fiction" (1901), in which Norris had urged fellow writers to venture into the squalid tenements of East Harlem and explore the "black, unsearched penetralia of the soul of man."[7] But to Roosevelt's Victorian mind, such searching must eventually reemerge from the underworld into the sunlit realm, as "Song of Myself" does, lest it result in nothing more than sordid "muckraking." And to Roosevelt, Zola and all other naturalists were mere muckrakers. Attempting to convince Wister (who, it is sometimes forgotten, began his writing career under the tutelage of Howells and always viewed his fictions as being truthful portraits of life) to remove a graphic description of violence from his story "Balaam and Pedro" (1894), Roosevelt argued: "I'm perfectly aware . . . that Zola has many admirers because he says things out loud that great writers from Greece down to the present have mostly passed over in silence. I think that *conscientious descriptions of the unspeakable* do not constitute an interpretation of life, but merely disgust all readers not afflicted with the hysteria of bad taste. There's nothing masculine in being revolting" (emphasis Roosevelt's).[8] And in a letter to Upton Sinclair, Roosevelt insisted that "the net result of Zola's writings has been evil. Where one man has gained from them a shuddering horror at existing wrong which has impelled him to try to right that wrong, a hundred have simply had the lascivious, the beast side of their natures strengthened and intensified by them." Roosevelt goes on to say that, while "radical" action is often necessary in the fight against "selfish greed on the part of the capitalist," a quarter century's experience in politics has led him to distrust those of a "hysterical temper."[9]

Illustrating once again why he defies the label of genteel, Matthews defended Zola's works against the charge that they were artless and morally pernicious. In *These Many Years* he remarks that he became an admirer of Zola's fiction in the 1870s, and that he and coauthor H. C. Bunner in 1879 sent the controversial French writer one of their short stories with a letter (written in French) expressing their support of the idea that fiction writers should draw on "human documents." Unable to read English, Zola never read their story, but he was stirred sufficiently by their letter to reply that he was "touched by the sympathy which you have kindly testified to me; and I am very happy to learn that my ideas—which are in fact only the ideas of every intelligent man of my age—are finding an echo in America."[10] Matthews engaged in more substantial efforts to promote Zola's fiction in the decades that followed. In *French Dramatists* as well as in several essays published in the 1890s,[11] he argues that there is no disputing the fact that the Frenchman is a novelist of the "most extraordinary fecundity and force," adding that the reader who fails (as Roosevelt did) to appreciate the strength and complex art of his fiction must be "feeble in perception." Zola's novels and plays, he states, may not be suitable for "clean-minded American women," but they are decidedly *not* obscene: although Zola's fictions are "indecent," they are no more immoral than a "clinic or a dissection is immoral." Nor are Zola's creative works, Matthews correctly observes, the "objective" representations of life that Zola calls for in critical essays such as "Naturalism in the Theatre." Like Henry James, Matthews knew that the verbal "reproduction of nature is neither possible nor desirable" and that "convention is the foundation of every art." However sincerely Zola propounded his theory that the artist must examine life with scientific detachment and avoid all artifice when recording his observations in his fictions, he was "an artist in spite of himself," creating harmoniously *structured* works from the welter of experience, works that are symbolic *interpretations* not duplications of "reality." As late as 1901, in his seminal work *The Philosophy of the Short-story*, we find Matthews expressing his chagrin that American readers are too repulsed by the "dirt" in Zola's novels to detect the "real beauty and firm strength" at their heart.[12]

Yet, despite such sympathetic criticism of Zola's work, Matthews essentially concurred with Roosevelt's charge that the French novelist and his fellow naturalists were too illtempered to produce fictions that capture the marvelous diversity and complexity of life. The "gloomy" Zola, he contends, is preoccupied with the "unclean, sordid, and despicable" facts of life; unable to see the good in man, he could produce only repulsive characters. Zola's attempt to arouse his readers' emotions against poverty and social injustice is laudable, but his zeal for social reform has robbed him of his sense of humor and has imbued his fiction with a "chill and lifeless" tone at times. (Speaking on the topic of humor in a different essay, Matthews states that one can hardly have enough good humor, "although an ardent reformer might find that an excess of it chilled the heart of his resolution.")[13] In the chapter added to the 1891 edition of *French Dramatists*, Matthews accuses the Zola-led naturalists of being not only zealous but arrogant: "The Naturalists, like all reformers, are inclined to be intolerant. They are prone to claim all virtue for their own party."[14] What is needed, he continues, is a mode of literature that stands midway between the "extreme Naturalists . . . on the one end, and the extreme Idealists at the other,—and, as usual, safety is in the centre" (302). Matthews seems unaware that his endorsement of "centered" realism—or what William James termed "meliorism"—was as ideological as Zola's theory of naturalism, only more conservatively so.[15] As we saw in the previous chapter, Matthews was himself wont to claim all virtue for Roosevelt and the "party" of progressivists who excluded blacks, women, and ethnic immigrants from the center of power.

Usually existing as a subtext in his essays criticizing naturalism or defending realism, Matthews's political values often push to the surface, as for example in an essay on Charles Dudley Warner in *Aspects of Fiction* (1896). After remarking that Warner's *Golden House*, especially its portrait of the money-obsessed millionaire, forces the reader to recognize the "strangely inadequate and startlingly imperfect" character of the American social structure, Matthews explicitly links literary realism and progressivism, and opposes both to radicalism: "Perhaps nothing is more harmful today," he maintains, "than the frequent denunciations of the existing order of things with the obvious inference that a society so deformed [by the inequities resulting from the capitalist system] needs to be rooted up and cleared away and made over. What ought to be clear to us is that, with all the defects of the social organization in our time, this organization is less defective than it ever was before; that there has been steady progress in the world from generation to generation; that there has never been a century in which the average man has not been better off than he was in the previous century." It is our duty, he continues, "to do all that in us lies to help forward this progress; and . . . nothing tends to retard this improvement more than violent and inflammatory declamation." Novels of social realism like Warner's, therefore, are valuable because they impel the reader to wish to "reorganize" rather than "destroy" society.[16]

The progressivist ideology underpinning Matthews's

advocacy of literary realism is equally evident in another essay in *Aspects*, "Two Studies of the South."[17] The two studies in question are Thomas Nelson Page's *The Old South* (1892) and William P. Trent's biography of William Gilmore Simms. Matthews's essay emphasizes the important contribution each book, especially Trent's, makes to the debate over why the literature produced by the New South should be superior to that of the Old South. Literature professor at the University of the South at Sewanee and editor of the *Sewanee Review* (which he helped found), Trent was viewed by the New Orleans–born Matthews as well as by Roosevelt as exemplifying the New Southerner who "has his face set resolutely towards the future." Trent needed such resolution; his assertion in *William Gilmore Simms* that slavery rather than states' rights was the primary cause of the Civil War incurred the wrath of apologists for the peculiar institution.

Matthews supports Trent's and Page's opinion that the inferior quality of antebellum southern literature was due primarily to the pernicious institution of slavery, which shackled white imaginations as well as black bodies. Slavery, Matthews argues (following Trent), was supported by and in turn helped to perpetuate the feudal character of southern culture; and in their efforts to keep alive feudal values, southern writers, instead of exploring their own ground, looked to English literature—to the Waverley novels in particular—thereby developing a "colonial dependence" on Great Britain at the very time that the northern states were nurturing their own writers. At this juncture, Matthews quotes Twain's well-known diatribe against Scott, whom Twain accused of checking the wave of "progressive ideas and progressive works" and reviving the "jejune romanticism of an absurd past that is dead." In the closing passage of his essay, Matthews states that the abolition of slavery freed southern writers to "speak the truth, with an eye to nature," the departure of feudal ideals allowing them to see that "life as it is—the every-day existence of the plain people—is the stuff of which literature is made." The suggestion here and in other of Matthews's essays that the literary realists were on the side of morality and progress, while the literary idealists were in the devil's camp, prompted the poet George Cabot Lodge to ask sarcastically: "And indeed what is this realism, this literature of the intelligent and virtuous? How does it differ from the Imaginative, primitive literature which according to Mr. Matthews is responsible for every crime from the Spanish Inquisition to the Civil War?"[18]

To begin to answer that pointed question—which Matthews never directly addresses—we must return to the influence of Hippolyte Taine, whose writings formed, according to Everett Carter, the "basis of conscious American realism."[19] They certainly formed the basis of Matthews's, for his judgments of what were "realistic" fictions were largely determined by the Tainean notion that serious writers project the distinctive traits of their race, moment, and milieu. We see this very clearly, for example, in such essays as "The Study of Fiction." Written for presentation to an audience of English teachers during the Spanish-American War, the essay defines "serious fiction" as "Realistic fiction, the fiction in which the author has tried to tell the truth about life as he sees it."[20] Since such fiction inevitably reveals the "race traits" of a nation, Matthews urges teachers of literature to analyze in their classes "the accuracy with which race-characteristics are recorded in the fiction of a language—how, for example, the energy and the humor of the Anglo-Saxon stock dominates the novels of the English language" (84), while such Spanish "race traits" as "empty honor, careless cruelty, and administrative corruption" are inscribed in Spanish novels. Matthews goes so far as to claim that anyone who had uncovered the racial characteristics projected in the fictions of Howells, Garland, Wister, and other serious/realist American writers of the day "might have made a pretty good guess at the way [the Spanish-American War] . . . would bring out the energy of the race, the tenacity, the resolution, the ingenuity—and even the good-humored and easy-going toleration which is perhaps our chief defect as a people" (99–100)!

Exactly *how* one uncovers and then gauges the accuracy of "race traits" embedded in fictional texts, Matthews does not say. As suggested by his statement above that realist writers *try* to tell the truth about life as *they see it*, Matthews did not naively accept the theory of mimesis which claimed that "objective" writers could reproduce "reality." Matthews did not seem to doubt that "reality" (including "race traits") was "out there," but he was astute enough to realize that no writer, not even the most scholarly historian, could reproduce it. Indeed, many of his remarks on writing and interpreting texts have a poststructuralist ring to them. For example, he anticipates the theory of intertextuality when he insists that writers' visions of history and reality are as influenced by the texts they have read as by personal experience, and that the critic can never make a completely independent analysis of a well-known text since "he can read only through the spectacles of the countless critics who have preceded him . . . and this makes it impossible for him to think for himself." Furthermore, he insisted, as today's New Historicists do, that all historical studies are reconstructions, not reproductions, of the past, and that we can get closer to historical *truth* by reading literary works of art rather than histories.[21] (Recall Taine's declaration that a great work of art can provide more historical understanding than a "heap of historians with their histories.")

There is clearly a fissure in Matthews's argument that one should search realist works for national "race traits." How can any reader—especially an English teacher whose analysis of a canonized work is inevitably constrained by the critical commentary he or she has read—test the "fulness and accuracy" with which age-old race-characteristics are inscribed in fiction if the enduring traits of a race are, as Matthews maintains, revealed most clearly in *texts*? Put another way, Matthews seems to be saying that to be considered a "serious" or "Realistic" work of art, a text must accurately record national "race traits"; and to determine which "race traits" are the "true" ones, we must study Realist literature. It does not take an expert logician to see that we have a circular argument here.

During the latter decades of the nineteenth century and the opening one of the twentieth, Matthews commended the fiction of many of his contemporary American writers who in his view offered true pictures of American life, including Garland, Wister, Mary Wilkins Freeman, and John W. De Forest.[22] The two realist writers he championed most often and vigorously, however, were Howells and Twain.

Recollecting his experiences as a member of the Saturday Club, Bliss Perry, after suggesting that Howells was never as happy in New York City as in Brahmin Cambridge, reports that the Dean complained to him in the 1890s: "No one ever drops in any more to talk about books, no one except once in a while Brander Matthews."[23] Perry continues his reminiscence without another word about Howells's book-loving visitor. Matthews in fact frequently appears on the scene in biographical and critical studies of Howells only to disappear, as in Perry's essay, almost as soon as he arrives, most scholars apparently considering his literary relationship with Howells too insignificant to merit much attention.[24] Yet that relationship, though obscured by the shadows of Twain, Henry James, Crane, Norris, and other prominent writers who occupied privileged positions in Howells's life, spanned four decades, and there can be no doubt that the Dean considered him one of the realist movement's sturdiest allies as well as a trusted friend. Howells, in turn, supported Matthews's literary activities by favorably reviewing his books, citing him in essays, and praising him—often in the most enthusiastic terms—in personal correspondence. Oddly enough, the two men held sharply divergent views on certain social and political issues. Indeed, one of the more intriguing aspects of their relationship is that, while he was defending Howells at the turn of the century against those who questioned both his literary doctrines and his patriotism, Matthews was, as we have seen, an ardent supporter of Roosevelt, the living symbol of the imperialistic ideology that Howells deplored.

Though Howells and Matthews did not meet in person until the early 1890s, after the Dean had taken up residence in New York City, their literary relationship had begun some fifteen years earlier, when Matthews was a fledgling drama critic. Howells had a lifelong passion for the theater; he was one of the leading drama critics in American during the late nineteenth century and author of some three dozen plays. And though his desire to achieve the same success as a playwright that he enjoyed as a novelist brought frustration and disappointment, he nonetheless remained, as he put it to Henry James, irresistibly attracted to the tormenting "blue fire of the theatre."[25]

Matthews's first published comments on Howells fanned that flame. In an unsigned review of *The Parlor Car* in *The Nation* (31 Aug. 1876, 136), twenty-four-year-old Brander expressed high praise for Howells's "bright little play," which, like the Dean's novels, struck "just the light-comedy key." (Howells's darker vision, of course, had not yet fully manifested itself in his fiction, but even after it did, Matthews preferred to emphasize the more "smiling aspects" of the Dean's writings.) Matthews continued and heightened his praise of Howells the playwright a year later in a review of the elder writer's comedy *Out of the Question* (*The Library Table*, 13 Sept. 1877, 174–75).

In his autobiography, Matthews remarks that it took him years to have an essay accepted for publication in Howells's *Atlantic*; but Howells's rejection letters apparently did not discourage the young New Yorker from fully committing himself as an ally to Howells and the realists during the late 1880s, after the publication of *The Rise of Silas Lapham*—which impressed Matthews with its "miraculous veracity"—drew the furor of Howells's adversaries.[26] By 1889, Hamlin Garland, who came to respect Matthews as much as he did Howells, was writing Matthews to praise his essay "The Dramatic Outlook in America" (*Harper's Magazine*, May 1889, 924–30) and to enlist his support in the campaign for literary realism.[27]

"The Dramatic Outlook in America" caught the attention of Howells as well as of Garland, and in fact it was the first of Matthews's writings to earn the Dean's public praise. The essay's central thesis is that, although the drama had been on the decline for a century and a half, it was showing signs of a revival. Put simply, Matthews attributes the decline to the pernicious influence of romanticism, and the revival to the healthy influence of realism. Great playwrights such as Shakespeare and Molière, he observes, have always attempted to reflect the life of their times. (Matthews would later stress the "realism" of Shakespeare and Molière in his books on each playwright.) In the early nineteenth century, however, the success of Scott's Waverley novels and of technically sophisticated but artificial French drama drove realism and therefore the life out of the theater in England and in the United States. But "the French dramatists of to-day are conscious of the realistic movement which dominates the fiction of France, of Russia, and of America. The younger playwrights especially are aware of the increasing public appreciation of the more exact presentation of the facts of life" (927). The more accurately a French play reflects French life, the less adaptable it will be to the English or American stage; thus, as "Realism, and its younger brother, Natural-ism, gain in power in Paris, fewer and fewer French plays will be fit for the American market" (928), and, consequently, the demand for native drama will increase.

Needless to say, Howells, who disdained the French-style "well-made play" and who encouraged the efforts of Edward Harrigan, James A. Herne, and other playwrights to inject re-alistic content and technique into American drama of the day, welcomed Matthews's views. "Mr. Matthews," Howells wrote in his July 1889 "Editor's Study," "is one of the very few people among us authorized by knowledge and experience to treat of a matter so many are willing to handle without either. His wide acquaintance with dramatic literature affords him the right critical perspective, and his ventures as a playwright enable him to conceive of the subject from the theatrical point of view, and to represent those claims of the stage which literary men are sometimes disposed to contemn."[28]

Matthews's review of *Criticism and Fiction* two years later left no doubt that he approached literature with what Howells considered to be the "right critical perspective."[29] As in virtu-ally all his defenses of Howells, Matthews's strategy is to dis-arm the opposition by insisting that the Dean's controversial views evolve from rather than revolt against traditional liter-ary theory. Matthews concedes at the outset that Howells tends to be combative in propounding his ideas, so much so that it at times seems as if he "longed to see all mankind wearing one coat that he might tread on the tail of it." But he then argues that, though good critics should, as a rule, avoid being po-lemical, Howells's militant posture in *Criticism and Fiction* is justifiable, for it is a counterattack against the assaults of sneering British critics and "colonial-minded" American ones. What Howells demands, Matthews emphasizes, is nothing more than truth in fiction. Even when Howells is wrong (as, for example, in his failure to fully appreciate the art of Thackeray), Matthews contends, his thoughtfully ex-pressed critical opinions are ever stimulating and force his adversaries to analyze more carefully their own views. Howells, Matthews asserts, has thus raised the level of critical discussion and done a great service to literature.

And, as Howells recognized, Matthews had done him a great service. His personal letter of appreciation to Matthews reveals the high esteem in which he had come to hold this young friend of the realists. "I have sometime had it in mind and heart to tell you what very fine work I thought you were doing in criticism for the *Cosmopolitan*," he opens, adding that the remark is sincere and not merely an attempt to repay a compliment. He goes on to say:

> I told Mr. [Henry] Alden, the last time I saw him . . .
> what I tell you now: that your work is better than that
> of any other critic of your generation among us. I had
> to make exception of your elders of course [such as
> Henry James]. I like your fighting in the open; I like
> your spirit, and I like your manner.[30]

During the two decades following his review of *Criticism and Fiction*, a period during which realism began to wane under the persistent counterattacks of the neoromanticists, Matthews continued to fight in the open for literature that would reflect the life and character (i.e., "race traits") of his contemporary America, and often received Howells's praise and appreciation for doing so. In, for example, "Text-Books of Fiction" (1896), an essay that promoted scholarly study of the modern novel at a time when the great majority of Matthews's academic colleagues held that genre in contempt, he declares that literary historians ought to trace

> the successive steps of the story-tellers who narrated
> at the first things quite Impossible; and then things
> only Improbable—in which stage the romanticists still
> linger even in this last decade of the nineteenth

century, when riper artists have already tried to pass from the description of the merely Probable to a depiction of the absolutely Inevitable.[31]

That "riper artists" refers to Howells and his fellow American realists is suggested earlier in the same essay when Matthews castigates the "colonial-minded" American professor William Edward Simonds for completely ignoring, in his survey of contemporary fiction, "the extraordinary skill with which almost every locality in the United States has been translated into literature. Nowhere does he praise the vigor with which American character has been presented by the best of our later writers of fiction" (227).

As we saw in the previous chapter, when war broke out with Spain in 1898, Matthews, though he condemned "frothy" jingoism and had mixed feelings regarding the annexation of the Philippines, was ideologically much closer to Roosevelt and the imperialists than to Howells and the anti-imperialists, whose ranks included that "hysteric old maid" Charles Eliot Norton. Yet, the political differences separating Howells and Matthews during the closing years of the century did not seem to strain their friendship and certainly did not alter Matthews's opinion that the Dean was a consummate craftsman. In 1894 Roosevelt wrote Matthews that Howells's fiction had begun to project a "jaundiced view of life"; such "morbidity," he further stated, was characteristic of the "reform spirit."[32] The Rough Rider probably had in mind *A Hazard of New Fortunes*, perhaps Howells's darkest fiction and one that clearly reflects the Christian Socialism he subscribed to at that time. Matthews, however, had a quite different reaction to *Hazard*: in an 1898 letter to Trent, he praised it as the "real thing," adding that he wished he could write half as well as Howells. In the same year, Howells thanked Matthews for praising a new novel of his (*The Story of a Play* apparently): "You make it worth one's while to do one's best," Howells wrote, adding "I would be willing to write a far more popular novel than mine will be for such advice as yours."[33]

Even as he was idolizing Roosevelt as war hero and president, Matthews was defending Howells and his realism credo as vigorously as ever. In, for example, "Romance against Romanticism" (an article that anticipates Louis J. Budd's "W. D. Howells's Defense of the Romance" by more than half a century), Matthews sought to exonerate Howells of the unjust charge that he was inimical to any work of literature that failed his test of realism.[34] Those who have accused Howells of being hostile to romance, Matthews argues, have failed to see that "it is only barren Romanticism he detests and despises" and that he "has more than once gladly recorded his delight in true Romance" (38), such as that created by Hawthorne and Stevenson. Howells might have cringed somewhat at Matthews's more "strenuous" remarks—his assertion, for example, that the heroes of the age-honored romances are "brave boys, all of them, hearty and honest and sturdy" (44)—but he must have appreciated the piece overall.

The Dean had even more reason to be pleased with Matthews's "Mr. Howells as a Critic," an essay that will be familiar to many students of Howells.[35] Gathering together arguments formulated in his earlier praises of Howells, Matthews constructs his most persuasive case for the Dean and the literary realism for which he stood. After declaring Howells the most multifarious of all American writers at the opening of the twentieth century, Matthews argues, as he had done in his 1891 review of *Criticism and Fiction,* that the controversy aroused by that book and other of Howells's earlier writings stemmed more from the often aggressive manner in which the Dean presented his views than from the views themselves. Matthews once again admits that Howells has at times been too blunt in pointing out the faults of earlier masters (of Thackeray, in particular) and has not always been judicious in his praise of contemporary writers, but he emphatically denies the charge—leveled by certain "stupid" and "malevolent" critics—that Howells elevates such realists as De Forest or H. B. Fuller to the rank of literary master. From the vantage point of the opening of the twentieth century, Matthews contends, *Criticism and Fiction* hardly seems iconoclastic: "At bottom all that Mr. Howells had done was to voice once again the demand that art, and more especially the art of fiction, should deal with life simply, naturally, and honestly. This has ever been the watch-cry of the younger generation in every century."[36]

Given these and the many other essays and reviews in which Matthews lauds him, it is no wonder that Howells would claim that he read and enjoyed virtually everything Matthews wrote.[37] Howells clearly did not, however, enjoy and agree with Matthews's "Ibsen the Playwright" (1905), an essay which, like his earlier defense of Zola, reveals the tensions inherent in his insistence that writers tell the truth as they see it while simultaneously projecting a "progressive" or Rooseveltian ethos.[38] Matthews declares that Ibsen is a "poet-philosopher who wishes to make people think, to awaken them from an ethical lethargy, to shock them into asking questions for which the complacent morality of the moment can provide no adequate answer." And he further argues that the Norwegian is a playwright of "surpassing technical dexterity" (253), who exhibits a genius for creating fully rounded and lifelike characters and for probing the "naked human soul, in its doubts and its perplexities" (254). But the line of argument takes a sudden turn when it focuses on the ideology underlying Ibsen's social dramas. Contending that the "romanticist is forever wrestling with the realist" in Ibsen, Matthews is disturbed by a "romanticistic clamor, a tocsin of anarchy" (274) he detects in several of the Norwegian's plays, especially in *Hedda Gabler*. If the essay begins in the tolerant voice of a Howells, it gradually hardens into that of a Roosevelt, with Matthews suggesting that Ibsen's plays reveal a "hint of abnormal eccentricity" and "morbid perversity." When we encounter derogatory phrases such as these in Matthews's writings, we can be sure that distempered social reformers are in the vicinity, and indeed they are: Ibsen's social dramas, he states, have won the "fulsome adulation" of the "cranks and freaks . . . the short-haired women and long-haired men" (267). (Matthews uses the same disparaging expressions, as earlier noted, in "Reform and Reformers.") Whereas some may consider Ibsen a progressive thinker, his criticisms of modern civilization expose him as one of the "most extreme reactionaries," one who is willing to "give up the chronometer and return to the sun-dial" (273). The "sun-dial" is a metaphor for the ideology of romantic individualism that progressivists were trying to *organize* out of existence. And since, Matthews continues, the average theatergoer will not be in sympathy with such an outmoded philosophy, Ibsen's plays, Matthews (wrongly) predicts, will not endure.

If the works of Ibsen, Zola, and other "reformers" were to be rejected on the grounds that their "frequent denunciations of the existing order of things" retard social evolution, Shakespeare's dramas were to be valued not only because of their aesthetic merits but because their themes were, in Matthews's interpretation of them, perfectly in tune with the progressivist ideology he was attempting to promote in his literary criticism. In "How Shakspere Learnt His Trade" (1903), for example, Matthews explains that Shakespeare was an "idealist, as a poet must be [and] a realist, as a successful playwright always is"—which is to say that he was a "practical idealist."[39] Since he was a product of his age, Shakespeare, Matthews concedes, was an adherent of the aristocratic system; nonetheless, he "could fellowship with common men," which explains the appeal his plays had to the common people of his age and to the democratic-minded audiences of Matthews's. Matthews's Shakespeare, moreover, was "not over-squeamish, and he never shrunk from plain speech"; yet he was "clean-minded beyond most of his fellow playwrights," and he was ever a "gentleman" toward women.

A decade later, Matthews would develop essentially the same image of Shakespeare in his influential book *Shakspere as a Playwright* (1913). Here he contends that, though the great playwright has a profound sense of the tragic, his overall attitude toward life and toward his fellow man is (in contrast to Ibsen's or Zola's) "always healthy and never morbid": he is "steadily sane, rarely bitter and never desperately misanthropic," even when reminding us of the "gorilla which lurks within us—the ancestral gorilla, selfish and bestial." Shakespeare's histories indicate that he was "ardently patriotic"; and though his plays never preach morality, yet their "temper" manifests that he was "profoundly moral." Finally, Shakespeare is no romantic idealist (i.e., reformer): he has a firm grasp on "wholesome realities," and by forcing us to see life as it is, he nerves us for the "struggles of existence." One gets the impression that if this Shakespeare were transported in time to Progressive-Era America, he would respond enthusiastically to the *Origin of Species*, champion literary realism (but not "morbid" naturalism), and vote for Theodore Roosevelt.[40]

Howells's opinion of Ibsen was diametrically opposed to Matthews's, and though he professed admiration for "How Shakspere Learnt His Trade," he was hardly convinced that the vision projected by the Bard's plays was "always healthy and never morbid."[41] Shortly after Matthews's essay on Ibsen appeared, Howells published in the *North American Review* a passionate defense of the Norwegian that is virtually a point-by-point refutation of Matthews's criticisms. Where Matthews indicted Ibsen as a romanticist, Howells claims him for realism; where Matthews saw morbidity, Howells finds a "wholly sanative" sense of integrity; where Matthews predicted that the Norwegian's plays would not pass critical inspection in the future, Howells closes his piece by declaring that "it would not be altogether impossible that some in the future should know him with the passionate joy with which a few in the present have had the courage to know him."[42] Moreover, in this essay and elsewhere, Howells attempts to defend Ibsen's plays against the charge that they are morbid and immoral by arguing that one finds in them scenes no more violent or morally offensive than can be found in Shakespeare's *Hamlet* or *King Lear*. In regards to the temperament that created such works, Howells was willing to accept George Bernard Shaw's assertion that Shakespeare had a pessimistic view of life, and he expressed scorn for "the foolish fanaticism of [Shakespeare's] worshippers, who would see no defect in him."[43] Though he does not attempt to place Shakespeare or his works on the altar of perfection, Matthews's re-visioning of him into a progressive-minded "practical idealist" comes very close to being the kind of hero worship that Howells deplored.

Yet, however much they disagreed on literary or political issues, Matthews and Howells remained warm friends until the latter's death in 1920. Three years earlier, in a review of Matthews's autobiography, Howells made his final public comment on the professor's literary abilities, proclaiming him the foremost American scholar of the drama, as well as a talented fiction writer. (We shall return, in chapter 5, to Howells's responses to Matthews's fiction.) Among all our men of letters, Howells declares in the review, there are "no truer Americans, no more genuine, than Mr. Matthews and Mr. Garland."[44] (Twain and Henry James, of course, were no longer alive.) In the same year (1917), on the occasion of Howells's eightieth birthday, Matthews returned the compliment by extolling him as the "most versatile and multifarious of all our writers," adding that his cosmopolitan perspective did not weaken his strong sense of nationalism.[45]

If Howells was the "eastern" realist whom Matthews most admired, Twain was the "western" one. From his 1885 review of *Huckleberry Finn*—one of the earliest and most favorable by an American critic—through the end of his career, Matthews defended Twain with the same vigor he did Howells, the two novelists' names often appearing side by side in his essays. He repeatedly insisted that the creator of Tom Sawyer and Huck Finn was not, as many English and "colonial-minded" American critics and academics charged, a "mere humorist," but a serious artist whose fictions, though they contained many of the most humorous scenes in American literature, probed the darker corners of American culture and the human soul. And though Twain might jestingly complain in "Fenimore Cooper's Literary Offences" that Matthews praised Cooper's novels without having read them, there can be no doubt that he shared Howells's high regard for their academic advocate.

In "Memories of Mark Twain" (1922)—a deeply affectionate portrait of Twain which emphasizes that the melancholic vision of life projected in *The Mysterious Stranger* and *What Is Man?* lies beneath the surface of the humorous early fiction—Matthews claims that he read "The Jumping Frog of Calaveras County" in 1867 and thereafter virtually everything that Twain published. Matthews did not make Twain's personal acquaintance, however, until 1883. The circumstances of their meeting are further illustration of the way in which Matthews's club memberships helped gain him access to the literary "center." Twain accepted an invitation to join the Kinsmen, a literary dining club that Matthews helped found; at the second dinner meeting of the group, Matthews had the good fortune (or perhaps it was by design of the host, Matthews's close friend Laurence Hutton) to be seated next to Twain. Matthews had many other opportunities in the future to socialize with Twain at the Authors Club, which Matthews also helped found.[46]

When *Huckleberry Finn* was published, Matthews, who was writing reviews (anonymously) for the London *Saturday Review*, leaped at the opportunity to inform British readers of the American writer's genius. Readers today will find much of what Matthews says in the review to be exactly what they would expect from a Victorian-era "genteel"—his description, for example, of the novel as a "tale of boyish adventure," or his remark that the portrait of Jim captures the "essential simplicity and kindliness and generosity of the Southern negro." But they will also find much to respect in the piece: the appreciation of Twain's narrative technique ("the skill with which the character of Huck Finn is maintained is marvellous. We see everything through his eyes and not a pair of Mark Twain's spectacles"); his assertion that Twain "draws from life, and yet lifts his work from the domain of the photograph to the region of art"; and the recognition that though the novel is not burdened by authorial discourses on moral, social, and political issues, such issues are nonetheless embodied in the dramatic action. In regard to the last point, Matthews calls attention to the Grangerford-Shepherdson feud and to Colonel Sherburn's murder of Boggs and subsequent confrontation with the lynch mob. In a remark that tells us more about Brander Matthews than Twain, he adds that such scenes reflect the violent and anarchic frontier life that, while not wholly gone, "is now rapidly passing away under the influence of advancing civilization and increasing commercial prosperity."[47] To what extent Twain at this point in his life agreed with that statement, we do not know; but he did like the review overall, and told Matthews so.[48]

During the years that followed, Matthews continued to laud Twain's fiction. In 1898, Twain responded to three essays Matthews had sent him by saying: "Compliments are sometimes pretty hard to hear, but these are not that sort. They are conspicuously and most pleasantly the other way."[49] (Matthews felt the same way about the hilarious but very flattering speech Twain delivered at his testimonial dinner in 1893.)[50] Twain does not identify the essays in question, but "The Penalty of Humor" (1896) was probably among them. As the title suggests, the essay is concerned with the penalty that writers suffer to their literary reputations for making people laugh; once branded a "humorist," the novelist who mixes the humorous and serious will likely find that the former will blind readers to the latter. Writers such as Cervantes, Rabelais, and Benjamin Franklin have paid this price in the past, Matthews observes, and some are paying it in the present, none more so than Twain. Then follow two pages of the kind of compliments that Twain liked to hear—along with a few honest criticisms which might have made him wince, such as the remark that he has "written too much that is little better than burlesque and extravaganza." Twain, Matthews contends, is a master of English prose, a marvelous storyteller, and a profound explorer of the springs of human action. Certain scenes in *Tom Sawyer*, *Huckleberry Finn*, and *Pudd'nhead Wilson* (such as the Grangerford-Shepherdson feud, the attempted lynching of Sherburn, and Chambers's selling of Roxy down the river) rank among the most powerful in English-language literature. Yet, despite these and many other scenes of pathos or tragedy in Twain's novels, he is generally dismissed, after a few patronizing comments, as a "funny man only," another Artemus Ward. No contemporary writer, Matthews concludes, has been treated so unjustly by the critics.[51]

Such attempts by Matthews to rescue Twain from the category of "funny man only" help explain why Twain, a month after expressing his appreciation for the three pieces Matthews sent him, would cite the professor as one of only two people (Howells being the other) to whom he would entrust the writing of the introduction to the Uniform Edition of his collected works. When Howells declined, Matthews took on the assignment, and the result was "Biographical Criticism."[52] In addition to providing a sketch of Twain's life to that date, Matthews restates views expressed earlier in "The Penalty of Humor" and other pieces: namely, that Twain is a consummate artist; that the humor in his novels is rooted in an essentially melancholic vision of human existence; and that he is a supreme realist, whose best fictions offer a true picture of American life and the American character. He also argues that *Tom Sawyer*, *Huckleberry Finn*, and *Pudd'nhead Wilson* are Twain's best novels because they are grounded in his firsthand knowledge of the places and people he was portraying, as a historical romance like *A Connecticut Yankee in King Arthur's Court* could not be.

In addition to praising Twain's talents as a novelist, "Biographical Criticism" celebrates his personal virtues: his "sterling ethical standard," his honesty and integrity, his fiercely democratic spirit, his deep humanity and compassion, and, most important, his patriotism. Though Twain has spent much time abroad, he has developed a cosmopolitan character without "enfeebling his own native faith." Matthews, recall, says virtually the same thing about Howells in his 1917 birthday tribute to him, and in both cases he implicitly draws the contrast with Henry James, that expatriate whose attraction to English culture did, according to Matthews, "enfeeble" his sense of Americanism. Unlike a James, Twain has the "very marrow of Americanism. He is as intensely and as typically American as Franklin or Emerson or Hawthorne." Or Roosevelt. Though Matthews never mentions the hero of San Juan Hill in "Biographical Criticism," the spirit of Roosevelt infuses the section lauding Twain's Americanism, so much so that by the end of the essay Twain has in a sense become Roosevelt's double. Is it Twain or Roosevelt that Matthews describes when he remarks that this "very embodiment of Americanism" is as optimistic as Emerson (a comment which contradicts the earlier assertion that Twain's vision is melancholic at heart), is a "manly" realist, and is a "practical idealist"?[53]

At the time Matthews wrote "Biographical Criticism," Twain was an opponent of President McKinley and his foreign policy but not of Vice-President Roosevelt, even though Roosevelt represented many things that Twain detested: jingoism, neoromanticism, political theatrics, even big-game hunting (which to Twain was a form of cruelty to animals). But when Roosevelt, after becoming president, continued the expansionist policies of his predecessor, Twain (who by 1901 had become a fervid anti-imperialist) came to despise him. To Twain, President Roosevelt was the "Tom Sawyer of the political world of the twentieth century; always showing off; always hunting a chance to show off; in his frenzied imagination the Great Republic is a vast Barnum circus with him for a clown and the whole world for audience." Roosevelt, for his part, admired *Huckleberry Finn* as well as other of Twain's roughing-it fiction, but not his politics. When Twain, for example, announced that he was on the side of the Boxers in their rebellion against European aggressors, Roosevelt (then vice-president) snapped that the situation in China was much more complicated than "all our prize idiots from Mark Twain and Godkin down" realized.[54]

Roosevelt's juxtaposition of Twain and Godkin serves as a reminder that Twain was a dyed-in-the-wool Mugwump. At about the same time that Matthews was enlightening readers of the London *Saturday Review* to the virtues of the "mugquomps," Twain was delivering a political address in Hartford in which he defended the Mugwumps against the charge that they were turncoats; the only traitorous Republicans, he countered, were those who betrayed the party's traditional principles by supporting the nomination of the corrupt Blaine. That charge, of course, applied to loyal-Republican Roosevelt. Long after Matthews had severed his connections with Godkin and the Mugwumps, Twain was declaring: "I was born a Mugwump, and I shall probably die a Mugwump."[55]

In 1898 Matthews wrote a friend: "But how [Clemens] can write! How he can say what he thinks! And how clear his thinking is—mostly."[56] Matthews does not clarify the "mostly," but if he had, he probably would have pointed to Twain's adherence to an outdated Mugwumpery and his failure to appreciate the "progressive" nature of the McKinley administration's "new statecraft." In any case, in "Biographical Criticism" Matthews implicitly defended Twain against any suggestions that he was un-American, by re-visioning him in the image of Roosevelt. Twain, one might assume, would have been somewhat embarrassed, if not perturbed, by the professor's attempt to portray him as the embodiment of "manly Americanism," but that assumption would be wrong, for he in fact loved the essay, exclaiming to Bliss Perry (who had commissioned Matthews to write it): "I told you Brander would do it well. . . . No one can beat his Introduction. It is as clear and compact and felicitous a piece of work as any man might wish to see." Howells was equally pleased by the introduction, publicly praising it as a "singularly intelligent" piece of work.[57] Twain's and Howells's enthusiastic response to Matthews's "Rooseveltian" praise of Twain would seem to be a telling example of Sacvan Bercovitch's claim that, however fiercely the "genteel 'reactionaries'" and "reform-minded Realists" debated their literary politics, those debates were conducted within the ideological boundaries of American "consensus."[58]

Matthews often put his felicitous pen to work for Twain in the years that followed publication of "Biographical Criticism." Though it contains no separate piece on Twain, Matthews's *The Historical Novel and Other Essays* (1901) is dedicated to Twain, whose name appears frequently in the essays, always to his advantage. The same is true of *Inquiries and Opinions* (1907), which reprints "Biographical Criticism."[59] In addition to the previously mentioned "Memories of Mark Twain," Matthews published several essays after

Twain's death, including a canonizing chapter in the 1918 edition of his textbook *An Introduction to the Study of American Literature.*[60] In "Mark Twain and the Theater," one of the essays in *Playwrights on Playmaking* (1923), he addressed a neglected aspect of Twain's literary career. Twain was as serious as Howells in his attempts to become a successful playwright, with the same futile results. Seeking to account for the great novelist's failure as a dramatist, Matthews argues (as he had in "Women Dramatists" and other earlier writings) that, where a loosely structured novel may be compelling if its characters are sharply drawn, a play requires a tightly woven plot in order to be successful when performed on stage. Though he possessed a theatrical personality and was a genius at creating complex, lifelike characters in his fiction, Twain, Matthews contends, lacked the "engineering draftsmanship" required of a playwright: he could create literary "diamonds," but could not "cut and polish and set" them for the stage.[61]

"Mark Twain and the Theater" is followed, significantly, in *Playwrights on Playmaking* by an essay examining the plays of another accomplished novelist who failed as a dramatist, Henry James. According to Matthews, he and James were first introduced in 1883, at the first meeting of the American Copyright League; during the years that followed, the two met occasionally at the London Athenaeum club, of which both were members.[62] As evidenced by his review of *French Poets and Novelists* in 1878—in which he proclaimed that James was, with the exception of Arnold and Lowell, the "foremost literary critic" of the English language—Matthews developed a great respect for James's literary criticism years before the two met, and he seems to have maintained that respect, for his later works frequently quote from James's critical writings.[63] Matthews had mixed feelings about James's fiction, however. In an 1892 essay he extols James's "talent, his flexibility, his subtilty, his delicate art, his extraordinary sensitiveness to

impressions," but then suggests that, when James transplanted himself to England and ceased writing about the
American scene, his artistic powers began to wane and his
literary style began to "stutter."[64] James, for his part, does
not seem to have taken much notice of Matthews's work,
and he certainly did not hold him in the same high regard
that Howells and Twain did. But he was sufficiently aware
of Matthews's influential connections with New York editors and publishers to seek his assistance, in 1914, in securing journalism employment for a friend, remarking then that
Matthews was "absolutely the authority" to consult on such
matters.[65]

On the issue of literary form or structure, Matthews was,
as many of his comments quoted above make clear, a Jamesian
rather than a Howellsian, and in "Henry James and the Theater," Matthews commends James's preoccupation with the
"whole stiff mystery of technic."[66] James, Matthews further
observes, clearly possessed the architectural skill demanded
of the playwright; moreover, his many critical essays on the
drama reveal that he had a thorough appreciation of the special conditions that the theater imposes upon the script writer.
Why then, Matthews asks, did this supreme craftsman fail
to produce successful plays? The answer, he suggests, lies
in James's instinctual feelings of revulsion toward the "vulgar herd." Great playwrights like Shakespeare and Molière,
Matthews argues, sought to appeal to the play-going public,
with whom they felt a sense of "solidarity." This is not to
say that Shakespeare and Molière succeeded by "writing
down to the mob, but by writing broad to humanity." At this
point Matthews suddenly shifts from an even-tempered to a
"strenuous" rhetoric: in order to appeal to the public, the
dramatist must be, as Shakespeare and Molière were, "stout
of heart and strong of stomach, with no drooping tendrils of
exquisite delicacy" (203). In short, James, who fled his "vulgar" native land to enjoy the more refined, aristocratic cul-

ture of England, possessed the technical dexterity but not the democratic temperament nor the "manliness" demanded by the egalitarian marketplace of the theater. Though he does not utter Roosevelt's contemptuous comment about James, Matthews insinuates that James's failure to win popular audiences for his plays and, by extension, for his "stuttering" novels was due to his being a "miserable little snob."[67] Thus, Matthews's essays on Twain and James in *Playwrights on Playmaking* combine to imply that, though the two writers may have been equal in their failure to construct successful plays, Twain was far superior in character.

By the time he wrote the pieces collected in *Playwrights on Playmaking*, Matthews had in fact abandoned the term "realism." His explanation for doing so sounds as if it were written by one of today's reader-response critics rather than by a "genteel." The meaning of any word, he observes in *These Many Years*, is not intrinsic but is rather the product of individual interpretation. "If this uncertainty and this variableness" of meaning, he continues, is "obvious in ordinary speech about ordinary things, it is intensified in all discussions of art." Thus, he concludes, literary categories such as "romantic" and "realistic" are "will-o'the-wisps and chameleons, changing color while one looks at them."[68]

Yet, if he moved theoretically "beyond realism," Matthews held to his conviction that, as he had asserted in *French Dramatists*, the most desirable mode of literature was that which positioned itself in the "safe centre," the progressivist-favored middle ground between the extremes of pessimistic determinism and naive optimism. Though he could appreciate the technical merits of Zola's and Ibsen's art, he ignored or depreciated American naturalist fiction. His numerous essays on contemporary realist writers make not a single reference to Dreiser, for example. When Stephen Crane sent Matthews a copy of *Maggie* in 1893, his response was to construct his own tale of Rum Alley that turned Crane's naturalistic vision upside down.[69] Matthews would not admit into the canon *all* those who strove to tell the truth about life as they saw it—as Dreiser, Crane, and other naturalists were doing—only those whose works projected (or, in the case of Twain, "mostly" projected) the manly courage, moral integrity, sense of humor, and faith in progress that were in Matthews's mind the distinctive traits of the "real" American character.

4   "On Deck" with Roosevelt during the Campaign for American Cultural Independence

It appears to us that at this stage of the proceedings, there is no such thing as nationality in the highest literary expression; but there is a universality, a humanity, which is very much better.
—W. D. Howells, "Editor's Study," *Harper's Monthly*, Nov. 1891

Yet the fact remains that the greatest work must bear the stamp of originality. In exactly the same way, the greatest work must bear the stamp of nationalism. American work must smack of our own soil, mental and moral, no less than physical, or it will have little of permanent value.
—Theodore Roosevelt, "Nationalism in Literature and Art," 1916

Writing to Matthews in 1889 when the Realism War was at high pitch, Garland remarked: "There are so few of us that we should be able to work together for 'Americanism in art'—If that phrase be less offensive than 'realism.'"[1] Garland's words remind us that, for many late nineteenth-century American critics, the battle for literary realism was part of the larger campaign for cultural independence. Underway since the Declaration of Independence, the quest for nationality reached full steam during the age of Emerson. But, in the post–Civil War decades, the legacy of Emersonian Americanism seemed in the eyes of many to be threatened by the new sense of cosmopolitanism which impelled thousands of Americans to travel across the seas to experience culture instead of seeking it—and helping to create it—at home. Garland and his fellow literary nationalists also feared that the influx of immigrants from southern and eastern Europe—the so-called "new immigrants"—would gradually supplant, by their sheer numbers, the Anglo-Saxons as the dominant American racial group, thus resulting in cultural "decadence."[2]

A particularly striking illustration of the way in which race, politics, and literature were entangled in the minds of the New Nationalists occurs in a letter that Roosevelt sent to Matthews in 1894. After complaining that the United States was "getting some very undesirable [immigrants] now," Roosevelt trumpets the cause of literary Americanism: "We must," he exclaims, echoing Emerson's "American Scholar," "strike out for ourselves, we must work according to our own ideas, and must free ourselves from the shackles of conventionality." In the next paragraph, significantly, he denounces Henry James, declaring that the expatriate writer's "polished, pointless, uninteresting stories about the upper social classes in England make one blush to think that he was once an American."[3] Two months earlier, in an article titled "What Americanism Means," Roosevelt had condemned the new cosmopolitanism in equally shrill language: "Nothing," he pontificated, "will more quickly or more surely disqualify a man from doing good work in the world than the acquirement of that flaccid habit of mind which its possessors style cosmopolitanism." These "Europeanized" Americans, he went on to say, demonstrate "incredible and contemptible folly" as they "wander back to bow down before the alien gods whom our forefathers forsook."[4]

From James's perspective, the contemptible folly was, of course, to turn one's back on the rich culture of Europe and become a narrow-minded provincial like Roosevelt, worshipping a country that, as James asserted in his oft-quoted passage in *Hawthorne*, had no history, no literature, no muse-ums—no culture. Carrying this cosmopolitan point of view into his fiction, James aspired to "write in such a way that it would be impossible to an outsider to say whether I am at a given moment an American writing about England or an Englishman writing about America."[5]

As we have seen, Matthews cultivated a cosmopolitan taste in literature, and he frequently traveled abroad, biting deep, as James would say, into the apple of Europe, of France in particular. Indeed, he became so "Frenchified" that, in a re-view of *French Dramatists of the 19th Century*, Francisque Sarcey charged that the book's only fault was that its point of view was "too Parisian."[6] And in 1907 the French expressed their gratitude to Matthews for his long service to their literature by awarding him the prestigious Legion of Honor. Thus, from one angle, Roosevelt's derogatory comment about "Eu-ropeanized" Americans would seem to apply as much to Matthews as to James. Yet, as previously discussed, Matthews shared Roosevelt's strong sense of nationalism, and the professor's essays on Howells and Twain repeatedly stress their Americanism (which is precisely why Garland deemed him an ally in the campaign for Americanism in art). As the controversy raged between the "flaccid cosmopolitans" like James and the jingoistic nationalists like Roosevelt during the late nineteenth and early twentieth centuries, Matthews's mind was, characteristically, divided. His strategy for re-solving the dilemma was to construct a theory that syncre-tizes the opposing principles of nationalism and internation-alism, and roots both in literary realism.

As David Hollinger observes, many prominent Ameri-can intellectuals of the 1940s and 1950s believed that, with Europe having been reduced to shambles by World War II, the United States, its culture enriched by its ethnically di-verse population, had become the most viable embodiment of the cosmopolitan ideal, even though it "would be an exaggeration to say that New York took the place of Paris as the cultural capital" of the world.[7] Actually, the notion that American culture was cosmopolitan rather than provincial had been around long before the 1940s. As Europe was being ravaged by World War I, for example, Randolph Bourne published an essay titled "Trans-National America" (1916), in which he argued that the United States was developing into the "first international nation," though most English-Americans were, because of their devotion to the Anglocentric concept of the "melting pot," unaware of the country's cultural pluralism.[8] Some twenty-five years before Bourne's essay appeared, Matthews (under whom Bourne would study dramatic literature at Columbia) had declared, in an essay published in *Cosmopolitan*, that American culture was the embodiment of the cosmopolitan ideal and that New York had indeed transplanted Paris as the world's cultural capital.

Titled "More American Stories," the essay is a review of short-story collections by contemporary American authors.[9] Yet Matthews begins with a comment not about American fiction but about Parisian culture. Though most Americans consider Paris to be the most charming and cosmopolitan city on earth, Paris is, upon close inspection, rather provincial; the French, he explains, care little for what is occurring outside France, and they tend to be resistant to foreign art. Few Frenchmen, he charges, have bothered to read such English writers as Browning or Tennyson, or such American ones as Hawthorne and Whitman. The compliment to Whitman—the poet whom Van Wyck Brooks and other anti-genteels would later honor as the father of modern American poetry—yet again demonstrates why Matthews resists the "genteel" label.

Matthews goes on to suggest, in a passage that Bourne must have taken special interest in if he read the piece, that with all its apparent narrowness New York City is "really more cosmopolitan than Paris," because New Yorkers are busily engaged in constructing a new tradition from the multitude of foreign ones that have been imported by the city's ethnic immigrants. Ironically, when he turns his attention to the works under review—works which he claims represent the cosmopolitan character of American literature—he discusses such writers as Ambrose Bierce, H. C. Bunner, Joel Chandler Harris, Henry James, and Mark Twain, but not a single ethnic (or woman) writer. As a Bourne or James Weldon Johnson would have immediately perceived, the list of white-male authors suggests that the "new tradition" touted by Matthews is as Anglocentric as the old one.

In an address entitled "American Literature" delivered four years later (1896) at a National Education Association (NEA) convention, Matthews amplified and refined the argument he had sketched out in "More American Stories." According to Matthews, the meeting drew about twelve thousand educators from across the country, and so many of them appeared at his session that he had to deliver his talk a second time for those shut out of the initial reading.[10] Matthews begins the essay on a cosmopolitan note, contending that, of the world's many literatures, which he categorizes by language rather than by nation, the three preeminent ones are Greek, French, and English.[11] Arguing, à la Taine, that literature projects the "inexorable" race characteristics of a people, Matthews asserts that Greek literature is characterized by sense of form; French, by intellectual seriousness; and English—of which American literature is a "branch"—by vigor and vitality. Americans, he proceeds, have much to learn from Greek, French, and English (i.e., British) literature, but only by studying their native writers can they learn the truth about *American* culture, which, while having much in common with that of its mother country, is nonetheless distinctly different.

Manifesting the imperialistic temper we have earlier examined, Matthews emphasizes that, since the "English-speaking stock" are civilizing the "waste places of the earth and [wresting] new lands from hostile savages," it seems inevitable that English literature will achieve world dominance. As the fastest-developing branch of English literature, American literature will one day share in that conquest. If, that is, its evolution is not stymied by two obstacles—provincialism and colonialism. Provincialism he defines as "local pride unduly inflated"; colonialism, as "timid deference to foreign opinion." The best guard against the provincial demon is to insist that American writers be judged by universal standards, while the surest antidote to pernicious colonialism is to stand "on our own two feet" and resolve (as Howells and the realist writers were then doing) to "survey life with our own eyes and not through any imported spectacles." In the essay's key passage, Matthews calls for an "American cosmopolitanism" and endorses Coleridge's assertion that the "cosmopolitanism which does not spring out of, and blossom upon, the deep-rooted stem of nationality or patriotism, is a spurious and rotten growth." Thus, the American-cosmopolitan writer will read and see the "best the world has to offer," but will then return a "loyal citizen of [his] own country."

Matthews returned often to the theme of "American cosmopolitanism" in subsequent writings, most notably in "Literature in the New Century" (1904).[12] His central thesis here is that twentieth-century writers should exploit the four major legacies from the nineteenth century: science; democracy; nationalism; and, finally, that "stepping across the confines of language and race" we call cosmopolitanism. "The deeper interest in expression of national qualities and in the representation of provincial peculiarities [by local-color writers] is today," he states, "accompanied by an increasing cosmopolitanism which seems to be casting down the barriers of race and of language." The cosmopolitanism Matthews has in mind here, however, concerns the borrowing of literary *forms* only; for it is the "national spirit," or racial identity, that breathes life into art. Thus, though literary works may be similar in their artistic formulae and structures, they differ in their "essence, in the motives that move the characters and in their outlook on life." In short, what accounts for the international appeal of great works of art is their nationalistic or racial core. This racial individuality, Matthews claims, is the best safeguard against "mere craftsmanship"; it permits a writer to "frequent the past without becoming archaic [as happens to all "historical novelists"] and to travel abroad without becoming exotic because it will supply him always with a good reason for remaining a citizen of his own country." Matthews cites Twain, among others, as an example of the realist-nationalist-cosmopolitan writer. (In "Biographical Criticism," he praised the author of *Huckleberry Finn* for developing a cosmopolitan personality without "enfeebling his own native faith.") And though he makes no mention of Howells here, he once described the Dean as the "most intensely national and the most truly cosmopolitan [of American writers], with that sound cosmopolitanism which burgeons bounteously because it is deeply rooted in the soil of its nativity."[13]

As such comments make evident, Matthews placed a higher value on the first term of the phrase "American cosmopolitanism" than on the second. Though he fused nationalism and internationalism in theory, he was in practice closely allied, as usual, with Roosevelt. Roosevelt had no doubts that his friend was a New Nationalist at heart: "Thank heaven," he wrote Matthews in 1891, "we *do* agree on Americanism"; two years later he remarked that, when it came to Americanism, "I guess we are both of us usually on deck."[14] From the 1890s until the end of his professional career, Matthews was "on deck" throughout the literary-political campaign to nationalize and professionalize American literature. The ultimate goal of that campaign was to ensure that the United States would be, not trans-national or culturally pluralistic, but "homogeneous . . . in speech, in law, in thought, and in our unattainable ideals."[15]

"I decidedly envy you your reputation as being the champion of American methods and American ways in literature, in spelling, and in all other directions," Roosevelt informed Matthews in 1894.[16] In Roosevelt's view, Matthews had earned that reputation with the publication of *Americanisms and Briticisms* (1892), a collection of essays whose table of contents illustrates the many directions in which Matthews's literary Americanism ran: in addition to its title essay, the book includes pieces on *Huckleberry Finn* (a reprint of Matthews's 1885 review of the novel, discussed earlier), James Fenimore Cooper's novels, the humor of H. C. Bunner, American spelling practices, and American literary independence. Despite their disparate subject matter, the essays as a whole form a concerted attack on the "colonial" mind as it manifested itself not only in English condescension toward Brother Jonathan but, even worse, in American deference to British opinion. (Chief of the American "colonials" was that "evil influence" at Harvard, Charles Eliot Norton, whom Matthews considered a hopeless Anglophile.)[17]

During the late nineteenth-century campaign for cultural independence, one of the major fields of conflict between the Americans and the British was the English language itself. The debate over American and British forms of English, a debate which had, of course, been going on since the Revolutionary War, was political as well as linguistic, since it centered on which nation had the *authority* to amend the language.[18] From the perspective of many British critics and journalists, "Americanisms" (deviations from British pronunciation, spelling, and vocabulary) were degrading or "mongrelizing" the once-pure English language; and since the corruption of culture, the argument ran (and still runs), inevitably follows the corruption of language, the British were certain that their former colony was on the road to moral and political ruin. The title essay of *Americanisms and Briticisms* is a spirited refutation of this view. Arguing that since language is always evolving, a fixed and "pure" English never has existed, and demonstrating that many of the alleged "Americanisms" cited by English critics are actually "Briticisms" (i.e., of British origin), Matthews proclaims: "The English language is not bankrupt that it needs to have a receiver appointed; it is quite capable of minding its own business without the care of a committee of Englishmen." The attacks from across the Atlantic, he charges, are the results not of linguistic inquiry but of England's supercilious attitude toward Americans.[19] What might be called the "manifest destiny" subtext of "Americanisms and Briticisms" surfaces when Matthews announces that "We may be sure that branch of our Anglo-Saxon stock will use the best English, and will perhaps see its standards of speech accepted by the other branches, which is most vigorous physically, mentally, and morally, which has the most intelligence, and which knows its duty best and does it most fearlessly." It is easy to see why the author of "The Strenuous Life" would recommend the essay to fellow imperialist Henry Cabot Lodge and would declare (in a review of another of Matthews's works) that "Americanisms and Briticisms" is "by far the most noteworthy critical or literary essay which has been published by any American writer for a score of years."[20]

Nor is it surprising that Roosevelt would admire Matthews's essay on Fenimore Cooper in *Americanisms and Briticisms*. Roosevelt delighted in Cooper's fiction, and the Leatherstocking novels were, as Richard Slotkin emphasizes, a shaping influence on Roosevelt's myth-ideological system.[21] Roosevelt's ideology, in turn, seems to have shaped Matthews's perceptions of Cooper. Ignoring Cooper's aristocratic temperament, his bitter quarrel with his countrymen, and the pessimistic vision of such later novels as *The Crater*,

Matthews recreates Cooper in Roosevelt's image when he states that Cooper's two defining traits are a "hearty, robust, out-of-doors and open-air wholesomeness" and an "intense Americanism—ingrained, abiding, and dominant" (93).

In "The Literary Independence of the United States," Matthews again applauds the Americanism of Cooper as he argues that, though the United States now stands on its own politically and commercially, it has not yet achieved full independence in the literary realm. Demonstrating the conjunction of realism and Americanism noted earlier, Matthews praises realist writers like Howells and Twain, whose novels bear not a trace of intellectual deference to British opinion. The realists, he notes with pride, have not only captured the reading public of their native land, they are "conquering abroad" as well (86), that conquest aided significantly by passage of the 1891 international copyright act (discussed below).

In contrast to the "stalwart Americanism" of a Cooper, Howells, or Twain, the essayist Agnes Repplier (1855–1950) represents the American "colonial" attitude at its worst. Philadelphia's most prominent woman of letters, Repplier was as erudite and articulate as any critic of her day, but her essays during the late 1880s and early 1890s virtually ignore native writers. As Anglophilic as her good friend Andrew Lang, Repplier chose not to participate in the campaign for literary Americanism. Matthews makes disparaging references to both Lang and Repplier in a review essay on Henry Cabot Lodge's *Studies in History* and Thomas Wentworth Higginson's *The New World and the New Book*, both of which deplore American intellectual dependence on Great Britain. He notes with satisfaction, for example, that one of Higginson's verbal "transatlantic darts" struck Lang, drawing a "cry of pain" from him.[22] Though he admits that Higginson's aggressive nationalism might seem excessive to some, Matthews nonetheless insists that all Americans would profit from reading the book, Miss

Repplier most of all. While acknowledging that Repplier's essays are often brilliantly expressed, they are marked, Matthews charges, by a groveling deference to English opinion. "Although a Philadelphian," he gibes at one point, "she has apparently never heard of the Declaration of Independence." Perhaps, he further sneers, some of Miss Repplier's Philadelphia friends could take this "British sparrow" hatched in the United States to Independence Hall the next Fourth of July and show her the Liberty Bell, then on the way home purchase her copies of Higginson's and Lodge's books.

As we have seen, the author of "'Those Literary Fellows'" held a patriarchal attitude toward women intellectuals. That Matthews's hostility toward Repplier may have been a reaction to her gender as well as to her "colonialism" is suggested when, belittling her literary taste, he asserts that "In literature as in some other things a woman's opinion is often personal and accidental; it depends on the way the book has happened to strike her" (148). Women, in other words, read capriciously rather than critically.

In his study of Repplier, George Stewart Stokes notes that, though Roosevelt and Repplier developed a mutual respect after she was introduced to the former president in 1914, he "may not have approved entirely" of her.[23] That is an understatement, for Roosevelt initially shared Matthews's disdain for Repplier's Anglophilism, and his contemptuous remarks about her, like Matthews's, reveal the fear of feminization lurking beneath the "manly Americanism" both men sought to promote. In one letter to Matthews, for example, Roosevelt declares that "Miss Repplier, whose original essays were no good, is beginning to write like Andrew Lang gone crazy"; in another, he refers to her as a "female idiot" and a "sporadic she-fool."[24]

Roosevelt did not limit his denunciations of Repplier to private correspondence. Upon reading a draft version of the essay in which Matthews sniped at Repplier, Roosevelt wrote to express his admiration for it, adding that the "cringing provincialism and lack of patriotism" of Repplier's recently published "The Praises of War" (*Atlantic Monthly*, Dec. 1891) so irritated him that he was about to launch his own attack against her in an article he intended to submit to Howells, editor of *Cosmopolitan* at the time. (Though he would later condemn Howells as a "feeble apostle of Tolstoi," Roosevelt and the Dean were on good terms at this point.) The piece, he adds, would not be merely a criticism of Repplier but rather a discourse on Americanism, "using her partly as a peg and partly as an awful object lesson." Several months later, Roosevelt informed Matthews that he had written Howells about "having you see the article—though I am ashamed of myself for doing so," a comment which suggests that Roosevelt sought (and no doubt received) Matthews's help in preparing the essay for *Cosmopolitan*, where it appeared under the title "A Colonial Survival" in December 1892.[25]

Roosevelt does not call Repplier a "female idiot" in "Colonial Survival," but that is precisely what he implies. After firing salvos at several of his favorite targets—Kipling, the vulgar rich, effete literary men, "brainless women of fashion," "émigré novelists," and all Americans who were "by education and instinct entirely un-American"—Roosevelt turns his attention to "The Praises of War."[26] Though in accord with Repplier's attempt to analyze literary treatments of war and patriotism, he complains that her critiques seem "unreal" because she delights "only in battles that are won by the expenditure of nothing more violent than rose-water"; her perspective, in other words, is feminine. Only a man who has the capacity to experience the "joy of battle," Roosevelt continues, "knows that he feels [that joy] when the wolf begins to rise in his heart; he does not then shrink from blood and sweat, or deem that they mar the fight; he revels in them, in the toil, the pain and the danger, as but setting off the triumph." Seeking to refute Repplier's argument that battles seldom generate first-rate literature, he points to such "immortal tales of prowess" as the *Nibelungenlied*, Chaucer's "Knight's Tale," Longfellow's "Saga of Olaf," and, of course, the battle fictions of Fenimore Cooper. Repplier's remark that the American Civil War evoked only doggerel poetry is, he exclaims, "colonialism gone crazy."

Roosevelt's and Matthews's skirmish with Repplier blazed for some time, but by 1894 Roosevelt felt that their female foe had been vanquished: "Do you know," he wrote Matthews, when calling attention to Repplier's complimentary allusion to one of the professor's short stories, "I think you have had a decidedly chastening effect on that young lady?"[27] Whether Matthews had, as Roosevelt implies, verbally beaten Repplier into submission to their views is arguable, but Repplier did in fact come to embrace the militant Americanism the two men advocated. Indeed, when Roosevelt later waged his campaign against Woodrow Wilson and the policy of neutrality before the United States entered World War I, Repplier was firmly on the side of the Warrior against the Priest. In her *Counter-Currents* (1916), a collection of nine essays previously published in the *Atlantic Monthly*, she stridently mocks Wilson's isolationism and pacifism; deplores American "loss of nerve"; argues that Christianity and war have "walked together down the centuries"; and, in the essay titled "Americanism," expresses her support for "Americanization Day" programs, warning that unassimilated immigrants threaten national security.[28] The author Roosevelt once disparaged for her lack of patriotism and "rose-water" view of battle was now writing like a Rough Rider.

In a remark cited earlier, Roosevelt mentioned spelling as one of the areas in which Matthews "championed" American methods and ways, and champion it he does in

"As to 'American Spelling,'" another essay in *Americanisms and Briticisms*. As he chides the British for behaving as if a "papal bull" had declared the infallibility of British orthography, Matthews observes that no philologist would defend the current English spelling system, which is so chaotic and "stupid" that it requires the "broom of reform." That broom, he goes on to say, has begun to sweep in the United States, where the "so-called 'American spelling' differs from the spelling which obtains in England only in so far as it has yielded a little more readily to the forces which make for progress" (53). Efforts to bring orthography more in line with pronunciation had been underway at least since Benjamin Franklin devised his phonetic alphabet in 1768, but the simplified-spelling movement, like the larger campaign for cultural independence of which it was a part, was at its peak during the late nineteenth and early twentieth centuries.[29] In 1906, American proponents of a more logical spelling system added yet another reform organization to the many that sprung up during the Progressive Era by establishing the Simplified Spelling Board. Once again, the energetic Matthews was at the center.

In fact, the meeting that resulted in the creation of the Simplified Spelling Board took place at Matthews's home, and he served as the board's first chair, until Professor Thomas Lounsbury of Yale was elected its president a year later. The board's activities were initially financed by a three-year grant from Andrew Carnegie, who was a staunch supporter of the movement and an admirer of Matthews. ("I am so much your admirer," he once wrote Matthews, "as to stand somewhat in awe of you," adding that the professor made the best speeches on simplified spelling.)[30] The board attracted a host of progressive-minded writers, publishers, scholars, and lexicographers, including such luminaries as Twain, William James, G. W. Cable, Henry Holt, Isaac K. Funk, Walter W. Skeat, and Richard Watson Gilder. As

Matthews explains in "Simplified Spelling and 'Fonetic Reform'" (1909), the board's central goal was to "accelerate the progress" of spelling simplification that had been occurring gradually in the United States for over a century. The board, he takes great pains to stress, was *not* aligned with the "radical 'fonetic' reform" movement, whose object was to demolish the existing spelling system and replace it with one in which there would be an exact correspondence between orthography and pronunciation.[31] While sympathetic to that goal, Matthews argues that the movement was doomed to fail because the Anglo-American "stock" have a "racial antipathy to revolutionary radicalism of any kind"—a remark which again reveals the essentially conservative nature of Matthews's "progressivism." Pursuing the "middle path of progress" between the retention of the absurd existing spelling system on the one hand, and its radical transformation on the other, the board decided to intervene in the natural evolution of spelling simplification by endorsing a list of three hundred words whose orthography had been made more rational, usually by striking out superfluous letters (e.g., "catl" instead of "cattle"). As Matthews notes, many of the spelling adjustments suggested by the board had previously been endorsed by the NEA.

To Matthews, the board's goal of streamlining the orthographic system was as important as other reforms championed by progressivists (civil-service reform, for example) because it attacked a problem that continues to haunt us today—illiteracy. That problem, he recognized, had (and still has) political implications. Convinced that the perplexing nature of the existing spelling system prevented large numbers of Americans, especially "foreigners," from becoming literate, Matthews believed that a victory for the board would be a victory for American democracy: "So long as the average voter can't read," he wrote Roosevelt in 1906, "he is prey of the henchman. . . . But anything which makes it

easier for him to read, helps just so much toward his thinking for himself, free from the semi-hypnotic appeal of the
oral argument."[32] As critics of progressivism have argued,
such democratic rhetoric might have been propelled by the
fear that the lower class, especially its immigrant members,
would use the ballot box to overthrow a power structure
dominated by educated, middle-class Anglo-Americans like
Matthews.

Whether we interpret Matthews's support of the spelling-
reform movement as a commendable attempt to achieve the
democratic ideal or as a self-serving effort to preserve "genteel"
hegemony (the truth, I suspect, lies somewhere in between),
there is no doubt that his advocacy of this particular reform
was, as with all his progressivist activities, undergirded by his
belief in Anglo-American racial superiority. As noted above,
Matthews was convinced that, since the United States and
Great Britain were spreading their civilization into the "waste
places" throughout the globe, the English language was des-
tined to become a world language. In the closing lines of
"Simplified Spelling and 'Fonetic Reform,'" he emphasized
that the simplified-spelling movement, which had advocates
in England as well as in the United States, deserved the support of the American public because the reforms it was promoting would help make English "fitter for its impending
adoption as a world-language,—that is to say, as the second
tongue of all educated men thruout the globe" (231).

In the same year in which the Simplified Spelling Board
was established, President Roosevelt invited Matthews to
the White House to "talk over everything from spelling to
the Japanese."[33] Whether Matthews had any influence on the
"Gentlemen's Agreement" that Roosevelt would reach with
Japan in 1907 is unknown, but there is ample evidence suggesting that he was largely responsible for Roosevelt's decision in August 1906 to issue an executive order directing the
Government Printing Office to employ in all its publications

the three hundred spellings endorsed by the Simplified Spelling Board. Roosevelt in fact sent a draft of the order to Matthews for comments and suggestions before submitting it to the government printer.[34] Roosevelt's modest action, however, generated a storm of controversy and gave his critics on the press an opportunity to ridicule him. Within four months of issuing the order, Roosevelt informed Matthews that he was withdrawing from the "undignified contest," but with no regrets for having entered the fray. The defeat, however, did not dissuade Matthews from persisting. Nor did a petulant letter from Carnegie several years later in which the philanthropist complained that he was tired of wasting his money on the enterprise.[35] (Carnegie eventually withdrew his financial support.) Matthews remained hopeful that the simplified-spelling movement would one day prevail, and he continued to employ the board's three hundred recommended spellings in his own writing "thruout" his life.

In "As to 'American Spelling'" Matthews, remarking that some British publishers objected to publishing American books because of the "barbaric" spellings they contained, yokes the simplified-spelling movement with the campaign for an international copyright law, implying that both reforms were part of the larger crusade for American cultural independence. The year before he wrote that essay, the American Copyright League had hosted a lavish banquet in celebration of its eighth anniversary and, more important, of the passage of the Platt-Simmonds Act, commonly referred to as the Copyright Act of 1891.[36] The signing of that bill into law climaxed one of the most dramatic literary-political battles in American history. Prior to passage of the new copyright law, American writers enjoyed copyright protection at home but were vulnerable to pirating abroad. Moreover, since many American publishers engaged in acts of piracy, the American market was flooded with inexpensive reprints of foreign books. This situation, as James Fenimore Cooper, among others, had complained earlier in the century, made it extremely difficult for American writers to support themselves from the proceeds from their writing, and thus helped perpetuate the dominance of Anglo-European literature in the United States.[37] Thus, while there can be no doubt that some supporters of the bill were acting out of economic self-interest, most did believe that an international copyright act was an essential weapon in the struggle for cultural independence. Senator Thomas Platt, one of the bill's cosponsors, declared that the "direct mission of the principle involved in the bill [was] to develop a distinctively American literature"; and in his banquet speech, Henry Cabot Lodge went so far as to tout the bill as a "monument and a milestone in the march of American civilization."[38] That milestone was reached, however, only after long and hard politicking by the bill's proponents, a coalition of writers, publishers, and politicians who crusaded under the twin banners of Americanism and progressive reform. Not surprisingly, Matthews and Roosevelt were "on deck" throughout the campaign.

Matthews was in fact as instrumental in establishing the American Copyright League as he had been in organizing the Simplified Spelling Board; the initial meeting of the league, like that of the board, was convened at his home (on April 16, 1883).[39] As earlier mentioned, Matthews was among the group of men who in 1882 founded the Authors Club. The league was its offspring: the idea of creating the league was first broached at a meeting of the Authors Club, and the men of letters who brought that idea to fruition were each of them club members.

As the league organized its lobbying efforts, Matthews served on the executive committee and became chair of the subcommittee on publicity. In that capacity, he in 1887 published an essay on the copyright problem in the *New Princeton*

Review.[40] Titled "American Authors and British Pirates," the article argued that, while book piracy by American publishers was prevalent, piracy perpetrated by British ones was more widespread and did much more injury to American writers than was generally admitted. Under British law at the time, American authors enjoyed copyright protection only if their books were initially published in England and only if the authors themselves were within the British Commonwealth at the time of publication. Though British pirates were the main targets of Matthews's criticism, he stressed that his own country's failure to grant copyright protection to foreign authors was a national disgrace, and he entreated his fellow Americans to support legislation then pending in Congress that would protect the property rights of *all* authors.

Its arguments logically expressed and thoroughly supported by data gleaned from publishers' catalogs and examples from literary history, "American Authors and British Pirates" makes a compelling case for reform of the copyright laws. It is easy to see why the Copyright League would in 1889 publish a revised and expanded version of it as a pamphlet under the same title. Ironically, the most severe criticism of the *New Princeton Review* piece came not from an Englishman but from a fellow league member and close friend, Mark Twain.

Shortly after publishing "American Authors and British Pirates," Matthews sent a letter to Twain explaining that William M. Sloane, editor of the *New Princeton Review*, had asked him (Matthews) to respond in a second essay to British criticisms of the piece. Reminding Twain that British publishing houses were selling books under his name that he did not write, Matthews appealed for information or suggestions that might bolster his case against the pirates across the sea: "I'd like a dozen lines from you bristling with facts," Matthews requested, "And a hand to keep on the good fight."[41] Twain delivered the fighting lines, but not quite in the manner Matthews had expected.

Before even reading Matthews's article, Twain wrote him a letter in which he *defended* British copyright law and chided him for laying blame on England when the United States Congress (which had not yet passed an international copyright act) was the main culprit. But instead of mailing the letter to Matthews, Twain sent it—without Matthews's knowledge—to Sloane, along with a multi-page "P.S. (of the feminine sort)" that he composed after he finally did read the *Princeton Review* piece. Sloane published Twain's letter (bearing the salutation "My Dear Matthews") and long post-script, followed by Matthews's response, in a subsequent number of the journal.[42]

Claiming that all the books he had published within the preceding fifteen years were protected under British copy-right, Twain argued in his "P.S." that Americans had no cause to criticize British law: "To-day the American author can go to Canada, spend three days there, and come home with an English and Canadian copyright which is as strong as if it had been built out of railroad iron." Thus, in Twain's opinion, "nine-tenths of the sin belongs with the American author." After taking some six pages to develop that point, Twain closed with the statement: "Matthews, I am your friend, and you know it; and that is what makes me say what I say." Those reassuring words, however, could not compensate for Twain having subjected his friend to the kind of verbal abuse in the preceding pages that is generally reserved for one's most detested enemies. Twain, for example, accused Matthews of having a "distorted mind" and suggested that as a lawyer Matthews should be ashamed of the "ragged case" he had constructed against British copyright law. Twain's rhetorical heat increased as he proceeded: "You are the very wrong-headedest person in America. . . . Why, man, you—well, you are geometrically color-blind; . . . And you are injudicious. . . . From your first page to your last one, you do not chance your hands on a single argument that isn't a boomerang." Matthews's essay, he declared (shortly before stating "I am your friend, and you know it"), was filled with "stupefying nonsense."

Reflecting, in "Memories of Mark Twain," on Twain's reaction to his *New Princeton Review* essay, Matthews states that, shocked as he was by Twain's vehement attack on him, he kept his temper as he prepared his retort, sending Sloane a letter that was "strictly legal in tone."[43] The eleven-page letter projects a good deal more verve and emotion than Matthews's description of it would suggest, but it does not contain the kind of inflammatory rhetoric and personal insults that Twain injected into his "P.S." Fair-minded readers of the exchange in the *New Princeton Review* would, I think, have to give the advantage to Matthews.

Matthews begins his rebuttal by expressing astonishment that Twain, in his "brilliant Postscript," should have so misapprehended the chief purpose of "American Authors and British Pirates"—to convince readers that an international agreement was needed so that American *and* British writers would receive just treatment. As to Twain's assertion that prior-publication and residency requirements of British law posed no significant obstacles to American authors seeking copyright protection, Matthews reminds the famous novelist that fledgling writers often find it very difficult to secure a British publisher for their book, especially if it is their first one. And should they find a British publisher, how easy is it, Matthews asks, for "poor authors who may chance to live in Florida or Texas" to travel to Canada—as though they were "fugitive aldermen"—so as to be within the Commonwealth on the day their book sees print? Defending himself against Twain's charge that only an inept lawyer could have prepared the case set forth in "American Authors and British Pirates," Matthews the attorney turns the tables on his accuser: "The training of the law-school," he advises Twain, "teaches us to consider a law broadly in all its bearings, to examine its working under different circumstances, to discover its effect not only on ourselves but on others, to determine whether its benefits and its hardships are distributed equally and equitably. And this—if you will allow me to say so—this is exactly what you have not done. Because the present British law protects you to your own satisfaction, you ask no more." He reminds Twain, moreover, that under current British law, books that are serialized in American periodicals before being published in volume form—as Twain's own *Innocents Abroad* was—can be legally pirated by British publishers. In addition to citing relevant court cases, Matthews supports his position by presenting anecdotal evidence received (as the result of the same request for information that he had made to Twain) from Charles Dudley Warner, George Haven Putnam, and other eminent American men of letters who did not share Twain's view that cases of British piracy were primarily the fault of American writers rather than of British copyright law. In the coup de grace, Matthews notes that certain British publishers are advertising such well-known books by "Mark Twain" as *Screamers* and *Practical Jokes*, adding that he would like to know how Twain feels about such piracy when it is practiced on himself.

According to Matthews, Twain was so enraged by the rejoinder that he held a grudge against him for several years, until 1890, to be exact, when the two men reconciled while vacationing near each other in the Catskills. Like most professional humorists, observes Matthews in "Memories," Twain quickly lost his sense of humor when *he* was the target of criticism.[44]

The year after *American Authors and British Pirates* was published, Matthews made another contribution to the "good fight": "The Evolution of Copyright," which appeared in the

December 1890 number of *Political Science Quarterly*. The essay may have been prompted by Civil Service Commissioner and fellow Copyright League member Roosevelt. In February of 1890 he had written Matthews: "Can't you get down here [Washington] some time this winter? I would like you to see some of our 'men in action' in congress. They are not always polished, but they are strong. . . . I swear by Tom Reed [Speaker of the House]; and I tell you what, all copy right [*sic*] men ought to stand by him." Frustrated by the opposition against Reed and his allies, Roosevelt appealed to Matthews again, in April: "I wish you would write a scathing article in the forum at the proper time holding up *by name* the chief congressional foes of copyright to merited ridicule" (emphasis Roosevelt's).[45] In composing "The Evolution of Copyright," Matthews wisely ignored the advice of his pugnacious friend; as he had done in his earlier essay rebutting Twain, he avoided ad hominem attacks and kept his argument legal and scholarly in tone. Beginning with pro-copyright statements by two revered men of letters— James Russell Lowell (president of the Copyright League) and Matthew Arnold—Matthews traces the history of copyright from 1469, when the Senate of Venice granted John of Spira the exclusive publication rights to the epistles of Cicero and Pliny, to 1890. Appealing to his readers' sense of national pride as well as of justice, Matthews notes that, where the United States was at one time leading the way in passing laws protecting the rights of authors and publishers, it had by the late nineteenth century fallen behind England and the major European powers in that respect. "Nothing," he observes in the closing lines, "could be more striking than a contrast of the liberality with which the American law treats the inventor and the niggardliness with which it treats the author."[46]

Though Matthews's essay is more polished than strong, it nonetheless greatly pleased Roosevelt, who wrote the author to express his admiration for it, and to register his disappointment in certain of their friends (Twain, perhaps) who had injured their own cause by their "curiously unintelligent deification of the English attitude on the subject." As regards copyright law, Roosevelt went on to say, the French were civilized, the English were "Barbarians," and the Americans were "downright savages." Roosevelt concluded his letter by stating that American resistance to copyright reform helped perpetuate "our condition of literary servitude."[47] Roosevelt was in fact so impressed by "The Evolution of Copyright" that he gave the article to Speaker Reed. If Matthews's account is correct, the piece was largely responsible for Reed's decision to grant the copyright bill a vote during the close of the 1891 congressional session.[48]

With the passage of the Platt-Simmons Act, the "good fight" was won. But, as Christopher Wilson has recently argued, the long-term effects of the new law were mixed.[49] Wilson concedes that during the late 1890s production of American fiction rose dramatically and that, as Matthews had predicted, many previously unknown American writers rose to prominence. Yet the new protection granted to writers had less desirable results as well: if literature was to be conceived of as being *property*, then its producers had to be viewed as *laborers*, subject to the supervision and, in many cases, control of their employer-publishers. Moreover, the frenzied competition among publishers to produce "bestsellers" put increasing pressure on writers to "write to the market" and to secure agents who could offer expert advice on how best to do so. Even Howells, who had in 1887 proclaimed the campaign for international copyright law "one of the most righteous causes that ever appealed to the justice of a nation," was by 1904 bemoaning the unforeseen consequences of the 1891 act: the disappearance of inexpensive books, the weakening of connections with foreign literary currents, and the new wave of sentimental fiction. As Wilson puts it: "Whereas authors had sought greater occupational stability and independence, the outcome [of the 1891 Copyright Act] had been greater risk-taking . . . ; whereas authors had secured their 'rights,' publishers had enlarged their power. Nowhere was this contradiction more evident than in the encroachment of publisher prerogative onto the very notion of 'invention,' a move that coincided with the denigration of the 'literary'" (88). In short, by winning the "good fight" in 1891, Matthews and his fellow copyright crusaders may have actually undermined their own efforts to promote American literary independence.

Roosevelt's and Matthews's literary politics on behalf of "true Americanism" extended beyond the halls of Congress and into the schoolrooms later in the decade, for both men strongly believed that students should study American literature from textbooks that would, as Roosevelt's and Lodge's *Hero Tales from American History* aimed to do, promote the "manly" virtues and a strong sense of nationalism.

When Matthews joined Columbia's faculty in 1891, American literature held the status of unwanted stepchild in the academy. Columbia, however, was one of the few colleges offering a course on American writers, and Matthews was the instructor. (Matthews was also responsible for teaching and developing a course in the modern novel, another subject virtually absent from college curricula of the period.) Roosevelt was greatly interested in Matthews's efforts to promote American literature at Columbia, and he responded enthusiastically to copies of syllabi and exams that the professor sent him.[50] Within a year after Matthews had assumed his position at the college, Roosevelt was urging him to write a "school hand book of American literature," a "series of reviews . . . of our different American authors and schools of literature. If you would only do this . . . you would make a book of the utmost permanent value of interest."[51]

Matthews undertook the project. First published serially

in the juvenile magazine *St. Nicholas,* the group of biographi-
cal-critical essays, their appeal to students enhanced by
sketches or photographs of the authors discussed and reproductions of original manuscript pages, appeared in textbook
form as *An Introduction to the Study of American Literature* in
1896.[52] In eighteen chapters, the book surveys the history of
American literature from the Puritans to the 1890s. Though
discussions of the writers give due attention to literary "technic," the bulk of the text is composed of biographical data and
general assessments of the writers' merits. Those assessments,
not surprisingly, often seem eminently Victorian to modern
eyes. For example, such poets as Fitz-Greene Halleck and Joseph Drake, Bryant, Longfellow, Whittier, Holmes, and Lowell,
as well as the historian Francis Parkman (whose inclusion reminds us that Matthews did not draw a sharp dividing line
between history and "literature"), enjoy full chapters unto
themselves, whereas Whitman and Melville receive only brief
mention in the section on "minor writers." Yet, many of the
writers Matthews privileges and his comments about them
would seem quite familiar to present-day teachers of Ameri-
can-literature survey courses. Though he slights Puritan writing overall, Matthews praises Jonathan Edwards's *Freedom of
the Will* as a "monument of intellectual effort" (20). He describes Emerson as the "foremost representative of the powerful influence which New England has exerted on American life and on American literature" (93). Hawthorne, he
avers, is the most "accomplished artist in fiction that
America has yet produced" (123). And if he relegates
Whitman to the ranks of the minor writers, Matthews nonetheless observes that some foreign critics consider Whitman
the greatest of all American poets, adding that though his
verse is "irregular," it is "beautifully rhythmic" (224–25).
Like Whitman and Melville (*Typee* receives a word of praise,
but *Moby-Dick* is ignored), women writers are slighted; but
Matthews does call attention to Margaret Fuller's abilities as

a literary critic and acclaims Stowe's *Uncle Tom's Cabin* as a novel of abiding value (226–27).

The year before his textbook appeared, Matthews had published a revised edition of his *Poems of American Patriotism* (1882; 1895), an anthology of such patriotic poems as "Paul Revere's Ride," "Old Ironsides," "O Captain! My Captain!" and "The Star Spangled Banner." When Roosevelt received the book, he exclaimed that it ought to be distributed, copy for copy, with his and Lodge's *Hero Tales* "as a missionary tract."[53] That *An Introduction to the Study of American Literature* is likewise a "missionary tract" for "true Americanism" is evident at the outset, for the introduction announces that, while American literature is a branch of English-language literature, the special "soil and conditions" of the United States have made an indelible mark on the writings of the American authors to be discussed: "We believe," Matthews proclaims, "that there is such a thing as Americanism; and that there have been Americans of a type impossible elsewhere in the world—impossible, certainly, in Great Britain" (13). Repeating remarks made in *Americanisms and Briticisms*, he informs his intended audience of students that a language can be only as strong and vibrant as its people are, and that since the English-speaking "race" is steadily spreading across the globe, English literature is bound to expand. Matthews's imperialistic ideology manifests itself once again as he contends that, since the people of the United States are as vigorous and aggressive as their British cousins, "it seems likely that hereafter the Americans, rather than the British, will be recognized as the chief of the English-speaking peoples" (11–13).

In promoting his nationalistic message, Matthews is preoccupied throughout with illuminating the admirable "race traits" he detects in the lives as well as the works of the authors he discusses. As a group, our literary ancestors are, Matthews implies, morally wholesome (with the excep-

Brander Matthews

tion, needless to say, of Poe, who is portrayed as a genius destroyed by his depravity), good-humored, sturdy, optimistic, idealistic yet practical, egalitarian, and, of course, intensely patriotic. Lowell, for example, is described as a "true American, not only in his stalwart patriotism in the hour of trial, but in his loving acceptance of the doctrine of human equality." Holmes is lauded for his kindliness and "sunny sagacity." Emerson's essays ever reveal a "sturdy and wholesome Americanism." Defending Thoreau against the charge that he urged men to return to the savage state, Matthews commends *Walden* as a "wholesome" warning against the pursuit of luxury. And Whitman is described as an "intense American" whose "stalwart verse" looks to the future with "splendid confidence."

Though among the earliest textbooks in the field, *An Introduction to the Study of American Literature* did have precursors, the two major ones being Moses Coit Tyler's *A History of American Literature, 1607–1765* (1878), and Charles F. Richardson's *American Literature, 1607–1885* (1887–89). Matthews cites both works. Since Tyler's study restricts itself to the colonial period, Matthews probably drew on Richardson in preparing his chapters on nineteenth-century American literature, but in doing so he revised Richardson's low opinion of the American realists.[54] In the closing chapter of his book, Matthews suggests that, while there is no towering figure on the field of American literature, the average of literary skill is higher than ever—especially in the South and West—because his contemporary writers practice the (Howellsian) credo of telling the "whole truth, and nothing but the truth" about American life (233). Though he does not mention specific names (citing living authors by name would have been unconventional at that time), photos of Twain and Edward Eggleston leave no doubt that he is alluding to the realists. Contemporary American literature and literary criticism are robust and flourishing, he declares, because they bear no traces of the "colonial attitude"; American writers no longer look toward England for approval. Yet, though they "know that American literature has to grow in its own way and of its own accord," these writers refuse to be judged solely as *American* authors, insisting that American literature be measured by the "loftiest standards" of world literature (234). Thus, as in his essays "American Literature" and "Literature in the New Century," Matthews conjoins realism-nationalism-cosmopolitanism, with the middle term of the triad receiving, as usual, heaviest emphasis.

Though Matthews's textbook is hardly the work of "utmost permanent value" that Roosevelt hoped it would be, it was clearly a success from the author's standpoint, its sales reaching the quarter-million mark within twenty-five years after its initial publication.[55] A significant portion of those sales, no doubt, resulted from the sterling review the text received in *The Bookman* shortly after publication. *An Introduction to the Study of American Literature*, asserts the *Bookman* reviewer, is "a piece of work as good of its kind as any American scholar ever had in his hands." Furthermore, "the principles upon which Mr. Matthews insists with such quiet force and good taste are those which must be adopted, not only by every student of American writings, but by every American writer if he is going to do work that is really worth doing." The reviewer finds the sketch of Cooper to be "capital," and concurs with Matthews's assertion that Parkman is the greatest of American historians. The author of the review, as the reader may have guessed by now, is Roosevelt—who wrote the critique at Matthews's request, and received his assistance in getting it published.[56]

Matthews's textbook received an equally favorable review in *Harper's Weekly* from a critic who seldom concurred with Roosevelt's literary or political opinions—Howells. The Dean may have had the jingoistic Roosevelt in mind when he wrote the critique, for he announces at the outset that nationalism in literature becomes a vice rather than a virtue if carried to extremes; he does not, he insists, value any book simply because of its "Americanism." Yet, after thus attempting to distance himself from those who would make patriotism a litmus test for a work of art, Howells reveals the pull that consensus nationalism had on his own criticism by admitting that the "Jingo" in him is touched by Matthews's study, which "heartens us with a true sense of the greatness of our native republic of letters."[57]

It would take roughly another quarter century before the greatness of our native republic of letters impressed a sufficient number of academicians to gain the study of American literature a firm foothold in the university curriculum. A momentous event in the struggle to clear space for American literature in the academy was the four-volume *Cambridge History of American Literature* (1917–21). Once again, Matthews was not far from the center. In fact, he would have been directly at the center if the project's initiator and publisher, George Haven Putnam, had had his way, for Putnam wanted Matthews to coedit the *CHAL* with William P. Trent.[58] As noted earlier, though Matthews and Trent did not see eye-to-eye on the issue of American imperialism, they were intimate friends and steady correspondents during the 1890s. Matthews in fact worked indefatigably during these years to promote Trent's professional career. In addition to citing him as an exemplary New Southerner in "Two Studies of the South," Matthews recommended, to his old friend William C. Brownell, that Scribner's publish Trent's collection of essays *The Authority of Criticism* (1899). In 1893, Matthews had urged Lounsbury to support Trent's application for a position at Yale; despite Lounsbury's efforts, Trent failed to get the job. When a position opened in his own English department several years later, Matthews again lobbied on Trent's behalf, successfully this time.[59] Trent's appointment to Columbia in 1900 owed a debt not only to the influence of Matthews but to that of New York's governor, Theodore Roosevelt.[60] An advocate of southern literature and of the *Sewanee Review*, Roosevelt shared Matthews's high opinion of Trent. Despite his opposition to United States expansionism in the 1890s, Trent equally admired Roosevelt, as suggested by Trent's dedicating *Southern Statesmen of the Old Regime* (1897) to him.[61]

Not long after taking up residence at Morningside Heights, Trent paid Matthews back, so to speak, for favors received by publishing an essay titled "Brander Matthews as a Dramatic Critic," in which he praised his benefactor in terms usually reserved for the deceased. America's foremost drama critic, Trent gushed, was "wholly fearless, remarkably suggestive, always clean-minded and sound-hearted, possessed of wide sympathies, and democratic in the best sense of the term."[62] But by the time Putnam conceived the idea, in 1914, of producing the *CHAL*, Trent and Matthews were no longer on speaking terms. The rupture between the two was caused by political rather than literary differences: as nationalistic strife in Europe was setting the stage for World War I, Trent was expressing pro-German sentiments at Columbia (in poetry as well as prose), while Matthews was, like Roosevelt, condemning the Germans and urging support for Great Britain. Putnam's suggestion that Matthews serve as Trent's coeditor was therefore rejected. Trent became senior editor of the project, which was headquartered at Columbia; Matthews settled for the role of contributor, writing the chapter (23) on Holmes, Lowell, and other poets of "familiar verse."[63]

However repulsed he was by Trent's political views, Matthews would have found little to complain about upon reading the essay that Trent and his three associate editors (John Erskine, Stuart Sherman, and Carl Van Doren) composed as the preface to the *CHAL*, for it espouses the same sort of nationalistic cosmopolitanism that Matthews had been promoting for more than a quarter century. Trent and his fellow editors announce that the *CHAL* is a "life of the American people as expressed in their writings rather than a history of *belles-lettres* alone," adding that such a comprehensive historical account of American literature would render the spirit of American literary criticism "more energetic and more masculine." Yet they nonetheless emphasize that "there never was and never can be an exclusively national literature," since any country's literature is indebted to the literature of other countries and of other ages. In constructing the framework of the *CHAL*, they insist, they sought to avoid the "temptation of national pride," of mistaking, as Matthews put it, a native goose for a swan of Avon.[64]

The *CHAL* was a major step toward establishing American literature as a profession. Its publication was followed in 1921 by the formation of the American Literature Group of the Modern Language Society, which in turn established the journal *American Literature* in 1929, the year of Matthews's death. Matthews thus died knowing that his lifelong campaign to make American literature a respected academic discipline had largely been won. Yet, it was a bittersweet victory for him overall, because even as the *CHAL* was implicitly "canonizing" many of the writers whom Matthews had privileged in his *An Introduction to the Study of American Literature* (e.g., Cooper, Lowell, Holmes, Whittier, Howells), the younger generation of Americanists was consigning them to the margins, redrawing the center around writers whom Matthews's textbook either slighted (Melville and Whitman) or completely ignored (Dreiser and Crane).

Refuting the notion, advanced by a long line of American scholars, that F. O. Matthiessen's *American Renaissance* almost single-handedly established American literature in the academy, Eric Cheyfitz has recently argued that Matthiessen's book was not the origin but the culmination of a movement,

initiated in the nineteenth century, to nationalize and pro-
fessionalize American literature; *American Renaissance*, as
Cheyfitz puts it, was thus a "classically corporate" project.[65]
If we accept Cheyfitz's metaphor, then the Columbia professor who in the 1890s authored such essays as "American
Literature" and "The Literary Independence of the United
States," lobbied for American spelling and the Copyright
Act of 1891, developed one of the first college courses on
American writers, and produced a textbook on American literature that eventually sold over a quarter-million copies
deserves recognition as a leading member of the board during the "corporation's" formative years. As we shall see in
chapter 6, however, Matthews's championing of "American
methods and American ways in literature" was completely
ignored by Bourne, Mencken, and other younger members
of the corporate board who caricatured him as a colonial-
minded genteel.

5   Ideological "Snap-Shots" of the New York Metropolis: Matthews's Fiction

In addition to his voluminous scholarship and criticism, Matthews produced a sizable and varied corpus of fiction: three full-length novels, several books of short stories, and a juvenile romance. Matthews admitted that many of his early stories, written during the late 1870s and early 1880s, were done purely for fun and were imitative of the "clever" but superficial fictions of Thomas Bailey Aldrich. But, as he crusaded for Howells and literary realism during the eighties, Matthews became increasingly interested in exploiting the "local color" potential of his beloved New York. As he explains in his autobiography:

> The field was here, and it was fertile, and furthermore, it had not been pre-empted. Yet there were very few of us who then [the late 1880s] recognized the richness of the soil or who had confidence in the crop that could be raised. London had been painted on the broad canvases of a host of robust novelists. . . . but New York had not yet attracted either the novelists [with the exception of Henry James, of course] or the tellers of brief tales. Her streets were paved with gold . . . but the men of letters who strayed here and there in her thorofares had not the vision to perceive they were living in a Golconda of opportunity.[1]

With this vision in mind, Matthews set out to "write short stories saturated with local color," verbal "snap-shots" that would capture and fix the "color, unending movement, and incessant vitality" of the great metropolis.[2] In 1894 he collected a dozen of these previously published "snap-shots" into a volume titled *Vignettes of Manhattan,* and followed it in 1897 with a second volume, *Outlines in Local Color.* Realizing that the short-story form could not contain the "movement of the mighty city," he approached his subject with a larger camera, producing three novels: *His Father's Son* (1895), *A Confident To-morrow* (1899), and *The Action and the Word* (1900). Though none of these works was the best-seller he hoped for, each was, he remarks, well-received by reviewers and by his "fellow-craftsmen in the practice of fiction."[3] Matthews's novels were not as well received as he suggests, but they did win praise from several literary fellows, including the craftsman he most wanted to please—Howells.

In 1893, as he struggled to overcome his penchant for producing "clever" stories and to create enduring "snapshots," Matthews, reflecting on a recent conversation with Howells, wrote him: "What you said the other night about my stories not being your kind of stories is true, I'm afraid. Not only is my natural gift less, but both my temperament and my training are very different from yours. Yet your kinds of stories are the stories I like best, read oftenest, praise most highly. From no American author have I learned as much as from you of the ways, customs, traditions, thoughts and characters of my fellow citizens." Matthews closed by declaring that, though his own works fell short of the realist mark, he did not "belong in the other [what Howells termed the "romanticistic"] camp."[4]

Why Howells would place Matthews's fiction in the "other camp" is suggested by a story like "Memories," which, as noted in chapter 2, is a thinly veiled tribute to Roosevelt and promotes the Rough Rider's code of the "strenuous life" and "manly duty." Roosevelt was very pleased also with *Vignettes of Manhattan,* which Matthews dedicated to him. No doubt the volume includes several of the pieces that prompted Howells to reprimand Matthews for being a romanticistic writer. In "Before the Break of Day," for example, Matthews responded to the copy of *Maggie* that Stephen Crane had sent him by re-visioning it into an improbable tale of heroism that celebrates the American Dream. The tale is set in the Bowery, and its heroine is named Maggie. Like Crane's, this Maggie's life has been hard and gets worse after she is jilted by a young tough. But Matthews's heroine does not slide into the naturalistic abyss; rescued from its edge by an honest bartender, she and her new beau get married, buy a saloon of their own, and feel confident that they will be rich if they keep working hard. In another vignette, a father succeeds in securing a governor's pardon for his son, who had been unjustly imprisoned for manslaughter. The youth, however, is killed in a prison riot the very day the pardon is granted; when the father reads the newspaper account of his son's death, he falls dead on the spot, "still tightly grasping the pardon."[5]

After receiving Howells's frank criticism in 1893, however, Matthews attempted to replace the melodramatic lens through which he had envisioned his vignettes with a realist one. His first success as a Howellsian "realist" was, in the Dean's as well as his own eyes, *His Father's Son*, a novel that was serialized in two parts in *Harper's Weekly* in 1895 before being published in volume form in 1896. As Howells had sarcastically observed in an 1891 "Editor's Study" piece, the millionaire had become the new subject for the romance.[6] The central character of *His Father's Son* is a millionaire, but he is no more romanticized than is Jacob Dryfoos of *A Hazard of New Fortunes*. In his fictions set in Fort Roosevelt or the ghetto, Matthews was swimming in alien waters; but in depicting the Wall Street scene he was in his own element. Before the Panic of 1873 financially ruined his father, young Brander spent a good deal of time at his father's business office on Wall Street, observing firsthand the making and breaking of millionaires. Those observations had convinced him that the majority of Wall Street tycoons were not heroes to be idolized but unprincipled materialists whose lust for profits was a cancer of the national spirit. That view was, of course, shared by Roosevelt and most other progressivists. In the opening chapter of *His Father's Son*, Ezra Pierce (the father) preaches to his son Winslow that, though some may consider investors to be mere gamblers, they are actually the "greatest benefactors of humanity the world has ever seen."[7] Subsequent events in the novel, however, refute that claim: under the well-intentioned but inevitably pernicious tutelage of his father—who refuses to see the immorality of many of his business dealings—Winslow gradually becomes possessed by the gambling demon and is transformed from a moral idealist into a selfish cynic. By the end of the narrative, he has destroyed his marriage and has fled to Europe to escape prosecution for fraud. There he marries a Parisian socialite and pesters his heartbroken father for more money.

Reviewing the first installment of the novel when it appeared in *Harper's*, Howells showered it and the author with praise. Matthews's essays and drama criticism have been consistently brilliant, states the Dean, but the fictions preceding *His Father's Son* are, as he had told Matthews personally in 1893, tainted by elements of the fantastic.[8] "I have had to ask myself," Howells continues, "Hasn't his knowledge of literature got the better of his knowledge of life at this point or at that [in his stories]? Will he be able to go forward in the light of the verity dear to his artistic conscience, or will he advance in the flicker of the trickery fancy that amuses him?" But with *His Father's Son*, Howells declares, Matthews seems to have abandoned the fanciful and sensational and has joined the American school of fiction best represented by the recent work of such accomplished realists as Henry B. Fuller. The first half of Matthews's novel reveals a "firm texture of character, a fidelity of circumstance, a quiet truth of local color"; this is Wall Street as never before depicted in American literature. If the second and final installment of the novel sustains the artistic virtues present in the first, then

Matthews, Howells contends, will have established himself as a novelist of true quality.

Matthews, needless to say, was greatly flattered and wrote Howells to say so. Admitting that most of his previous fictions—even those that "pretended to be realistic"—were essentially "fantastic," he declares that *His Father's Son* is his attempt to face life seriously and truthfully, as writers such as Turgenev and, of course, Howells himself have done. "I hope," Matthews states, "you will like the story to the end; however much it may fall off, it does not change its manner at all. The end is too sad, I fear, for the study ever to be popular; and so your praise of it is doubly precious."[9]

Though one particularly uncharitable critic dismissed the completed novel as a "sad dog,"[10] most reviewers praised the book's theme and its detailed depiction of the Wall Street scene. But they also faulted Matthews for creating characters lacking psychological depth, and at least one critic found Winslow's slide from moral idealism to selfish cynicism improbable.[11] Most critics today would, I think, concur with these complaints. Howells's review, however, offers a much more positive perspective: filled with superlatives, it grants the high marks that Matthews had hoped for. Announcing that Matthews "kept faith with me to the last word" of the novel, Howells reports that he has not read a "cleaner, finer, straighter piece of work" in a long time; *His Father's Son* is a "tragedy of principles, of conditions, of moral forces, but so livingly embodied that it is too intensely human, too like us all, to suffer us to be very self-confident in condemning this or that person in it."[12] In seeking to present a truthful vision of Wall Street, argues Howells, Matthews could not help but accuse the "whole economic system," though "that is scarcely what the author meant [to do]." Significantly, further on in the same review essay, Howells only lukewarmly recommends Crane's *The Red Badge of Courage*, judging it psychologically realistic but somewhat immature.

Works of art, Theodor Adorno has written, achieve greatness only insofar as they "let speak what ideology conceals. They transcend, whether they want to or not, false consciousness."[13] Adorno's proposition helps explain, I think, why Howells—who at this point in his life was a socialist in his politics, if not in his life-style—would value Matthews's banal novel over Crane's masterpiece of psychological impressionism. As his admiration for and friendship with Andrew Carnegie testifies, Matthews did not share the Dean's view of capitalism as an "infernal" economic system; like Roosevelt, he condemned plutocracy but not the economic system that created plutocrats. Thus, from a Marxist perspective, Matthews was clearly a prisoner of "false consciousness." But, in conceiving *His Father's Son* he had, Howells suggests in the review, transcended his bourgeois ideology and produced a work whose subtext indicts capitalism, though that was "scarcely what [he] meant [to do]." (Howells may have preferred *Maggie* over *The Red Badge of Courage* because the ghetto tale, too, implicitly condemns the "whole economic system.") Yet Howells's interpretation—one might say appropriation—of *His Father's Son* as an attack on socioeconomic principles that Matthews himself embraced did not, apparently, chafe the professor, for he expressed his deep appreciation for the review, remarking, "You were in my mind always as I wrote. I was trying to tell the truth according to your precepts and was hoping that you would like the tale."[14]

When Matthews undertook writing his second novel, *A Confident To-morrow*, four years later in 1899, Howells was again in his mind, so much so that the book contains a thinly disguised portrait of him. But the portrait is not entirely flattering, and the novel overall projects Matthews's growing disenchantment with Howells's praxis, if not theory, of literary realism. In this book Matthews sought not to "keep faith" with his literary father but to rid himself of what Harold Bloom would diagnose as the "anxiety of influence."

Described as a "determined realist," Frank Sartain, the novel's central character, comes from Topeka, where he had spent several years as a journalist, to New York City in hopes of publishing his first novel, titled *Dust and Ashes*.[15] Mirror image of *His Father's Son*, Sartain's fictional study of the metropolis focuses all its attention on the villains of Wall Street and their victims (67). Having had no firsthand experience with the New York scene, however, Sartain based his depiction of it entirely on other books as well as on his unpleasant boyhood experiences at Narragansett Pier, where as a hack-driver for the rich during summers, he was exposed to the "hollowness of our boasted civilization" (17) and to social snobbery. The shortcomings of American culture and social snobbery are, of course, two prominent themes in Howells's novels, including *A Hazard of New Fortunes*, which was, one suspects, among the urban fictions that shaped Sartain's perceptions of big-city life. Upon arriving in New York, Sartain immediately seeks the acquaintance of Meredith Vivian, a novelist whose "delicate art" Sartain admires with the same "profound reverence" (10) as Matthews did Howells's. That Howells was the model for Vivian seems beyond question. Like Howells, Vivian, who advises Sartain to write about what he knows best rather than what seems interesting "literary" material, rose from humble beginnings to become the most successful and influential novelist of his era (37) and a sort of father figure to the younger generation of writers. Howells, as his six volumes of *Selected Letters* reveal, wrote numerous letters of encouragement and advice to fledgling writers and critics. Matthews's essays and reviews praising Howells's works earned him many notes of appreciation and support, including the one in which the Dean proclaimed: "your work is better than that of any critic of your generation."[16] The description of Vivian's relationship and correspondence with his literary sons suggests, however, that Matthews may have suspected that ulterior motives lurked beneath the surface of such flattering remarks. Vivian, one character sarcastically observes, has

> a habit of attaching to him by bonds of gratitude for favors received all the rising young men of letters in the country. [He] writes one of his clever little notes to every man who reviews one of his books—and if the fellow who did the notice is young, he takes it as a great compliment to himself and as proof that his critical faculty is singularly acute. (139)

Sartain, who upon reviewing one of Vivian's novels receives a letter from him commending the review for its "justice both in the praise and the blame" (208), wonders if all those "clever little notes" are Vivian's self-seeking attempts to maintain his prominent stature among upcoming writers like himself. In a letter expressing his appreciation for Matthews's "Mr. Howells as a Critic" in 1902—three years after *A Confident Tomorrow* was written—Howells, curiously enough, echoed Vivian's urbane note to Sartain: "Your praise," the Dean remarked, "seems the more reasonable because your blame is so just."[17] Emerson Adams, a painter whose character fuses the idealism of an Emerson with the prickly cynicism of a Henry Adams, assures Sartain, however, that the elder writer is by nature kind, sincere, and generous—just as Matthews assured his contemporaries that Howells was a man "large of nature and of a transparent sincerity."[18] These qualities, not any manipulative practices on Vivian's part, have kept him "solid" with the younger writers, declares Adams (139). Sartain accepts Adams's assessment, but by merely raising the question of Vivian's sincerity, Matthews plants in the reader's mind the seed of doubt about Vivian's character and, by implication, about Howells's as well.

Subsequent events in the narrative deepen the ambivalent image of Vivian and therefore of Howells. *Dust and Ashes*, Sartain admits, was an attempt to follow in Vivian's footsteps (21); not surprisingly, though he finds its art rather immature, Vivian responds favorably to the Wall Street novel (187), just as the author of *A Hazard of New Fortunes* had to *His Father's Son*. But the longer he investigates the city for himself, the more Sartain is "seized by a sense of the beauty inherent in modern life" (50). Influenced by Emerson Adams, who is at his most sarcastic when castigating those who denigrate the modern and idealize the ancient (Matthews, we recall, disparaged Ibsen for desiring to return to the "sun-dial"), Sartain comes to equate the metropolis with vitality and progress rather than with degeneracy. In an epiphanic moment brought on by Adams's passionate outburst celebrating the city, Sartain discovers that his "realism had been rather sordid," that he had "looked down for his facts rather than up" (66). His second novel, he therefore determines, will offer a much more positive perspective on New York than did his tale of Wall Street villains and victims.

An upbeat perspective on New York is precisely what Matthews provides in *A Confident To-morrow*, for this novel, in contrast to *His Father's Son*, is a success story with a happy ending. After Sartain comes to New York and meets Vivian, he falls in love with the charming Esther Dircks, whose father is a socialist radical. Intellectually vacuous, ignorant of political issues, and not interested in gaining the right to vote, Esther is a far cry from the "New Woman." When her father, Raphael, inherits a large sum of money, he launches a reformist newspaper and offers the editorship to Sartain, whose disdain for the plutocrats appeals to the cranky old man. Sartain, however, is as opposed to Dircks's anarchism as he is to laissez-faire capitalism and crass commercialism. Sartain's politics are unmistakably progressivist; he supports abolition of the patronage system, subsidized housing, and other social and political reforms that Roosevelt and the progressivists championed in real life. As one who believed that "public opinion, if only sufficiently enlightened and aroused, is equal to the necessary regenerative tasks and can yet dominate the future," Roosevelt must have been delighted by Sartain's exclamation, in the passage that embodies the novel's central theme, that "It has always seemed to me that the way to make the world better is to tell people it is getting better, and to prove it to them; to encourage them and not to discourage them; to inspire hope and confidence and energy to fight a good fight, with certain victory in the distance" (178). And Roosevelt—who in 1894, the year of the bloody Pullman riots in Chicago, admitted to Matthews that he liked to see a "mob handled by the regulars, or by good State guards, not over-scrupulous about bloodshed"—would without doubt have concurred with Sartain's condemnation of the strikers' violent actions against the police during the New York street-car strike.[19] Though Dircks's sympathies are entirely with labor, Sartain—who has come to believe that the "boyish iconoclasm" he brought with him to New York was "rather foolish" (284)—feels morally compelled to write an editorial in which he argues that "If we attack the robber barons because they set themselves above the law, we must also call the strikers to order when they put themselves outside the law" (274). Outraged, the fanatical Dircks refuses to put another cent into a tabloid that "stood up for law" (281). (Since he has by this point gone bankrupt, he could not provide more money for the enterprise even if he wanted to.) The paper goes under. Sartain is unemployed but not dismayed; he remains confident about tomorrow. His optimism is borne out when he is hired—at a larger salary—by a New York publishing house, this stroke of good fortune allowing him to marry the fair Esther. And Sartain's faith in the common sense of his fellow New Yorkers is vali-

Brander Matthews

dated by their electing an honest reformer to the mayor's office (229), as reform-minded New Yorkers had done in 1894 by voting for William L. Strong and against the Tammany machine. In the novel's closing lines, as Sartain and his new bride gaze, arm in arm, at the New York skyline, we are told that, whereas two years earlier the mighty city seemed a "frowning fortress" to the callow young man, it now appears "friendly and inviting" (300).

Noting the obvious parallels between Dircks and the anarchist Lindau of *A Hazard of New Fortunes*, Matthews's Columbia colleague Harry Thurston Peck suggested in his review of *A Confident To-morrow* that "Mr. Matthews's well-known admiration for the work of Mr. Howells has led him unconsciously to assimilate some of Mr. Howells's material."[20] Peck missed the point: Matthews indeed assimilated material from *A Hazard of New Fortunes*—not only Dircks's portrait but major plot elements as well—but he acted intentionally. As he had earlier done with Crane's *Maggie*, Matthews transformed a grim work that seeks to subvert the status quo into a middlebrow celebration of the American Dream. Where Howells's novel portrays the strikers sympathetically and condemns the brutality of the police, Matthews's puts the strikers in a negative light and insists that the police had to meet violence with violence in order to prevent anarchy. Where the plutocrat Jacob Dryfoos is the central target of Howells's scorn, the anarchist-socialist Dircks is the butt of Matthews's. Looking down rather than up for the facts when constructing his first New York novel, Howells produced his darkest fiction; turning his gaze upward—as Sartain physically does in the book's closing—Matthews created a progressivist novel that aims to "inspire hope and confidence and energy to fight a good fight."

Matthews's re-visioning of Howells's *Hazard of New Fortunes* should not, however, be interpreted as a repudiation of the doctrine of literary realism, which, as we have noted, he defined as the attempt to render life honestly and truthfully, for he believed that *A Confident To-morrow* presented a more accurate cross-section of New York life than did Howells's novel. It was Howells, after all, who in that famous quote of 1886 urged the American writer to dramatize the "more smiling aspects of life" since they were the "more American." The Haymarket tragedy of 1886 and the terrible death of his daughter in 1889 darkened Howells's vision, as *A Hazard of New Fortunes* testifies. Matthews, however, never wavered in his conviction that the "smiling aspects" *were* the more American. As previously discussed, Matthews was ideologically much closer to the jingoistic Roosevelt than to the deeply distressed Dean in the late 1890s. When he embarked upon his first novel in 1895, Matthews set out to produce a somber "Howellsian" critique of Gilded Age commercialism, the result, as Howells observed, being an implicit denunciation of capitalism. But the Spanish-American War fanned the flames of Matthews's burning sense of patriotism, and *A Confident To-morrow*—the title itself implying Matthews's "bully" Americanism—projected, as such essays as "The Study of Fiction" also did, his belief that the "race traits" most manifest in the "typical" Anglo-American were courage, tenacity, energy, good humor, and so on. Put simply, Matthews's quarrel with Howells was not over the aesthetic of realism, which Matthews, we recall, vigorously defended in "Mr. Howells as a Critic" (1902) and in other post-1900 essays, but over the Dean's vision of America and the ideology in which that vision was grounded.

In 1894 Roosevelt, who admired Howells's early works, complained that the Dean's view of life had turned "jaundiced."[21] As he breaks away from Vivian's influence in *A Confident To-morrow*, Matthews's persona employs a synonymous metaphor in describing the "damning defect" of the elder writer's novels: they lack, he says, the "ruddy drop of human blood" (250). By the end of the novel Sartain, though

Brander Matthews

he maintains his friendship with and respect for Vivian, discovers that he "could no longer assign to the elder author so high a place as he had hitherto given him. It came upon him with a certain shock that he had outgrown Vivian, that he had passed beyond the stage in which such writing as Vivian's was to be admired inevitably, and that perhaps, after all, he had been setting too high a value upon Vivian's work" (250). With that comment, Matthews completed the figurative slaying of his literary father.

Surely Howells, who had reviewed Matthews's first novel with such enthusiasm and who commented, either publicly or privately, on virtually every book his friend published, must have read *A Confident To-morrow*, yet he does not mention it in any of his published writings or in any of the numerous letters he wrote to Matthews after 1900. Assuming he did read the book and recognized, as he could hardly avoid doing, its ambivalent portrait of him, he apparently did not allow the experience to sour his relationship with Matthews; the two men remained close friends until Howells's death. Matthews was one of many writers, most notably Garland and Wister, who drifted from Howells's to Roosevelt's camp during the late 1890s, and in such cases the Dean generally proved to be a tolerant literary mentor.[22] In his 1917 review of *These Many Years* Howells was as generous as ever with his praise: not only did he laud Matthews's accomplishments as a scholar and educator, he also expressed admiration for Matthews's "two . . . best novels."[23] Two, not three; since Howells, as explained below, considered Matthews's final novel, *The Action and the Word*, to be an even better work of art than *His Father's Son*, the novel he tactfully excluded must be *A Confident To-morrow*.

The Action and the Word (1900) concerns itself with one of Howells's favorite themes, the Woman Question; and, as in several of his marriage novels, that question is implicitly answered by affirming the value of marriage as a bulwark against anarchic desires that threaten both self and society.[24] But if Matthews followed Howells in this respect, he sought to go "beyond" the elder writer's "jaundiced" fiction by injecting his narrative with the element of passion he felt was wanting in the Dean's novels. In "Of Women's Novels" Matthews, as noted, had observed that women writers were "more willing than men [such as Howells?] to suggest the animal nature that sheathes our immortal souls; they are bolder in the use of the stronger emotions; they are more willing to suggest the possibilities of passion lurking all unsuspected beneath the placidity of modern fine-lady existence."[25] In *The Action and the Word*, Matthews, one might say, sought to write passionately "like a woman"—but the result would hardly have pleased feminists like Charlotte Perkins Gilman.

The novel's central character is Carla, a beautiful, dark-eyed Creole whose "supple" and "undulating" walk never fails to attract an admiring male eye. Daughter of a race-horse breeder, she spent her youth in an environment where "animal nature" could hardly be more apparent—a stud farm. When she marries into the upper stratum of Manhattan society, she becomes bored with her role as a wife and mother. The source of her frustration, Matthews all but explicitly states, is sexual repression. Dr. Brookfield (Carla's father-in-law), who represents the wisdom that comes with maturity, suspects that she is dissatisfied with domestic life because she did not "sow her her wild oats" as a youth, as males have the opportunity to do. She finds an outlet for her suppressed desires in amateur acting. Like her contemporary fictional actress, Carrie Meeber, Carla thrills her audiences with her ability to "exert the potent fascination of sex" on stage.[26] That acting is for Carla, as for Carrie, a sublimation of her sexual urges is vividly suggested when, in an agitated state after a successful performance, she remarks that the experience on stage reminded her of an exciting adventure she had when she was fifteen years old: in an act of intentional disobedience, she had gone bare-back riding on one of the studs, "astride like a man." Describing how her horse broke into a wild gallop, she exclaims: "There we were, flying down the pike, and I couldn't hold him, and my hair got loose, and I didn't know whether he was running away and whether he'd even stop. That was splendid, too! Excitement and success,—just like to-night,—for I conquered him after a while; and I rode him home on the snaffle" (149).

Though Matthews could be bold enough to reveal the passions lurking beneath the placidity of modern fine-lady existence, he nonetheless shared Howells's fear of the "unbridled" libido in women. As the story proceeds, it becomes clear that, if Carla's mild-mannered husband, Evert, does not take the reins, she will ride roughshod over him, thus destroying their marriage and jeopardizing the future happiness of their infant son. When she broaches the idea of going on the road as a professional actress and placing the baby under the care of a governess, Evert seeks counsel from Dr. Brookfield, who informs him that, however passionately they cry for independence, women desire to be *mastered* by their man (183). Inspired by his father's advice, Evert takes his stand. A bitter quarrel ensues, with Carla crying out: "I was a woman before I was a mother, wasn't I? And I think a woman has some rights, after all. She has a right to live her own life, hasn't she?" She further exclaims that she will be no "slave," no "talking doll, to be wound up and dressed and undressed [!] again" (218–19). Carla of course speaks— or rather screams—here in the voice of the New Woman, but though her arguments may sound persuasive to feminist ears, they are dismissed as the rantings of a spoiled child by her husband, and, clearly, by the novel's author, who once complained that the ending of *A Doll's House* was improbable because Ibsen denied Nora the "most permanent and most overpowering of woman's characteristics—the maternal instinct."[27] In the end, that instinct does indeed over-whelm Carla: after nursing her child through a serious ill-ness, she decides, as Dr. Brookfield knew she would, that she prefers the nursery to a room of her own. The closing scene finds her disparaging the author of *A Doll's House* as an "old bore" who knows nothing about "American girls," and chirping that "It's a wife's duty to wait on her husband" (239–40).

The reference to *A Doll's House* suggests that Matthews meant his novel to be a rebuttal of Ibsen's "unrealistic" play. But he may also have been targeting Kate Chopin's *The Awakening*, which had appeared a year before *The Action and the Word*. The many parallels between these works suggest that Matthews—who, as a native of New Orleans, had a spe-cial interest in fictional portraits of Creole life—had Chopin's novel in mind as he composed his own.[28] Both works dra-matize the struggle of a passionate woman to break the constricting bonds imposed by American Victorianism, and both set in opposition the Creole and Anglo (Puritan) atti-tudes toward sexual desire. Like Carla, Edna came to New Orleans from Kentucky, where her father bred race horses.[29] Finally, the title that Chopin chose for her novel would fit Matthews's perfectly, for the climactic event of *The Action and the Word* is Carla's "awakening" to her responsibilities as a wife and mother, responsibilities that Edna escapes through suicide.

The Action and the Word no doubt struck a responsive chord in those "manly" readers who shared Theodore Roosevelt's fear that *fin de siècle* American culture was be-coming dangerously feminized. Yet the most lavish praise of the book came not from the Rough Rider but from Howells, who must have somehow discovered in it the "fidelity to ex-perience and probability of motive" that he demanded in the realist novel. In an essay in *Literature and Life*, Howells placed *The Action and the Word* in the good company of

Crane's *Maggie*, Abraham Cahan's *Yekl*, and James's *Washington Square*; after speaking of the "masterly skill" with which Matthews had sketched New York's genteel society in *His Father's Son*, the Dean lauded Matthews's third novel as "one of the best American stories I know."[30] In a letter to Garland he called it "a capital story about a stage-tempted wife—the best thing [Matthews] has done." To Matthews himself, Howells gushed that the work was "one of the most perfect pieces of fiction in the language," adding: "The delicate beauty of such a book as The A[ction] and the W[ord] is obscured in a brute time for a while, but it will count you 12 in minds of true critics." And when he was asked to be general editor of a series of novels by prominent American and British writers (a project later aborted), Howells solicited a book from Matthews, asking him if he could produce "a novel of 50,000 words as good as 'The A[ction] and the W[ord]?'"[31]

From his own day to the present, Howells's attitude toward women has generated heated debate. To such admirers of Howells as Edwin H. Cady, the Dean's support of the suffrage movement, his well-known statement that women were, in general, morally superior to men, and the many sympathetic portraits in his novels of women trapped in the patriarchal net of Victorian American culture qualify him for the title of "ardent feminist." But Gail Thain Parker and other feminist critics have argued that the subtexts of Howells's works endorse male hegemony and reveal his unconscious fear of the independent woman.[32] Critics on both sides of the fence have been vexed by Howells's silence on *The Awakening*. We know that he admired "Boulet and Boulotte," one of Chopin's vignettes of Creole life, for he sent her a letter telling her so. No other correspondence between the two writers exists, however, and Howells makes no mention of Chopin or *The Awakening* in his writings.[33] But if *The Action and the Word* is, as I have suggested, a patriarchal re-visioning of *The Awakening*, then Howells's exuberant praise of Matthews's novel may be read as an implicit comment on Chopin's. In any case, Howells's discovery of "delicate beauty" in Matthews's crude caricature of the New Woman provides telling evidence for those in Parker's camp.

"Don't you be down-hearted; you are all right, and your day is coming," Howells assured Matthews in the letter commending the "delicate beauty" of *The Action and the Word*.[34] By that time, however, a thoroughly discouraged Matthews had faced the fact that his day as a novelist would never come; in 1900 he abandoned novel-writing, complaining to Trent (before the breach of their friendship occurred): "I don't sell—and I don't get praised."[35] A year earlier (1899), Howells had composed his lecture essay "Novel-Writing and Novel-Reading," perhaps his most thoughtfully expressed proclamation of his realist credo. In it he stated that "truth to life is the supreme office of the novel," and he contended that the novelist "is rarely the victim of such a possession, or obsession, that he does not know when he is representing and when he is misrepresenting life. If he does not know it fully at the time, he cannot fail to be aware of it upon review of his work."[36] The naïveté of that theory is clearly exposed by Matthews's assessment of his work. Though the reception of his novels (outside the flattering reviews provided by Howells, Trent, and other close friends) disheartened him to the point that he ceased writing fiction, Matthews never came to recognize what seems obvious to a contemporary critic: that his supposedly "objective" representations of the great metropolis were mediated by his race, class, gender, and ideology. In his retrospective analysis of why his novels failed to achieve the popularity and critical acclaim he had hoped for, Matthews insisted that the "picture I painted [in the novels] was true to life." The main reason his "snapshots" had not won a wide readership, suggested the creator of such cardboard stereotypes as Ezra Pierce, Raphael

Dircks, and Carla Brookfield, was that they were "too quiet in tone, too subdued, too moderate, to thrust themselves into the favor of the general public"; the merits of his novels, he was convinced, could be appreciated only by the "inner circle" who "relish deliberate workmanship."[37] That progressive-minded inner circle, one can be sure, included no Wall Street plutocrats, socialists, or "New Women."

In the Arena with Mencken, Bourne, and the "Juvenile Highbrows"

After devoting more than 460 pages of *These Many Years* to detailing the "pleasanter memories" of his life, Matthews brings his autobiography to a close by declaring that he remains a "man of cheerful yesterdays and of confident tomorrows."[1] As he penned those sanguine words in 1917, the world was embroiled in a war that would deprive thousands of young Americans of their opportunity for any tomorrow whatsoever. Matthews escaped the bloody battles "over there" but not the cultural conflict that had been raging in the United States even before the war produced the so-called "lost generation" of writers, and that conflict greatly aggrieved him in his later years. The modernist revolt in literature and art was already underway when Matthews assumed the presidency of the Modern Language Association in 1910; and while he was confidently presiding over the National Institute of Arts and Letters (1912–14) and composing his cheerful autobiography, H. L. Mencken, Randolph Bourne, Van Wyck Brooks, and other Young Intellectuals were storming the gates of the literary establishment, seeking to wrest cultural power from the hands of an older generation whose ideology seemed reactionary rather than progressive and whose literary canon seemed timidly "colonial" rather than vibrantly American. In the words of Bourne, the rebellious young were "pro-democratic, pro-hyphenate, pro-Negro, anti-Puritan, anti-English Americans."[2] Had he extended his list of descriptors (not all of which apply to Mencken, of course), he could have added "pro-Socialist," "pro-feminist," and "anti-war." Tacitly acknowledging Matthews as one of the literary establishment's most powerful figures, the Young Intellectuals made him one of their favorite targets. As the anonymous author of a "Literary Spotlight" essay in *The Bookman* put it in 1923, Matthews was a "welcome signpost for the younger generation. That much maligned group is glad to have him there, for he stands for the outworn things that have hardened, that have perished from a spiritual arteriosclerosis." The author goes on to say that, though the "young warriors" find Matthews's literary taste archaic and his temperament dogmatic, they cannot help but admire him as he "sallies into the vexed arena of modern letters bearing his frayed gonfalon."[3]

Frayed as his gonfalon was, Matthews carried it into battle with the same energy and tenacity he had demonstrated in the earlier campaigns for literary realism and Americanism, despite the fact that physical infirmities ravaged him during the last decade of his life.[4] "I think it is well for scholars who happen also to be men of letters," seventy-year-old Matthews advised a younger colleague, "to go down into the arena now and again and fight with the beasts."[5] During the 1910s and 1920s, Matthews ventured into the arena to do combat with the "beasts" over a variety of literary and political issues: the suppression of Dreiser's *The "Genius,"* the attempted affiliation of the Authors' League of America with the American Federation of Labor, the admission of women to the National Institute/Academy, the country's entry into World War I, and, as always, the literary canon. When not fighting in the open by publishing his arguments, Matthews, as he had so often done before, wielded his considerable influence behind the scenes on behalf of the "progressive" side.

Matthews was as prolific a writer as ever during the years surrounding World War I, publishing more than a dozen books and innumerable articles and reviews. The key work, however, is *The Tocsin of Revolt*. Though the volume was published in 1922, most of the essays in it had appeared in journals during or shortly after the war. First published in 1918, the title essay is Matthews's most fully developed counterattack against the young warriors who were trying to drive him from the literary center to the margins. From the opening sentence, in which he refers to his "three-score-and-ten" years of age, to the last, Matthews speaks self-consciously as the representative of the older generation that has been declared moribund and repressive by the younger. Alluding to the early nineteenth-century revolt of the Romantics against the Classicists, Matthews readily admits that the "conflict between youth and age, between conservatism and radicalism, is unending, because it is eternally necessary to the vitality of the several arts, which need to be reinvigorated generation after generation."[6] But where he had in 1881 championed the Hugo-led rebels in their contest against their elders—those scholars who were "full of years and honors"—the septuagenarian professor now chides the rising generation for its excessive individualism and rejection of tradition. Morally irresponsible and technically undisciplined, the leaders of the "modern movement" in the arts have failed to learn that "Progress can be made, not by disregarding what has already been discovered and invented," but by assimilating and re-visioning traditional ideas and forms. Making no attempt to conceal his feelings of revulsion and disgust, he charges that many modernist art works are little more than "indecent exposures of the nudity of their producers' minds," and expresses his hope that young artists sounding the tocsin of revolt will "tire of facile eccentricity and of lazy freakishness, of unprofitable sensationalism and of undisciplined individualism" (20). Two subsequent essays in *Tocsin of Revolt*—"Memories of Mark Twain" and "Theodore Roosevelt as a Man of Letters"—lavish praise on a pair of writers who embody the sound sense and manly discipline that Matthews found wanting in the arrogant and anarchic modernists. Since we earlier discussed its eulogizing of Twain, we shall pass over "Memories" here. The essay on Roosevelt, however, deserves attention, for it was the culminating effort of Matthews's attempt to inscribe his friend into the literary canon.

After Roosevelt's death in 1919, Matthews published several essays and reviews extolling the Rough Rider's literary as well as political accomplishments. In "Roosevelt as a Practical Politician" (1919), for example, he presented Roosevelt as the equal of Jefferson and Lincoln in practical idealism, erudition, devotion to democracy, and moral character. Matthews also delivered the commemorative tribute to Roosevelt at the Academy of Arts and Letters; the former president of the American Historical Society, he informed his audience, demonstrated in his best writings a "plumbing vision" and a "masculine and vascular" style.[7] In "Theodore Roosevelt as a Man of Letters"—which would later be reprinted as the introduction to the volume of literary essays in Roosevelt's *Works*—Matthews drew together the threads of praise he had woven into earlier adulations. Surveying the Roosevelt literary corpus, Matthews declares that Roosevelt's career was fuller and richer than Benjamin Franklin's, that his *Great Adventure* equals Lincoln's "Gettysburg Address" in its attainment of the "serener heights of pure literature," that his *Winning of the West* was exemplary in its "absolute impartiality" and "manly" prose, and that the "pure fires of patriotism" stoking his political essays and addresses roused the American people to do their "full duty in the war which saved civilization from the barbarian."[8]

This was precisely the kind of "gush" that Mencken, who viewed the progressivist crusade with aristocratic disdain, derides in the opening pages of his verbal "autopsy" on the deceased Roosevelt in *Prejudices: Second Series* (1920).[9] Mencken's Roosevelt was an "absolutist wearing false whiskers of a democrat," a saber-rattling militarist who had more in common with the political philosophy of the Kaiser than his admirers would care to admit. He was also a clownish "mob-master" and a xenophobe. Yet, despite all the debunking, Mencken's dissection of Roosevelt's character is, on balance, favorable. Roosevelt, Mencken asserts, often exhibited acute vision, especially in his desire to curb the power of corporate trusts, increase military preparedness, and awaken the nation to the dangers of isolationism. Despite his faults, Roosevelt was a "genuine leader of the nation"; unfortunately, in a nation composed predominantly of "third-rate" men, Roosevelt was forced to play the part of the clown when speaking from the bully pulpit. When his actual ideas are disentangled from the "demagogic fustian" in which he had wrapped them, Mencken avers, they will be given the "canonical honors" they deserve (131).

Matthews, though he would have been incensed by Mencken's criticisms of Roosevelt, would have been delighted by the contention that certain pronouncements of the Square Deal president should be canonized. He would, however, have found little to his liking in "The National Letters," the essay that opens *Prejudices: Second Series*. In it Mencken not only assails many of Matthews's favorite writers and cherished literary notions but makes disparaging personal remarks about him and several of his fellow professors. Beginning with a glance back at Emerson's "The American Scholar," Mencken argues that Emerson's call for a vibrant and truly American literature had yet to materialize. According to Mencken's diagnosis (and Bourne's and Brooks's as well), the blame lay with a literary establishment controlled by such "grave and glittering fish" as Brander Matthews, William C. Brownell, Stuart Sherman, Paul E. More, and Irving Babbitt (11). By privileging writers such as Owen Wister and Hamlin Garland who produce genteel and patriotic works, and by excluding those who, like Whitman, Dreiser, and O'Neill, exude a "sturdy animality" and challenge the Victorian ideals of moral wholesomeness, the "canon lawyers" (31) have created a feeble, timid, and hollow American literary canon. In addition to taking a Puritan attitude toward sexual matters, these elderly professors cling stubbornly to the notion of Anglo-Saxon racial superiority. Mencken, with his German roots and great admiration for Germanic culture, did not share Matthews's and Roosevelt's insistence that immigrants discard their Old World heritage and Anglo-Saxonize as soon as possible. In fact, he turns the Anglo-American theory of "race decadence" on its head in "The National Letters" by contending that the "Anglo-Saxon strain, second-rate at the start, has tended to degenerate steadily to lower levels" (47). Thus it was up to the hyphenate writers, whose sensibilities had not been warped by a desiccated Puritanism, to revitalize American literature. But before they could rescue American literature from its decline into flaccid gentility, they had to overcome the aging Anglophiles guarding the gates. "Despite all the current highfalutin about melting pots and national destinies," Mencken charges, "the United States remains [in 1920] almost as much an English colonial possession, intellectually and spiritually, as it was on July 3, 1776" (91). Thus does Mencken turn the rhetoric of Americanism against Matthews, indicting him and his fellow "schoolmasters" for being colonial-minded impediments to the development of a robust American literature.

As his whole career demonstrates, Matthews, though he embraced the theory of Anglo-Saxon racial superiority, was hardly "colonial" in his thinking about American literary independence. In fact, one of the essays in *Tocsin of Revolt* represents arguments on the subject that he had been trumpeting since *Americanisms and Briticisms*. Titled "What Is American Literature," the piece decries the "self-abasing attitude of colonialism," the "timid deference to the opinions of the mother country and . . . blank disbelief that anything good can come out of our own."[10]

However much he may have despised Matthews's literary and political values, Mencken respected his linguistic scholarship, as *The American Language* testifies. In investigating the differences between the American and British versions of the English language—and in defending the legitimacy of the former—Mencken quotes from or cites for support *Americanisms and Briticisms* and several essays that Matthews had recently published.[11] In one of them, "Is the English Language Degenerating?" (1918), Matthews took a laissez-faire stance and urged the American Academy of Arts and Letters and other "upholders of authority and tradition" *not* to attempt to preserve, as did the French Academy, the "purity" of the language. The best thing the academy could do for the English language—which was evolving quite competently on its own, thank you—was to help stimulate public interest in literature and to publish writings exemplary in their style and diction. The essay hardly projects the image of the "pedagogical Prussian" that Mencken caricatures in "The National Letters," at least not until its closing page, where Matthews cannot resist the impulse to chastise the "eager and ardent youngsters" for their rebellion against tradition.[12]

Mencken was undoubtedly one of the "youngsters" Matthews had in mind. Yet, when he reviewed *The American Language* in the *New York Times*, Matthews did not allow his personal feelings toward Mencken to prejudice his critique. Correctly observing that he himself had voiced many of Mencken's arguments (which included an endorsement of the simplified-spelling movement), Matthews praised the book as an interesting, well-documented, and lively study from which he had derived both pleasure and profit.[13] His only complaint concerned the author's sometimes discourteous treatment of the American Academy (whose members Mencken disparaged as "gifted philologs of the sanhedrin") and of older scholars in the field, including Matthews himself. Expressing his resentment at being branded a pundit, Matthews queries Mencken at the end of the review: "What have I ever done to deserve this stigma?" Mencken's uncharitable response to Matthews's complimentary critique was to inform his friend Ernest Boyd that *The American Language* had "suffered the ignominy of being favourably reviewed by Brander Matthews. The truth is that the academic idiots are all taking it very seriously, greatly to my joy."[14]

What, specifically, had Matthews done to draw such mean-spirited remarks from Mencken? Stuart Sherman offered a response to that question in "Brander Matthews and the Mohawks." Sherman asserts that the "Mohawks'" image of Matthews as a prudish pedagogue was a distortion: "They may charge you on technical grounds with being a professor," states Sherman (himself a professor at the University of Illinois), "but in your own conscience you know that you have never been that. You were formed before pedagogy had a chance to deform you. You were forty before you ever told anecdotes in a professorial chair or brought the intoxicating airs of Bohemia and the great world of letters within the drab walls of a classroom"; indeed, "no Mohawk hates the pedantries of scholarship more sincerely than you do."[15] Moreover, Matthews's wide knowledge of world literature, his advocacy of cosmopolitan literary standards, his numerous travels and acquaintances abroad have, ironically, made him what the Mohawks are "howling for, a man of letters who is also a man of the world" (259). Matthews has done nothing to warrant the abuse heaped upon him by the "Mohawks"; in truth, his "unpardonable sin" is that he is old (around seventy at the time Sherman wrote the essay). In a passage that would fit easily into any number of essays by today's traditionalists who feel threatened by the aggressive young proponents of newer literary theories, Sherman charges that, whereas previous generations of critics acted respectfully toward their elders, Matthews's detractors "fear the past as an enemy at their rear"; they hold that "military considerations demand the devastation of the territory behind their lines [especially of the National Academy, which the rebels had been trying to destroy for years], and the destruction of all able-bodied men who will not actively enlist in their band" (255).

There is a good deal of truth in Sherman's remarks. But his portrayal of Matthews as an academic Lear wronged by his selfish and spiteful literary children was as biased in favor of Matthews as Mencken's debunking remarks were against. An admiring pupil of Irving Babbitt and Paul Elmer More during his Harvard days, Sherman (1881–1926) was a young intellectual but a staunch traditionalist nonetheless. Matthews had ambivalent feelings toward Babbitt and More. He shared their admiration for classical literature and respected their scholarship, but he was put off by the aristocratic ideology underlying their New Humanist critical theory, and he especially objected to their condescending attitude toward American literature. (The New Humanists' disdain for contemporary American literature eventually proved too much even for Sherman, who distanced himself from Babbitt and More during the last few years of his life.) But an aristocratic New Humanist was far preferable to an anarchic "Mohawk." Matthews therefore welcomed Babbitt and More as allies in his conflict with the young rebels: "We mossbacks," he wrote More in 1921, "must stand together."[16]

In a letter thanking Sherman for coming to his defense against his detractors, Matthews quipped that the essay would put "the Mohawks and *les Apaches* hot on your trail."[17] Actually, the "Mohawks" had been on Sherman's trail at least since 1915, when his "The Naturalism of Mr. Dreiser" ignited a long and bitter feud not only with Dreiser but with his champion Mencken. As the Dreiser essay and such later ones as "Mr. Mencken, the Jeune Fille, and the New Spirit in Letters" make clear, Sherman's feelings of revulsion toward the young rebels stemmed in large part from ethnic and class prejudice. In "The Naturalism of Mr. Dreiser," for example, he insinuates that the "degenerate" vision under-lying novels like *Sister Carrie* and *The "Genius"* is a natural out-growth of the immigrant mind: emphasizing Dreiser's German lineage, the Anglophilic Sherman snarls that the novelist rep-resents that "'ethnic' element of our mixed population which, as we are assured by competent authorities [such as Mencken, Bourne, and Brooks] is to redeem us from Puritanism and in-sure our artistic salvation." In the Mencken essay he conde-scendingly describes the new generation of American writers and critics as the vulgar and sensual descendants of European laborers who, "toiling inarticulately in shop and field," never mastered the fundamentals of English grammar. As in the Dreiser piece, he does not allow his reader to forget that the subject of his vitriol is *German*-American: Mencken, he sneers, is a "Nietzschean aristocrat" (which was true) and a member of the "Loyal Independent Order of the United Hiberno-German-Anti-English-Americans."[18]

Though he applauded Sherman's denunciations of the "immature and ill-informed advocates of exotic eroticism," Matthews did not join in the attack on Dreiser (who had, we recall, made satirical use of Matthews's play *The Gold Mine* in *Sister Carrie*).[19] Perhaps interpreting this silence to mean that Matthews was not as hostile toward Dreiser as Sherman and other Anglo-Saxon academics were, Mencken sought to enlist his support in 1916 when the New York Society for the Prevention of Vice threatened to file criminal charges against the John Lane Company if it did not censor *The "Ge-nius."*[20] After drawing up the petition protesting the attempted suppression of the novel, Mencken advised Dreiser that the best way to proceed was to have the document circulated among the best-known American authors. Much as he de-spised Matthews, Mencken could not overlook his high sta-tus in the literary establishment: "the signature of such an old ass as Brander Matthews," he wrote Dreiser, "would be worth a great deal."[21]

Matthews, however, refused to sign (as did Howells and Garland). Mencken promptly, and rather hypocritically, sent a cordially worded letter to the "old ass" pleading with him to reconsider. He informed Matthews that more than four hundred American authors had already signed the petition, including (the American) Winston Churchill, president of the Authors' League of America. (As Mencken knew, Matthews was an honorary vice-president of the league and a close friend of Churchill.) Mencken emphasized that the petition was not an endorsement of *The "Genius,"* which he in fact considered an inferior literary work, but a protest against censorship. American men of letters, he hoped, would stand behind Dreiser in the same manner in which French ones had stood behind Zola.[22]

That last argument should have been a compelling one to the author of "'Those Literary Fellows.'" In developing his thesis that men of letters should come down from the Ivory Tower and involve themselves in practical affairs, Matthews had praised the French writers who, to their "undying honor," had stepped forward during the Dreyfus iniquity "to insist on the duty of doing right even tho the heavens should fall."[23] Matthews nonetheless rejected Mencken's plea, apparently on the grounds that the threatened prosecution was merely a publicity stunt aimed at increasing the book's sales. Since many people did in fact believe that the whole affair was an advertising gimmick, Matthews may have been sincere, but his disdain for the "exotic eroticism" of the new realism seems a more likely reason for his decision not to sign the petition.[24] Whatever his motive, his refusal to support Dreiser and defend the principle of free expression was to Mencken an act of moral cowardice that encouraged the excesses of Comstockery.[25]

Interestingly, at the same time he was refusing to sign Mencken's petition protesting censorship, Matthews was circulating a petition of his own, one that helps clarify his "progressive" attitude toward labor unions. As mentioned above, Matthews was an honorary vice-president of the Authors' League of America, as were Roosevelt, Garland, Julian Street, and several other of Matthews's close friends. Founded in 1912, the organization aimed to develop, as its president Churchill expressed to Matthews, into a "great democracy of letters."[26] In reality, the league was, like the Institute/ Academy of Arts and Letters and most other literary organizations, controlled by elderly Anglo-American males who defined democracy in very exclusive terms. In 1916, shortly after Matthews assumed his vice-presidency, several members of the league's Executive Council who were sympathetic to the labor movement urged that the organization affiliate with the AFL, as certain teachers' and actors' groups had done. The suggestion greatly distressed conservative members of the organization, none more than Matthews, who along with Street directed the successful campaign to block the proposed affiliation.

Informed by Street in June 1916 of the Executive Council's action, Matthews replied that he would actively oppose the affiliation, and that if their protest failed and the "dark deed" were done, he would resign from the league. "More power to you," he closed his letter.[27] Power was, of course, the central issue, and Matthews did not want any of it to fall into the hands of the socialists or their fellow travelers. Though he claimed that his protest against affiliation was not motivated by anti-labor sentiments, he had, as we have seen, offered a negative portrait of labor unions and socialist radicals in *A Confident To-morrow*, and he once recommended a novel to Street because it was "very American and it did not display the cloven hoof of radicalism."[28] Street himself was fiercely anti-socialist: the novelist Walker Prichard Eaton, he once wrote Matthews, was an "infernal ass of a Socialist crank" and admirer of Eugene Debs.[29] Churchill was similarly ill-disposed toward unions, as was, somewhat surprisingly, Garland. Though he had in earlier years been assailed as a radical for his advocacy of a land tax and for his support of Henry George, Garland joined Matthews's protest with enthusiasm, writing him: "[Our opponents] may call us all Old Foagies but I don't feel any call to line up with engineers and cloak-makers." "I am a radical," he went on to explain, "but not that kind. . . . I have never had much faith in the union idea."[30] As his contemptuous reference to the "cloak-makers"—the majority of whom were, of course, Jews and their fellow "new immigrants"—suggests, Garland was as xenophobic as Roosevelt. So was Street, who in a letter to Matthews refers to New York as "Yiddish City."[31] Matthews, whose attitude toward Others has already been discussed at length, often made anti-Semitic remarks in personal letters, as for example when he wrote that his fellow passengers on a ship were "genteel and gentile (thank heaven)."[32] Clearly, the "Old Foagies'" opposition to the proposed alliance with the AFL was at least in part rooted in ethnic as well as class bias.

Street suggested that Matthews lead the protest movement, but he deferred on the grounds that to do so would be inappropriate since he had been a league member for only several months. But he promised to pour all his energies into the "good fight," which in his mind was inextricably linked to the continuing campaign for Americanism: the "Spirit of '76," he exclaimed to Street, would carry their side to victory.[33] Matthews advised Street to draft a petition to be signed by as many of the "elder men" as possible.[34] Though he thought the draft that Street produced made the right points, Matthews faulted it for being too tame. Violating his cardinal rule that a writer's rhetoric should always be temperate, he sharpened Street's language—so much so that he was later forced to accept blame for making the petition too caustic even for some supporters of their cause.[35] Matthews mailed copies of the toned-down version of the protest letter to men he knew he could count on: in addition to Churchill and Garland, he appealed to Wister, John Burroughs, George Haven Putnam, and Roosevelt. Roosevelt lent his support to the cause by providing his own letter of protest to be read before the Executive Council.[36] When the council met to discuss the issue in July, Matthews presented the petition he and Street had coauthored and demanded that it be sent to all league members, as the statement endorsing affiliation with the AFL had been.[37] The council agreed, and the petition received the large number of signatures that Matthews had hoped for. In October 1916 the council voted to drop efforts to ally the league with the AFL. "We did it with *our* little hatchets!" a jubilant Street wrote Matthews when the decision was announced.[38]

Matthews, we recall, had in 1902 assured Roosevelt that the National Institute of Arts and Letters could wield power on the "right side." During his tenure as president of the institute he used the influence of his office to ensure that the organization (the "morgue of the senile and respectable," Mencken called it) would remain a stronghold of traditionalism in the canon war. An example of how he exploited the powers of his office, as well as his personal relationship with Roosevelt, to promote literature that was ideologically "right" occurred in 1913 as the institute began planning its annual convention, which was for the first time to convene outside the East, in Chicago. Matthews appointed Garland chair of the program committee. Garland was a passionate foe of modernist literature, which in his eyes glamorized "incest, adultery, and other forms of sexual lawlessness," and he shared Matthews's admiration for Roosevelt.[39] After Roosevelt's defeat in the 1912 election, Garland told him that he (Garland) intended to form an "informal club of your friends to carry on the Progressive campaign."[40] Though Roosevelt had failed in his bid to retake the White House, he was nonetheless one of the most popular figures in the

United States at the time. Roosevelt's presence at the speakers' table, Garland believed, would gain national recognition for the institute as well as for Chicago literary culture. Thus he sought Matthews's help in persuading Roosevelt to deliver the keynote address at the convention. The suggested topic was "The Best in Literature": "only you," Matthews wrote Roosevelt, "can say what needs to be said on the subject."[41]

Since he was to be traveling in South America during the Chicago convention, Roosevelt was forced to decline Matthews's invitation; but at the combined meeting of the institute/academy in New York two years later, he did speak on literary value in an address titled "Nationalism in Literature and Art."[42] Matthews must have felt that Roosevelt said exactly what needed to be said on the subject, for the speech develops the theme of "American cosmopolitanism" that Matthews had been trumpeting since he delivered his address on "American Literature" to the National Education Association twenty years earlier (see chapter 4). Echoing Matthews, Roosevelt argued that the best literature "must bear the stamp of nationalism"; thus American work "must smack of our own soil, mental and moral, no less than physical, or it will have little of permanent value." In amplifying that argument, Roosevelt extolled writers such as Walt Whitman who felt a sympathetic identification with the common man, and condemned expatriate artists who could not decide if they were English or American (he had that "miserable little snob" Henry James in mind, of course). While he urged American artists to study and learn from world art and literature, he warned that a desire to be cosmopolitan could too easily degenerate into a servile imitation of the fashionably foreign. Such worship of European modernists, he further cautioned, could corrupt one's political as well as artistic values: "I care little more for the Cubist school in patriotism than I care for it in art or in poetry," he exclaimed, implying—correctly—that the modernist movement in art posed a threat to political authority. According to Garland, Roosevelt's speech was heartily applauded by the audience, many of whom were, of course, members of Garland's informal club of Roosevelt-admiring progressivists.[43]

During Matthews's presidency of the institute, its gates were being assailed not only by the "Mohawks" but by feminists who objected to the institute's exclusion of women. Since its inception, the organization had admitted only one woman (Julia Ward Howe, in 1907). In 1913 Matthews—who, as we have seen, had sought to exclude women from his English classes at Columbia and who had slighted women intellectuals in "'Those Literary Fellows'"—was publicly called upon to respond to the charge that the institute barred women. He acknowledged, in a newspaper interview, that no woman had succeeded in making it through the institute's secret nomination and election process in years, but he denied that the organization had a policy prohibiting women from becoming members. Indeed, he stated that in his opinion Edith Wharton, Mary Wilkins Freeman, and several other women writers were well qualified for membership, a statement that led the reporter to title the article "Women as 'Immortals' Favored by Matthews." The article, however, would have been more accurately titled "Matthews Favors Separate Society for Women"; rather than encouraging the institute members to nominate women, he urged women writers to "form a society of their own," and gallantly offered his assistance if they chose to do so.[44]

Matthews's private correspondence reveals that he was in fact as opposed to having women admitted to the institute as to his English classes. To Robert Underwood Johnson, for example, he expressed his hope that the institute members would not be "fools enough" to let in the "unfair sex." Among the "fools" was Garland. Husband of a suffragist and father of a daughter who studied literature and history at Columbia after Matthews's efforts to bar women from doing so failed, Garland was much more sympathetic to the women's movement than to the labor one. In their exchange of letters over the issue, Matthews wrote Garland that opening the gates to women would bring derision upon the institution (an argument with which Mrs. Garland, oddly enough, concurred). When the members voted down the election of women nominees in 1918, Garland wrote Matthews: "You won!—The fellows turned down the women for [admission]," adding that he bore no ill will. Not until 1926, when Edith Wharton was elected, did another woman make it in.[45]

In portraying Matthews as an innocent and rather perplexed victim of "Mohawk" attacks, Sherman neglected to mention Matthews's refusal to sign the Dreiser protest, his campaign against the affiliation of the Authors' League with the AFL, and his efforts to maintain the National Institute of Arts and Letters as a bastion of patriarchal authority—actions that, needless to say, alienated him from the rebellious young. Sherman also completely ignored Matthews's stance on the political issue that more than any other separated the younger and older generations, World War I. The "Mohawks" were not, of course, of one mind on the subject. Some, like Mencken, were sympathetic toward Germany and were thus infuriated by America's alliance with England; others, most notably Bourne, objected to the war on pacifist grounds. But they could all agree with Mencken's indictment of American intellectuals, especially academics, for their failure to provide moral leadership during the crisis. Instead of acting as a restraining influence on the "mob run wild," Mencken bitterly contended in "The National Letters," most professors were the "loudest spokesmen of its worst imbecilities. They fed it with bogus history, bogus philosophy, bogus idealism, bogus heroics" (83).

Most universities did in fact rally round the flag during

the war, none more fervently than Columbia; its leader, Nicholas Murray Butler, was an intimate friend of Roosevelt and one of the most hawkish of university presidents. After a large patriotic rally on campus two months before the United States declared war on Germany, Butler wired the White House to assure President Wilson that the university would fully commit its human and material resources to the war effort should the country enter the conflict. When the United States did go "over there," Butler urged all students to join in military drills, and he assured the board of trustees that the whole university was on "war footing."[46]

Butler's patriotic zeal resulted in one of the most shameful events in the institution's history. Determined to stifle dissident voices, he summarily fired two pacifist faculty members, J. McKeen Cattell and Henry W. L. Dana (grandson of Henry Wadsworth Longfellow). His action was supported by the trustees as well as by the standing committee of the alumni association, which asserted that no action could be too extreme to protect the institution from "foolish, prejudiced, irresponsible, unconsidered, emotional, ill-digested, or immature utterances or writings, not to mention those that openly breathe treason, sedition, or resistance to duly constituted authority."[47] The administration's blatant suppression of free speech and violation of university procedures (Cattell and Dana were denied their right of a hearing in front of a faculty committee) outraged many of the institution's most eminent professors, including Beard, Boas, and even Dewey, who supported Wilson's decision to go to war. Dewey resigned from the Committee of Nine (the faculty's advisory committee to the board of trustees) in protest. Beard went further and resigned from the university, his statement of resignation drawing adverse criticism from the *New York Times* as well as from the university authorities.[48]

Though Matthews does not specifically mention the Cattell-Dana incident in his published writings or private letters, there is evidence suggesting that he supported Butler and the trustees. For example, in *These Many Years*—which was published the year after the two professors had been fired—he offers a veiled justification of the dismissals when he writes, in describing his experiences as a Columbia professor, that the faculty's "relations with each other and with the several deans and the president and the trustees are ever friendly. So long as we do our work faithfully we are left alone to do it in our own fashion." He follows that claim, which must have astounded Cattell, Dana, and their advocates on the faculty, with the assertion that Columbia professors enjoy the *Lernfreiheit* and the *Lehrfreiheit* that once characterized the German universities but that has recently been crushed under the heel of "Prussian autocracy."[49] Matthews's private correspondence with Butler reveals, moreover, that he never wavered in his support of his president and that Butler held him in the highest esteem: "There is no one whose appreciation and approval I value as much as yours," Butler wrote Matthews in 1914. The commemorative tribute to Matthews that Butler delivered before the American Academy fifteen years later suggests that his high opinion of the professor never diminished.[50]

If his mind had been somewhat divided in response to the Spanish-American War, Matthews saw World War I in black-and-white terms: he damned the German "barbarians" and fully concurred with Butler's conviction that literary fellows had a patriotic duty to help defeat them. Writing in the *New York Times* shortly after the United States declared war on Germany, Matthews leveled his guns at those who charged that the spirit of militarism prompted the declaration. No nation, he argued, was more peace-loving than the United States. That claim is, of course, open to dispute. But Matthews was certainly correct in asserting that the United States had made determined efforts to remain neutral, and that when finally forced into the conflict, the country found itself "piteously unprepared" to wage war. When a foreign nation, he goes on to say, has been foolhardy enough to challenge the country in the past, American soldiers have consistently demonstrated that they possess the same steely resolve that characterized the adventurous pioneers who conquered the continent. Curiously, after thus suggesting that Anglo-Saxon "race traits" have given the advantage to Americans in all their wars, Matthews closes the article by quoting a black soldier—not, obviously, a descendant of the "selected stock" that defeated the English, Mexicans, and Spanish in earlier conflicts—who is reported to have exclaimed during a Civil War battle: "I will bring these colors back—or report to God the reasons why!"[51]

Among the soldiers of "selected stock" who reported to God was Roosevelt's son Quentin, killed in action in 1918. Attempting to console his old friend, Matthews actually congratulated him on the "costliness of the sacrifice you have laid on the altar of patriotism."[52] If those words seem insensitive, if not callous, to us, they would not have seemed so to Roosevelt. Though he was deeply saddened by his son's death, the sacrifice did not quell his war fever, nor his romantic desire to raise a brigade of volunteers and replay the combat experiences in which he had reveled two decades earlier in Cuba.[53]

While Roosevelt was futilely attempting to secure President Wilson's permission to become a combatant, Matthews continued his activities on the verbal battlefield by producing essays such as "The Duty of Intellectuals," originally published in 1918 and later reprinted in *Tocsin of Revolt*.[54] He apparently had Mencken in mind when he penned the piece, for he begins by observing that critics of American culture have complained (and Mencken certainly did) that Americans have no respect for the "aristocracy of intellect" and that members of this elite class seldom occupy high places in government. When elected political leaders are derelict in their duties, he proceeds to argue, the intellectual aristocracy has a moral obligation to step down from its "lofty isolation" and provide leadership to "the mob," as, to their credit, Lowell and Whittier had after the passage of the Fugitive Slave Act. America's foremost critic of the "booboisie" would have found little to fault in Matthews's line of reasoning thus far, but he would have been nettled by what follows. Where Mencken urged American intellectuals to oppose the "mob" that supported war against Germany, Matthews devotes the remainder of his essay to excoriating the German intellectuals. "Not only did the Intellectuals of Germany," he avers, "fail to urge moderation upon their fellow-subjects and to use their influence to modify as far as might be the fierceness of popular feeling . . . but they allowed themselves to be cajoled or coerced into signing a manifesto of which the sole effect in Germany was to intensify the spirit of hate." This was precisely the kind of attack on the German intelligentsia that Mencken would a year later attempt to rebut in "The National Letters," contending there that the manifesto signed by the German professors was relatively mild in its statements and that the American professors were far more involved in their government's propaganda campaign than German ones were in the Kaiser's (84–86). (Matthews continued his vituperative attacks on the Germans during the postwar years. In, for example, his reviews of Owen Wister's *Straight Deal* [1920] and *Neighbors Henceforth* [1923], he applauded Wister's denunciations of the "Huns" and derided pacifists and other "unthinking" individuals who urged Americans to adopt a forgive-and-forget attitude toward the Teutonic "barbarians.")[55]

Of course Mencken—whose admiration for Teutonic culture, especially for Nietzschean philosophy, would later blind him to the evils perpetrated by Hitler and his mob of

Nazis—was no more capable of speaking dispassionately on the duty of intellectuals during World War I than was Matthews.[56] Placed in historical context, Matthews's hatred of the "Huns" during and after the conflict is, moreover, understandable. Like millions of his fellow citizens, he was revolted by the U-boat sinkings of the *Lusitania* and other passenger ships and by the treachery of the German government revealed by the notorious Zimmerman telegram. Add to these well-publicized facts the enormously successful propaganda campaign conducted by George Creel and the Committee on Public Information, and it is easy to see why Matthews and a great many other writers and intellectuals (including Henry James) became infected by the war fever.

To understand Matthews's hostility toward the Kaiser's Germany is not, however, to deny Mencken's charge that Matthews and his fellow professors contributed to rather than resisted the "imbecilities" that followed President Wilson's reluctant decision to go to war. As United States troops were marching abroad to make the world safe for democracy, thousands of Americans on the home front were being deprived of their civil liberties. Though Matthews harshly condemns Prussian autocracy in his writings, he is silent on the suppression of free speech that resulted from the Espionage Act (1917) and the Sabotage and Sedition Acts (1918). Acting under the banner of "Americanism," government witch-hunters and vigilante groups often targeted innocent citizens whose only crime was having a German surname or being a socialist, a union member, or, as Cattell and Dana discovered, a pacifist. Matthews may not have sanctioned some of the more extreme measures advocated by Roosevelt—such as the suppression of German-language newspapers and the establishment of military tribunals for dissenters—but his apparent support of Butler and the trustees during the Cattell-Dana affair and his statement in 1918 that the country "must take the measures necessary to make us homogeneous and united" suggest that he was willing to sacrifice civil liberties on the altars of military preparedness and patriotism.[57]

The lack of moral leadership exhibited by Matthews, Butler, and other Columbia progressivists during the war may not have disturbed the vast majority of Columbia students, but it did repulse Randolph Bourne, the man whom Van Wyck Brooks called the "flying wedge of the younger generation."[58] A committed socialist, Bourne never completely embraced the ideology of the "gradual progress men," to use his phrase; but when he entered Columbia in 1909, he chose Dewey, Boas, and other progressivists as his mentors, and he voted for Roosevelt in 1912.[59] If perhaps not as impressed by Matthews as he was by Dewey and Boas, he seems at least to have had a cordial relationship with Matthews. In 1911 Matthews sent a note to Bourne, then editor of the *Columbia Monthly*, congratulating him on producing "one of the very best numbers of a college magazine that I have ever seen."[60] In addition to his editorial, in which he emphasized that the *Columbia Monthly* aimed to be a serious literary magazine and not the typical compound of "college humor, athletic and alumni news, short stories and freshman themes that passes in some colleges for the college magazine," Bourne offered a glowing review of Boas's *The Mind of Primitive Man*, the book that Matthews would later recommend to Roosevelt.[61] In a letter written during his visit to England in 1914, Bourne mentions that Matthews had given him a card of introduction to the British critic William Archer.[62]

Apparently, then, Bourne's criticism of the elder generation of critics and academics in "The Two Generations" (1911), one of the first missiles launched by the Young Intellectuals, had not alienated Matthews. But "The Professor" (1915) and several other pieces Bourne published during the war must have convinced Matthews that his former student had been poisoned by the rebellion virus that infected Mencken. Mencken (who respected Bourne's intellect but not his socialist-pacifist ideology) would have relished the caustic irony with which Bourne paints his portrait of the young genteel professor (Stuart Sherman, perhaps) in "The Professor," especially his remark that the early 1900s, when the young professor attended college and developed his literary taste, was a time when "Brander Matthews still thrilled the world of criticism with his scintillating Gallic wit and his cosmopolitan wealth of friendships."[63] Bourne does not mention Matthews by name in "The History of a Literary Radical," "The Art of Theodore Dreiser," "Those Columbia Trustees," "The War and the Intellectuals," "Trans-National America," "This Older Generation," or the other essays that Brooks included in *The History of a Literary Radical and Other Papers by Randolph Bourne* (1956), but they would have stung Matthews nonetheless, for they form a withering assault on the literary and political opinions he espoused. In "History of a Literary Radical," for example, Bourne details how, once exposed to the fiction of Hardy, Tolstoi, and other modern writers ignored in his Columbia literature classes, he revolted against the orthodoxies preached in the classrooms and sought to apply "pick and dynamite to the whole structure of the canon" (29). In "This Older Generation" he castigates the elder generation of critics and academics who, comfortably nestled in the "ramparts of privilege," completely ignore the "barriers of caste and race and economic inequality" (299) as they pursue their agenda of moral reform. "Those Columbia Trustees" indicts the trustees and Butler for their shameful persecution of Cattell and Dana, while "Twilight of Idols" condemns his former idol Dewey for supporting America's entry into the war and for being more concerned about the excesses of pacifists than of the militarists. Where Matthews's "The Duty of Intellectuals" assailed the German intelligentsia for failing to oppose the Kaiser,

Bourne's "The War and the Intellectuals" (originally published in 1917, the year before Matthews's essay appeared) raps American intellectuals—most notably Roosevelt and other eastern patricians who justified war in the name of "true Americanism"—for opening the "sluices and flood[ing] us with the sewage of the war spirit" (206–7).[64] The most important duty of the American intellectual class, he insists, is to prevent the war from passing into "popular mythology as a holy crusade" by revealing it to be the "most noxious complex of all the evils that afflict men" (221).

If after reading such essays by his former pupil, as he likely did, Matthews had any doubts as to what Bourne's personal opinion of him was, those doubts were removed by Bourne's review of *These Many Years*. Titled "A Vanishing World of Gentility," this piece was perhaps more effective than any other in pinning the label "genteel" on Matthews. Though Bourne gives an approving nod to Matthews's studies of Molière and Shakespeare and expresses admiration for his international-copyright and simplified-spelling crusades, the essay's tone is predominantly contemptuous. Likening Matthews to Peter Pan at one point and to Tiny Tim at another, Bourne portrays him as the representative man of letters of a literary era that "never grew up." After quoting in full the passage, cited above, in which Matthews describes Columbia as a harmonious institution dedicated to fostering *Lernfreiheit* and *Lehrfreiheit* in its faculty and students, Bourne offers this critique:

> Anyone who gets the full flavor of this passage, recalling all there is to be said on these matters, will be nearer the secret of that American race of men of letters of whom Mr. Matthews is one of the naiver specimens, a race to whom literature was a gesture of gentility and not a comprehension of life. There is a

fascination about that brilliant literary world of the seventies and eighties when the "Nation" and the New York "Tribune" and "World" monopolized the younger generation of critical talent. But what on earth can a younger generation of today do with the remains of this gentility? In his account of the atrocious college education [at Columbia] that the best of money could buy in America in 1868, Mr. Matthews gave me a guess at the secret of the continuance of the genteel tradition. Was it because you could get no education at all unless you got it from foreign travel or from cultivated relatives? Only the genteel, apparently, had these opportunities, so that the creation of a proletarian man of letters in America became automatically impossible, until universities and libraries improved and diffused the raw materials of the spirit.

If ever there was a man, Bourne continues, whose mind moved "far submerged below the significant literary currents of the time," it was Matthews.[65]

Within several months of writing those words, Bourne, victim of the flu epidemic of 1918, was dead, and the world war that had physically and psychologically devastated his generation was over. The end of the fighting in Europe did not, of course, bring about any cease-fire in the cultural conflict between the generations, and Matthews had by no means vanished from the battlefield. During the postwar years he was a regular book reviewer for the *New York Times*, a position he used as a sort of "bully pulpit" for preaching against the "Mohawks," or "juvenile highbrows," as he labeled them in a review of Harold Stearns's *America and the Young Intellectual* (1921). Stearns was one of the ringleaders of the Young Intellectuals. In the opening section of his book he disparaged Sherman's "The National Genius" and admitted that the young rebels for whom he spoke disliked the elder generation "almost to the point of hatred" for their hollowness, hypocrisy, Puritan self-righteousness, hysterical behavior during the war, and so on.[66] Titled "America and the Juvenile Highbrows" (readers of Brooks's "'Highbrow' and 'Lowbrow'" would not have missed the implied reference to that landmark of Young Intellectualism), Matthews's review of Stearns's book makes clear that he had by this time completely lost his temper with the young rebels. Speaking with the authorizing voice of a respected and productive scholar (he calls attention to his having published more than two-score books in his long career), he declares the book immature and incoherent. He is especially critical of Stearns's introductory essay, which he faults for being carelessly written, ponderously solemn, and marred by the "reckless overstatement and rash generalization" characteristic of the "juvenile highbrow": "Difficult indeed," he snaps, "will it be for the least mature of the juvenile highbrows to surpass the intolerant contempt in which [Stearns] . . . holds the immense majority of his fellow-citizens," i.e., the Lowbrows.[67] Weary of being informed that American civilization is such a blank failure that its brightest young minds must flee to Europe, Matthews asserts that the younger intellectuals with whom he is intimately acquainted (Sherman would certainly have been among them) have no such urge to become expatriates; they acknowledge the country's ills but also appreciate its merits.

Writing Sherman a week before "America and the Juvenile Highbrows" appeared, Matthews informed him that he had "spanked" Stearns, that "smart aleck kid," again in a forthcoming review of *Civilization in the United States* (1922). Edited with an introduction by Stearns, the book is a collection of essays on American culture, or the lack of it, by the gang of "Juvenile Highbrows," including Mencken and his *Smart Set* coeditor George Jean Nathan; those two names,

Brander Matthews

Matthews confided to Sherman, would not appear in the review—not because Matthews feared offending them but because he knew they would "writhe under 'absent treatment.'"[68] As in his review of *America and the Young Intellectual*, Matthews excoriates Stearns, charging that his prefatory essay—which deplores the "emotional and aesthetic starvation" of American social life and contends that "whatever else American civilization is, it is not Anglo-Saxon"—exhibits the "same recklessness in misstatement, the same inability to think clearly, and the same carelessness in the use of French" that marred the earlier volume.[69] Expressing his displeasure with the fact that the book devotes a chapter to examining American radicalism (by George Soule) but none to conservatism or religion, Matthews defiantly proclaims what the Young Intellectuals suspected all along: "I am myself a conservative, a reactionary, a standpatter, and a mossback."

Stearns is not the only one whom Matthews "spanks" in the review; he also applies his verbal paddle to the ethnologist Elsie Clews Parsons, who authored the chapter "Sex" (309–18). A former student of Boas and companion of Bourne, Parsons was a radical feminist whose book *The Family* (1906) had shocked genteel readers with its very un-Victorian notions of that institution.[70] As she had in the book, Parsons suggests in her essay that the boundary separating marriage and prostitution is not at all sharp, since many women marry for economic security rather than for love. (Charlotte Perkins Gilman had, of course, developed that thesis several years earlier in *Women and Economics*.) Exhibiting her indebtedness to Freudian theory, Clews suggests that sexual repression is the root cause of war, and that repressed sexual desires may account for "that herd sense which is so familiar a part of Americanism." She closes with a bold call for acceptance of artists who come out from "under cover" to engage in "variant" love relationships. Ignoring Clews's arguments, Matthews summarily dismisses the essay for being "inadequate, formless, and awkwardly written."

As Matthews had informed Sherman, the review does not mention by name Mencken, who contributed the chapter on American politics, or Nathan, who wrote on Matthews's major field of expertise, the American theater. Nor does Matthews refer directly to Brooks, who authored the chapter on American literary life and whose advice and assistance Stearns acknowledges in the preface. But Matthews surely had Brooks as well as Mencken and Nathan in mind when he remarked that his review would ignore the "more emotional contributions" by young intellectuals who "seem to be suffering from moral biliousness." As Brooks himself warned in the preface to *Letters and Leadership* (1918)—the central theme of which is that the United States lacked both literature and culture—most readers would find his critique "all too largely negative."[71] Matthews would have readily agreed with that assessment and would have extended it to include Brooks's earlier work, *America's Coming-of-Age* (1915), which opens with "'Highbrow' and 'Lowbrow.'"[72] In arguing his thesis that American culture had bifurcated into a desiccated, anemic "highbrow" or idealist tradition at one end and a starkly utilitarian or "lowbrow" one at the other, the American mind drifting chaotically in between the two extremes, Brooks, like Mencken and Bourne, upbraided the academic community. Universities, he complained, were islands of remote, lifeless ideals that had no application to the dominant culture of industrialism. Brooks scoffed at the New Nationalism and at Progressivism: "How can one speak of progress," he asked in *America's Coming-of-Age*, in a people obsessed with the pursuit of material wealth (176)? Brooks never mentions Matthews, but he does make disparaging comments about Matthews's New Humanist allies. During his Harvard days (1904–7), Brooks was influenced by Babbitt (though he was repulsed by the professor's dogmatic temperament) and was an avid reader of More's *Evening Post* essays.[73] But he soon became disenchanted with the New Humanists (Stuart Sherman included), complaining that their literary criticism was all intellect and no emotion; "arctic frigidity" was how he described More's criticism.[74] Matthews may have been responding to Brooks's charge when he (Matthews) contended, in a review of More's *A New England Group and Others* (1921), that More's unpopularity with the "vociferous youngsters" could be explained by their immature minds being made acutely uncomfortable by his wide and deep scholarship and his quiet insistence upon the value of authority and tradition.[75]

To focus only on the differences, sharp as they are, between the "genteel" professor and the "juvenile highbrow," as each saw the other, is to distort the picture, however, because the two men's literary criticism demonstrates remarkable similarities. Like Matthews, Brooks was greatly influenced by Arnold's discourses on criticism and culture, and by Taine's theory that literary inspiration is rooted in racial instincts: "an artist," Brooks asserts in *The Wine of the Puritans* (1908), "can produce great and lasting work only out of the materials which exist in him by instinct and which constitute racial fibre."[76] Like Matthews, also, Brooks sought to synthesize nationalism and cosmopolitanism; indeed, Matthews might have written the passage in *Wine of the Puritans* in which Brooks argues that American writers would not develop great works of art until they shed their "colonial" dependence on English models and allowed themselves to "simply be American, teach [their] impulses to beat with American ideas and ideals, absorb American life" (136). Finally, Matthews, as we have seen, was as hostile as Brooks to "highbrow" idealism (which both Matthews and Brooks associated with Harvard) and to "lowbrow" materialism. Since Matthews was a conservative and Brooks a socialist (another form of vaporous idealism to Matthews), the two men had quite different conceptions as to where the cultural middle ground they sought was located, but they believed that it lay somewhere between Boston and Wall Street on the symbolic map, and that it was well worth searching for.

Matthews's contemptuous comments in the *New York Times* about the younger generation drew the ire not only of local "juvenile highbrows" but of at least one expatriate who would become a leading force in literary modernism, Ezra Pound. In a *New York Times* review of John Matthews Manly's and Edith Rickert's *Contemporary British Literature: Bibliographies and Study Outlines* (1921), Matthews wrote that, while the two respected scholars deserved to be complimented for their conscientious work, their guide—*any* guide—to contemporary literature was a waste of time.[77] Forgetting, it seems, that he had spent years promoting the works of Twain, Howells, and other of his contemporary realists, Matthews—who titled his review "A Study of the Temporary"—opined that there was "no more patent absurdity in our education today here in America than the devout attention we are paying to the contemporary literature" that has no permanent value. Manly and Rickert, he regretted to report, would have performed a much more valuable service to literary studies had they restricted their focus to the "departed worthies" instead of living small fry. Matthews would permit critics and literature teachers to read current writers—for pleasure and relaxation—but they should reserve their critical faculties for the classics. How the "permanent value" of a literary work could be discovered if it was ignored by critics and scholars, Matthews doesn't explain; particular works, one might infer from his remarks, make their way into the canon without any debt to human agency. Ironically, many of the "temporary" writers who appear in Manly and Rickert's book are today considered "classic"—Conrad, Hardy, Joyce, Lawrence, Yeats, Virginia Woolf. Responding to the review from Paris, Pound implied—in the bilious tone Matthews had come to expect from the "juveniles"—that it was Matthews, not the Young Intellectuals, who was suffering from mental strabismus: literature, Pound informed Matthews, had not ceased in the year 1900, as Matthews and other critics of his generation would discover if they bothered to read younger writers.[78]

After the death of his wife in 1924, a forlorn and physically enfeebled Matthews decided to lay down his tattered gonfalon; he retired from Columbia, resigned his chancellorship (to which he had been elected in 1920) of the Academy of Arts and Letters, and stepped down from his *New York Times* post. In 1926 his once-vigorous voice was all but silenced by a stroke that affected his powers of speech. (Brooks suffered his nervous collapse in the same year.) Victim, like Bourne, of the flu, Matthews died on March 31, 1929, just months before the stock market crash would grimly mock his belief in progress and in confident tomorrows. In a front-page article announcing his death, the *New York Times*, referring to him as "one of the last 'eminent Victorians' of American origin," noted his friendships with Twain, Howells, and Kipling (but not, curiously, with Roosevelt) and quoted reactions from Butler, Garland, and others who had known him intimately.[79] On April 2 the paper reported that President Hoover had telegraphed his condolences to Matthews's sister, Florence.[80] The notices of his death might have also observed that Matthews's departure from the literary-political arena deprived More and other defenders of tradition and authority of a pugnacious ally, and deprived the "juvenile highbrows" of one of their most "welcome signposts" of a "vanishing gentility."

Epilogue

The younger generation's figuring of Matthews as a "signpost" of a decaying Victorian culture did not cease with his death. In 1932, Ludwig Lewisohn, another Young Intellectual who had studied—rather respectfully, it seems—under Matthews at Columbia, advanced Mencken's and Bourne's earlier efforts to depict him as an effete genteel. In his influential *Expression in America*, Lewisohn announces that he will examine "that entire group of writers, from Longfellow to Brander Matthews, which created what has come to be known as the genteel tradition in American letters."[1] Denouncing that tradition as venomously as Sinclair Lewis had two years earlier in his Nobel Prize acceptance speech, Lewisohn takes several opportunities to savage his former professor by name. In, for example, a passage describing the Young Intellectuals' revolt against the "shining facade of the genteel tradition," Lewisohn pauses to reflect: "one can imagine the scorn with which Mr. Brander Matthews would have received the information that in 1905 the future of our letters was implicated with nothing that took place in his noble drawing-rooms on West End Avenue and with everything that had its faint but definite beginnings" in the editorial offices of *The Smart Set* and other magazines quartered in less fashionable surroundings.[2] Matthews would have greeted that information with scorn, and he would not have been pleased by Lewisohn's portrait of him as a member of a "polite" society who believed that literature was a "decorous illustration of a system of ethics, manners, and economics fixed and frozen for all time somewhere in England, sometime in the nineteenth century" (418). Matthews did, especially in his later years when he was in the arena doing battle with the "juvenile highbrows," exhibit many of the traits generally ascribed to the Genteel Tradition: a belief in Anglo-Saxon racial superiority and in Manifest Destiny; a seemingly unshakeable confidence in "progress"; a tendency to privilege writers whose works projected a consensus ideology and to ignore those whose texts seemed to subvert the status quo; a paternalistic attitude toward women; an anxious ambivalence—and at times blatant prejudice—toward ethnic minorities, including Jewish Americans like Lewisohn; a fear that the younger writers' rejection of tradition and authority would lead to cultural barbarism. But, if we return to Santayana's "The Genteel Tradition," it becomes immediately clear that Matthews does not epitomize the sensibility that Santayana assails.[3] As we have seen, Matthews shared Santayana's disdain for academic idealism and his respect for Mark Twain, whom Santayana credits for half-escaping the constricting bonds of the genteel orthodoxy. If he did not entirely concur with Santayana's high opinion of Henry James and Whitman, he held the former's literary criticism in high regard and offered reserved praise of the latter's poetry. Santayana, moreover, would have been pleased to learn that Matthews admired William James's theory of psychology. If Matthews was incapable of being, as Santayana says of William James, the spokesman and representative of all those who were marginalized by the "stolid majority," he did champion James Weldon Johnson and praise women novelists when his fellow white male critics ignored them. And what kind of "genteel" would advise his middle-brow readers, as Matthews did, that Zola was a "most extraordinary" novelist whose fictions were *not* obscene?

Matthews, moreover, would have been delighted to read Santayana's review of *Civilization in the United States*, for it echoes many of the criticisms that Matthews leveled at the "juvenile highbrows" in his review of the book four months earlier. "I foresee," Santayana remarks at the outset, "that I am to hear the plaints of superior and highly critical minds, suffering from maladaptation [what Matthews called "mental strabismus"]; and that I shall learn more about their palpitating doubts than about America and about civilization."[4] Where Stearns, Brooks, and the other Young Intellectuals saw themselves as cultural radicals, Santayana suggests that they were in fact rather "genteel," their plans for cultural reform springing from a sensibility that is easily shocked and offended. The cultural distance between Matthews's fashionable West End Avenue drawing rooms and the less fashionable editorial offices of *The Smart Set* and the *Seven Arts* was not, Santayana implies, nearly as far as Lewisohn and his peers wanted to believe. Certainly the ideological differences were substantial; but if one is to speak, as Lewisohn does, about the "faint but definite beginnings" of modern American literature, one ought to go back much further than 1905, back to the late nineteenth century when Matthews and many of his fellow "anti-Victorians," to borrow Robert Falk's term, were protesting against the crass commercialism, provincialism, and timid gentility of their age.[5]

In any case, by the 1940s the abusive treatment of America's eminent Victorians had begun to subside to the point that even Brooks—whose later works would have, one suspects, found a receptive audience in Matthews had he been alive to read them—had become "heartily sick" of the term "genteel," which had "run in so many directions that it was as useless as old elastic."[6]

On those few occasions when he has been resurrected from the graveyard of the genteels, Matthews has usually been offered as a "signpost" of some other concept or ideology. His friendly contemporary Clayton Hamilton, for example, represented him shortly after his death as being the epitome of that "great group of men of letters which, on both sides of the Atlantic, made the latter half of the nineteenth century illustrious in the annals of our English literature."[7] Henry May, on the other hand, assures us that Matthews, in attempting to synthesize the contradictory philosophical stances of high idealism and hard-headed pragmatism, was "an exact exponent" of the "practical idealism" that marked the "end-of-innocence" era in American history.[8] In his analysis of the tensions existing in late nineteenth- and early twentieth-century America, T. J. Jackson Lears consigns the professor to the group of "antimoderns"—including Bourne, Brooks, and Santayana—who recoiled from materialistic and "over-civilized" culture.[9] Most recently, Gerald Graff, in his history of academic literary studies in the United States, groups Matthews with the mugwumpish "generalist-professors" who practiced an impressionistic criticism and revolted against specialized scholarship; the supreme example of this type, according to Graff, was the Harvard idealist whom Matthews absolutely detested, Charles Eliot Norton.[10]

As the present study suggests, Matthews may, in addition to the above, be construed as a signifier of the "divided mind" that Peter Conn posits as the defining trait of progressivism. Or of the essentially conservative ideology that Marxist critics inevitably detect at the heart of all attempts to "reform" the status quo. Or of the academic racism and sexism that produced an American literary canon which was, until recently, almost exclusively WASP and male. Or of the rhetoric of American consensus. Or of a heroic attempt to defend tradition and authority, and oppose what Allan Bloom would call the "closing of the American mind."[11] The point here, as any semiotician would be quick to argue, is that Matthews, like all signs, is free-floating; what he represents is determined by the context in which he is embedded and the aims and interests of the observer-namer.

But, if his complex life and writings can be re-visioned and appropriated for different and even contradictory uses, one assertion seems indisputable: Matthews, as Nicholas Murray Butler perfunctorily observed in his eulogy before the Academy of Arts and Letters, wished to be "where power was generated."[12] For over four decades he had his wish. Whether one admires, disdains, or has a divided mind about Matthews's literary criticism, one must grant that he was among the most prolific and influential figures at the center of the academic-literary establishment during his age, ever ready to wield power on behalf of his—and, almost invariably, Roosevelt's—"progressive" ideals. For those who claim that academic proponents of the New Historicism, feminism, multiculturalism, and other contemporary literary or cultural theories are guilty of politicizing the criticism and teaching of literature, Matthews's career stands as a vivid reminder that English departments in the United States were just as political in 1890 as in 1990; the main difference is that what some might term the "correct political thinking" of Matthews's day leaned not to the left but, as Matthews said, to the "right side."

Brander Matthews

Notes

Introduction

1. Mark Twain, *Mark Twain Speaking*, ed. Paul Fatout (Iowa City: Univ. of Iowa Press, 1976), 269.
2. George Santayana, *The Genteel Tradition: Nine Essays by George Santayana*, ed. Douglas L. Wilson (Cambridge, Mass.: Harvard Univ. Press, 1967), 38–64.
3. See Wilson's "Introductory" to *The Genteel Tradition*, 17–25, and Robert Falk, *The Victorian Mode in American Fiction, 1865–1885* (East Lansing: Michigan State Univ. Press, 1965), 9–16.
4. John W. Rathbun and Harry H. Clark, *American Literary Criticism, 1860–1905* (Boston: Twayne, 1979), 32–34.
5. Alfred Kazin, *On Native Grounds: An Interpretation of Modern American Prose Literature* (New York: Reynal and Hitchcock, 1942), 61; Henry F. May, *The End of American Innocence: A Study of the First Years of Our Time, 1912–1917* (New York: Knopf, 1959), 63; Larzer Ziff, *The American 1890s: Life and Times of a Lost Generation* (New York: Viking, 1966).
6. T. J. Jackson Lears, *No Place of Grace: Antimodernism and the Transformation of American Culture, 1880–1920* (New York: Pantheon, 1981), 320, 115; Peter Conn, *The Divided Mind: Ideology and Imagination in America, 1898–1917* (Cambridge, Eng.: Cambridge Univ. Press, 1983); Brenda Murphy, *American Realism and American Drama, 1880–1940* (Cambridge, Eng.: Cambridge Univ. Press, 1987), 48. A notable exception to the general neglect of Matthews is Nancy Barrineau's commendable essay on him in the *Dictionary of Literary Biography*, ed. Rathbun and Monica M. Grecu (Detroit: Gale, 1988), vol. 71: 153–62.
7. Thomas Bender, *New York Intellect: A History of Intellectual Life in New York City, from 1750 to the Beginnings of Our Own Time* (New York: Knopf, 1987), xvi.
8. See, for example, Robert M. Crunden, *Ministers of Reform:*

The Progressives' Achievement in American Civilization, 1889–1920 (New York: Basic Books, 1982); Daniel T. Rodgers, "In Search of Progressivism," *Reviews in American History* 10 (Dec. 1982): 113–32; Christopher P. Wilson, *The Labor of Words: Literary Professionalism in the Progressive Era* (Athens: Univ. of Georgia Press, 1985); and John D. Buenker, "Sovereign Individuals and Organic Networks: Political Cultures in Conflict During the Progressive Era," *American Quarterly* 40 (1988): 187–204. I use the term "progressive" loosely in this study to refer to the Rooseveltian branch of the reform movement that began in the 1880s and culminated in the formation of the Progressive party.

9. Herbert Croly, *Progressive Democracy* (New York: Macmillan, 1914), 19.

10. Frank Lentricchia, *Criticism and Social Change* (Chicago: Univ. of Chicago Press, 1983), 6.

Chapter 1

1. Brander Matthews, *These Many Years: Recollections of a New Yorker* (New York: Scribner's, 1917), 24. Subsequent references will appear parenthetically within the text.

2. Matthews to William P. Trent, 16 May 1899, Brander Matthews Papers, Rare Book and Manuscript Library, Columbia Univ.; subsequent references will be to "Matthews Papers."

3. Matthews, "Matthew Arnold and the Drama," *The Bookman* 44 (Sept. 1916): 1–8.

4. Matthews to Trent, 12 Aug. 1897, Matthews Papers.

5. *Matthew Arnold's Essays in Criticism, First Series*, ed. Sister Thomas Marion Hoctor (Chicago: Univ. of Chicago Press, 1968), 31–52.

6. Matthews, "American Literature," in *Aspects of Fiction and Other Ventures in Criticism* (New York: Harper, 1896), 18.

7. Qtd. in John Henry Raleigh, *Matthew Arnold and American Culture* (Berkeley: Univ. of California Press, 1961), 12.

8. Leo Weinstein, *Hippolyte Taine* (New York: Twayne, 1972), 29.

9. Hippolyte Taine, *History of English Literature*, trans. H. Van Laun (New York: William L. Allison, 1895), 1. Subsequent references to Taine's *History* are to this edition and will appear parenthetically within the text.

10. Michel Foucault, *The Archaeology of Knowledge* (New York: Pantheon, 1973), 10.

11. René Wellek, *A History of Modern Criticism: 1750–1950* (New Haven: Yale Univ. Press, 1965), vol. 4: 29.

12. Qtd. in Weinstein, *Hippolyte Taine*, 17.

13. Hayden White, *Metahistory: The Historical Imagination in Nineteenth-Century Europe* (Baltimore: Johns Hopkins Univ. Press, 1973), 24.

14. Weinstein, *Hippolyte Taine*, 22–24.

15. See Rathbun and Clark, *American Literary Criticism*, 94–102.

16. William D. Howells, "Recent Literature," *Atlantic Monthly* 29 (Feb. 1872): 241.

17. Everett Carter, *Howells and the Age of Realism* (New York: Lippincott, 1954), 95.

18. Theodore Dreiser, *Sister Carrie* (New York: Bantam, 1982), 248. This edition is a reprint of the 1900 Doubleday, Page text.

19. Frank Luther Mott, *A History of American Magazines* (Cambridge, Mass.: Harvard Univ. Press, 1951), vol. 3: 334; William M. Armstrong, *E. L. Godkin, A Biography* (Albany: State Univ. of New York Press, 1978), 75–88.

20. Armstrong, *E. L. Godkin*, 93.

21. Matthews, *French Dramatists of the 19th Century* (1881; New York: Scribner's, 1914), v. Subsequent references to this (the fifth) edition will appear parenthetically within the text.

22. Arnold, "The French Play in London," *Nineteenth Century* 6 (Aug. 1879): 228–43. Matthews expresses admiration for this essay in his "Matthew Arnold and the Drama" (5).

23. American reaction to Arnold's 1883–84 tour is detailed by Raleigh, *Matthew Arnold*, 47–87.

24. John G. Sproat, *"The Best Men": Liberal Reformers in the Gilded Age* (New York: Oxford Univ. Press, 1968), 79–85.

25. Ibid., 111–41.

26. Matthews, "Mugwumps," *Saturday Review* (London), 58 (24 Nov. 1884): 658–59.

27. Henry Adams, *Henry Adams and His Friends*, ed. Harold Dean Cater (Boston: Houghton Mifflin, 1947), 67.

28. Matthews, "The Future Literary Capital of the United States," *Lippincott's Magazine* 37 (Jan.–June 1886): 106.

29. Gerald W. McFarland, "The New York Mugwumps of 1884: A Profile," in *Moralists or Pragmatists? The Mugwumps, 1884–1900*, ed. McFarland (New York: Simon & Schuster, 1975), 62–80.

30. Qtd. in Michael E. McGerr, *The Decline of Popular Politics: The American North, 1865–1928* (New York: Oxford Univ. Press, 1986), 56–57.

31. McFarland, *Moralists or Pragmatists?* 11.

32. Theodore Roosevelt, *The Letters of Theodore Roosevelt*, ed. Elting E. Morison, 8 vols. (Cambridge, Mass.: Harvard Univ. Press, 1951–54), vol. 1: 177. Subsequent references to these volumes will appear parenthetically within the text.

33. The elitist and conservative character of the Mugwump and other liberal reform movements of the Gilded Age and Progressive Era has received much attention. See, for example, Sproat, *"The Best Men"*; McFarland, *Moralists or Pragmatists?*; Conn, *The Divided Mind*; and Bender, *New York Intellect*, chap. 5.

34. Armstrong, *E. L. Godkin*, 94, 99, 123–24, 158.

35. Qtd. in Crunden, *Ministers of Reform*, 70; Armstrong, *E. L. Godkin*, 124, 181.

36. Lionel Trilling, "The Van Amringe and Keppel Eras," in *A History of Columbia College on Morningside* (New York: Columbia Univ. Press, 1954), 24–25. Apparently relying on reports by those who had taught with or studied under Matthews at Co-

lumbia, Trilling (who did not join Columbia's faculty until 1932, three years after Matthews's death) describes Matthews as a "member of the self-sufficient New York society which Edith Wharton has described. . . . He was flamboyantly a worldling, at home wherever elegance, comfort, and distinguished company were to be found, a man of club lounges and theater green rooms. He held his University post with some irony and gave the same amusing lectures from the same notes year after year. . . . He was consciously and conscientiously a snob, and his snobbery was touched with malice." Matthews's only redeeming trait, Trilling suggests, was his ability to stimulate his students' interest in comparative drama. In an essay recounting the history of the Columbia English Department—including Matthews's feud with Woodberry—Oscar James Campbell is equally unkind to Matthews, whom he labels a "prima donna" ("The Department of English and Comparative Literature," in *A History of the Faculty of Philosophy, Columbia University*, ed. Jacques Barzun [New York: Columbia Univ. Press, 1957], 72–79). Though Matthews does indeed seem to have been something of a snob and prima donna, many of his contemporaries portray him with fondness and respect (see, for example, Clayton Hamilton's "Brander," *Scribner's Magazine* 86 [July–Dec. 1929]: 82–87). Attempting to determine which accounts most accurately portray the "real" Brander Matthews would be a futile endeavor, and one that I have no wish to undertake.

37. Matthews makes the "abscess" remark in a letter to Trent, 7 July 1910, Matthews Papers.

38. Matthews, "'Those Literary Fellows,'" in *The American of the Future and Other Essays* (1909; rpt. Freeport, N.Y.: Books for Libraries Press, 1968), 309–30. Subsequent references will appear parenthetically within the text.

39. Howard R. Bowen and Jack H. Schuster, *American Professors* (New York: Oxford Univ. Press, 1986), 55; anon., *A History of Barnard College* (New York: Barnard College, 1964), 117–26.

40. Lentricchia, *Criticism and Social Change*, 1–20.

41. Matthews, *Aspects of Fiction*, 170.

42. Matthews to Edwin R. Seligman, 26 Mar. 1910, Matthews Papers.

43. Matthews, "The Economic Interpretation of Literary History," in *Gateways to Literature and Other Essays* (1912; rpt. Freeport, N.Y.: Books for Libraries Press, 1971), 35. Subsequent page references will appear parenthetically within the text.

44. According to Raymond Williams (*Marxism and Literature* [Oxford: Oxford Univ. Press, 1977], 83–89), "setting bounds" or "setting limits" is in fact what Marx meant by "determine" (*bestimmen*); if so, then Matthews's assertion that economic factors limit literary development was in essential agreement with Marx's theory of economic determinism.

Chapter 2

1. Roosevelt, *The Works of Theodore Roosevelt: National Edition*, ed. Hermann Hagedorn, 20 vols. (New York: Scribner's, 1926), vol. 13:19. Subsequent references to Roosevelt's *Works* will appear parenthetically within the text.

2. See David H. Burton, "Theodore Roosevelt and Edwin Arlington Robinson: A Common Vision," *The Personalist* 49 (1968): 331–50; and John W. Crowley, "'Dear Bay': Theodore Roosevelt's Letters to George Cabot Lodge," *New York History* 53 (1972): 177–94.

3. Owen Wister, *Roosevelt: The Story of a Friendship, 1880–1919* (New York: Macmillan, 1930), 106, 134.

4. Roosevelt's attempt to fuse in his own personality the best aspects of the eastern aristocrat and western cowboy is explored by Richard Slotkin, "Nostalgia and Progress: Theodore Roosevelt's Myth of the Frontier," *American Quarterly* 33 (1981): 608–37.

5. Roosevelt's literary career has been the subject of scholarly

interest from his own times to the present. See, for example, Joseph B. Gilder, "A Man of Letters in the White House," *Critic* 29 (1901): 401–9; Henry A. Beers, *Four Americans: Roosevelt, Hawthorne, Emerson, Whitman* (1919; rpt. Freeport, N.Y.: Books for Libraries Press, 1968); Charles Fenton, "Theodore Roosevelt as an American Man of Letters," *Western Humanities Review* 13 (1959): 369–74; and Aloysius A. Norton, *Theodore Roosevelt* (Boston: Twayne, 1980), passim.

6. Matthews's literary relationship with Roosevelt is discussed at length in my "Theodore Roosevelt, Brander Matthews, and the Campaign for Literary Americanism," *American Quarterly* 41 (1989): 93–111.

7. Roosevelt to Matthews, 5 Oct. 1888, Matthews Papers.

8. Conn, *The Divided Mind*.

9. Matthews and Roosevelt may have met when they were children, for Matthews remarks in his autobiography that during his boyhood he lived for a time on the same street as the Roosevelts (*These Many Years*, 165).

10. Matthews, "Memories," *Scribner's Magazine*, 6 Aug. 1889, 168–75.

11. Roosevelt, *Letters* 1: 177. Matthews apparently conceived of the story in 1887, for Roosevelt remarks in this letter that Matthews had mentioned the story to him two years earlier.

12. Thomas G. Dyer, *Theodore Roosevelt and the Idea of Race* (Baton Rouge: Louisiana State Univ. Press, 1980), 6–7.

13. Matthews to Roosevelt, 10 July 1903, Theodore Roosevelt Papers (on microfilm), Library of Congress; subsequent references will be to "Roosevelt Papers."

14. Franklin H. Giddings, *Democracy and Empire* (New York: Macmillan, 1900), v.

15. Giddings, "The American People," *International Quarterly* 7 (June 1903): 281–99.

16. Matthews to Roosevelt, 10 Apr. 1904, Roosevelt Papers.

17. Thomas F. Gossett, *Race: The History of an Idea in America* (Dallas: Southern Methodist Univ. Press, 1963), 114.

18. Matthews to Roosevelt, 10 Apr. 1904, Roosevelt Papers.
19. John W. Burgess, "Germany, Great Britain, and the United States," *Political Science Quarterly* 19 (1904): 1–19.
20. Gossett, *Race*, 318–20.
21. Matthews to Roosevelt, 27 Nov. 1904, Roosevelt Papers.
22. Matthews, as earlier noted, was born in New Orleans, home of his mother's family. Martha Bulloch Roosevelt, Theodore's mother, grew up on a Georgia plantation; though she spent most of her married life in New York, she remained an "unreconstructed rebel" who delighted in telling her son romanticized accounts of life in the antebellum South (see Dyer, *Theodore Roosevelt*, 93–94).
23. Roosevelt to Matthews, 1 Jan. 1913, Matthews Papers.
24. Dyer, *Theodore Roosevelt*, 102.
25. Roosevelt to Matthews, 11 July 1903, Roosevelt Papers.
26. Dyer, *Theodore Roosevelt*, 122.
27. Franz Boas, *The Shaping of American Anthropology 1883–1911: A Franz Boas Reader*, ed. George W. Stocking, Jr. (New York: Basic Books, 1974), 307.
28. Ibid., 316.
29. Ibid., 313.
30. Ibid., 317.
31. Ibid., 318–30.
32. Quoted in Wister, *Roosevelt*, 66.
33. Roosevelt to Matthews, 3 Feb. 1915, Matthews Papers.
34. Matthews to Roosevelt, 7 Feb. 1915, Roosevelt Papers. Matthews's strong sense of Americanism did not, however, prevent him from telling anti-Semitic "jokes" to Roosevelt (letter to Roosevelt, 2 Apr. 1917, Roosevelt Papers).
35. Boas, *The Mind of Primitive Man* (New York: Macmillan, 1911), 26. Subsequent page references will appear parenthetically within the text.
36. Robert E. Fleming, *James Weldon Johnson* (Boston: Twayne, 1987), 106–11.
37. Ibid., 14.

38. Johnson, *The Autobiography of an Ex-Coloured Man* (1912; rpt. New York: Hill and Wang, 1960), 162–63. Subsequent page references will appear parenthetically within the text.

39. See Eugene Levy, *James Weldon Johnson: Black Leader, Black Voice* (Chicago: Univ. of Chicago Press, 1973), 178 ff.

40. Johnson to Roosevelt, 2 Apr. 1918, Roosevelt Papers. Roosevelt responded to Johnson's appeal as follows: "I wish I could comply with your request, but, my dear sir, you have no conception of the multitude of similar requests made of me almost every day. I am awfully sorry but it just is not possible for me to attempt anything additional" (Roosevelt to Johnson, 19 Apr. 1918, Roosevelt Papers). The exact nature of Johnson's request is not known, nor is it clear what previous action Roosevelt had taken.

41. Johnson, *Along This Way: The Autobiography of James Weldon Johnson* (New York: Viking, 1933), 192–93.

42. Ibid., 238, 193.

43. Fleming, *James Weldon Johnson*, 23–24.

44. Johnson to Matthews, [Nov. 1908], James Weldon Johnson Collection, Collection of American Literature, Beinecke Rare Book and Manuscript Library, Yale Univ.; subsequent references will be to "Johnson Collection."

45. Matthews, *Americanisms and Briticisms: With Other Essays on Other Isms* (New York: Harper, 1892), 1–31 et passim.

46. Joseph T. Skerrett, Jr., "Irony and Symbolic Action in James Weldon Johnson's *The Autobiography of an Ex-Coloured Man*," *American Quarterly* 32 (1980): 554–55.

47. Bernard W. Bell, *The Afro-American Novel and Its Tradition* (Amherst: Univ. of Massachusetts Press, 1987), 86.

48. Matthews, "American Character in American Fiction," *Munsey's Magazine* 49 (Aug. 1913): 794–98.

49. Matthews to Johnson, 2 Jan. 1913, Johnson Collection.

50. Roosevelt, *Letters* 1:439; Kipling to Matthews, 23 Oct. 1921, Matthews Papers.

51. Matthews to Roosevelt, 4 Jan. 1913, Roosevelt Papers.

52. Ibid.
53. Matthews to Johnson, 8 Jan. 1913, Johnson Collection.
54. In *Along This Way*, Johnson claims that he was a "non-resident member" of Roosevelt's "Black Cabinet" (239).
55. Roosevelt to Matthews, 7 Jan. 1913, Matthews Papers.
56. Johnson, *Fifty Years & Other Poems* (1917; rpt. New York: AMS Press, 1975), 1–5. In his autobiography, Johnson explains that he cut the last fifteen stanzas of the initial draft of "Fifty Years" because the despairing vision they projected was at odds with the inspirational tone of the preceding stanzas. If he were to rewrite the published version of the poem, he goes on to say, he would "question the superiority in the absolute of so-called white civilization over so-called primitive civilization" (*Along This Way*, 291).
57. See *Along This Way*, 290–91.
58. Matthews to Johnson, 8 Jan. 1913, Johnson Collection; Elihu Root to Matthews, 21 Feb. 1913, Johnson Collection.
59. Matthews to Johnson, 21 May 1913, Johnson Collection.
60. Matthews to Johnson, 27 Sept. 1916, Johnson Collection. The editorials in question have not been identified. Johnson offered no new or radical ideas on the "Negro problem" during his first few years with the *Age*, and his essays on nonracial topics were often quite conservative. For example, he spoke against the formation of the League of Nations (which he dismissed as "utopian") and also against the Adamson Act, which mandated an eight-hour workday for railroad employees (see Levy, *James Weldon Johnson*, 159, 185).
61. Howells, "An Exemplary Citizen," *North American Review* 173 (Aug. 1901): 283.
62. Levy, *James Weldon Johnson*, 151–52.
63. Though he did not share Booker T. Washington's fond feelings toward Roosevelt, Du Bois nonetheless sought on at least one occasion to gain his support. When in 1905 he learned that President Roosevelt was traveling to Atlanta, Du Bois wrote from Atlanta University to ask: "You are coming to our

very threshhold—will you not step in a moment and tell us and the world that you have the same faith in the right sort of college-bred black men that you have in the right sort of artisans and workingmen?" (*The Correspondence of W. E. B. Du Bois*, ed. Herbert Aptheker [Amherst: Univ. of Massachusetts Press, 1973], vol. 1: 123). Roosevelt did not accept Du Bois's invitation (but did, as earlier noted, deliver a speech at Tuskegee in 1905).

64. Matthews, introd. to Johnson's *Fifty Years*, xiii.

65. Roosevelt to Matthews, 17 Apr. 1918, Johnson Collection; Matthews to Johnson, 21 Apr. 1918, Johnson Collection.

66. Matthews to Johnson, 6 June 1922, Johnson Collection.

67. Matthews to Johnson, 23 Mar. 1922, and 14 Oct. 1925, Johnson Collection.

68. Matthews, introd. to Johnson's *Fifty Years*, xi–xiv.

69. Matthews, *A Book about the Theater* (New York: Scribner's, 1916), 229, 240. Matthews's private letters reveal that he harbored racist feelings. Several years before he had met Johnson, Matthews made a blatantly racist remark in a letter to his friend Laurence Hutton: "the service," he said, referring to the hotel at which he was vacationing, "is inadequate and African ('All coons smell alike to me,' as the song says)" (Matthews to Hutton, 19 Sept. 1897, Hutton Correspondence). In a 1905 letter to Roosevelt he makes a disparaging reference to the "coons of Khartoum" (11 June 1905, Roosevelt Papers). One can imagine how Johnson would have reacted to such comments had he been aware of them.

70. Johnson, *Along This Way*, 305–6; Richard Wright, *Black Boy: A Record of Childhood and Youth* (1945; rpt. New York: Harper, 1966), 271–72.

71. Johnson, *Along This Way*, 306. In his introduction to *The Diary of H. L. Mencken* (New York: Knopf, 1989), Charles A. Fecher states that Mencken's diary entries reveal a deeply ingrained conviction that blacks are inferior to whites (xviii–xix). Fecher's observation and the evidence upon which it is based should not have generated the uproar they have,

for scholars have been aware of Mencken's racist side for decades (see, for example, Douglas C. Stenerson, *H. L. Mencken: Iconoclast from Baltimore* [Chicago: Univ. of Chicago Press, 1971], 23). Mencken's positive influence on Johnson and other African-American writers is detailed in Charles Scruggs, "H. L. Mencken and James Weldon Johnson: Two Men Who Helped Shape a Renaissance," in *Critical Essays on H. L. Mencken*, ed. Stenerson (Boston: Hall, 1987), 186–203.

72. See Dyer, *Theodore Roosevelt*, 123–42.

73. Qtd. in Gossett, *Race*, 238; see also Dyer, *Theodore Roosevelt*, 69–88.

74. Matthews, *An Introduction to the Study of American Literature* (New York: American, 1896), 67.

75. Matthews, "Americanism," *Harper's Round Table*, 6 July 1897, 873–74; Roosevelt praises "Americanism" in a letter to Matthews dated 27 Sept. 1897, Matthews Papers.

76. See William M. Gibson, *Theodore Roosevelt Among the Humorists* (Knoxville: Univ. of Tennessee Press, 1980), 9–23.

77. Howells, "The Modern American Mood," *Harper's Monthly* 95 (July 1897): 199–204.

78. Howells, *Selected Letters of W. D. Howells*, ed. Thomas Wortham et al. (Boston: Twayne, 1981), vol. 4: 153.

79. Roosevelt's remark is quoted in Edmund Morris, *The Rise of Theodore Roosevelt* (New York: Coward, McCann & Geoghegan, 1979), 12.

80. Matthews to Trent, 9 May 1898, Matthews Papers.

81. Ibid. Godkin opposed annexation of the Philippines on essentially the same grounds, arguing that the United States would be burdened with governing an "inferior" people (Armstrong, *E. L. Godkin*, 108).

82. Matthews to Trent, 27 Aug. 1898, Matthews Papers.

83. Gossett, *Race*, 335–36; Everett Emerson, *The Authentic Mark Twain: A Literary Biography of Samuel L. Clemens* (Philadelphia: Univ. of Pennsylvania Press, 1985), 233–34.

84. Kermit Vanderbilt, *Charles Eliot Norton: Apostle of Culture in a Democracy* (Cambridge, Mass.: Belknap Press, 1959), 96–98.
85. Ibid., 213–16.
86. Charles Eliot Norton, *Letters of Charles Eliot Norton*, ed. Sara Norton and M. A. DeWolfe Howe (New York: Houghton Mifflin, 1913), vol. 2: 313.
87. Ibid., 352.
88. Qtd. in Vanderbilt, *Charles Eliot Norton*, 220.
89. Vanderbilt, *Charles Eliot Norton*, 211–16.
90. Matthews to Trent, 2 Mar. 1896, and 27 Aug. 1898, Matthews Papers.
91. Matthews to Roosevelt, 16 Mar. 1905, Roosevelt Papers.
92. Matthews, *The American of the Future*, 4. Subsequent page references to this volume will appear parenthetically within the text.
93. Roosevelt to Matthews, 27 Sept. 1906, Roosevelt Papers.
94. Matthews to Roosevelt, 22 Sept. 1906, Roosevelt Papers.
95. Roosevelt delivered his "Muck-Rake" address on 14 Apr. 1906; Matthews's essay appeared in the Sept. 1906 number of the *North American Review*. Upon reading Roosevelt's speech, Matthews correctly predicted that the term "muck-raker" would gain popular currency, adding that "It is not a bad thing for a country to have a President who knows how to read and write" (Matthews to Roosevelt, 22 Apr. 1906, Roosevelt Papers).
96. Matthews to Trent, 16 May 1899, Matthews Papers.
97. Henry James, *The Bostonians* (1886; New York: New American Library, 1979), 57.
98. See Roosevelt, *Works* 16: 164–226, and Dyer, *Theodore Roosevelt*, 150–54.
99. Matthews, "Of Women's Novels," in *Americanisms and Briticisms*, 169–77.
100. Charlotte Perkins Gilman to Matthews, 19 Oct. 1892, Matthews Papers. I have not located Matthews's response to Gilman, if one exists.

101. Matthews, "Women Dramatists," in *A Book about the Theater*, 113–25.

102. Matthews to Roosevelt, 23 Mar. 1915, Roosevelt Papers.

103. See Campbell, "The Department of English and Comparative Literature," 80; Blanche Colton Williams, "Brander Matthews—A Reminiscence," *MS*. 1 (July 1929): 1, 19.

104. Matthews to G. B. Cortelyou, 26 Apr. 1902, Roosevelt Papers.

105. Charles A. Fenton, "The American Academy of Arts and Letters vs. All Comers," *South Atlantic Quarterly* 58 (1959): 572–86.

106. Matthews to George Washington Cable (15 Sept. 1917, Matthews Papers) and Paul Elmer More (9 June 1922, Paul E. More Papers, Princeton Univ. Library; subsequently referred to as "More Papers").

Chapter 3

1. Warner Berthoff, *The Ferment of Realism: American Literature, 1884–1919* (1965; rpt. Cambridge, Eng.: Cambridge Univ. Press, 1981), 2.

2. Frederic is quoted in Austin Briggs, Jr., *The Novels of Harold Frederic* (Ithaca, N.Y.: Cornell Univ. Press, 1969), 111. June Howard discusses the affinities between progressivism and the naturalist branch of literary realism in *Form and History in American Literary Naturalism* (Chapel Hill: Univ. of North Carolina Press, 1985), 126 ff.

3. Matthews, *The Historical Novel and Other Essays* (1901; rpt. Freeport, N.Y.: Books for Libraries Press, 1968), 106.

4. Matthews, *The Theatres of Paris*, 208.

5. Matthews, *French Dramatists of the 19th Century*, 270–74.

6. Roosevelt, *Works* 12: 98–105.

7. Frank Norris, *The Literary Criticism of Frank Norris*, ed. Donald Pizer (Austin: Univ. of Texas Press, 1964), 78.

8. Wister, *Roosevelt*, 34. Roosevelt's success in persuading Wister to remove the violent details from "Balaam and Pedro" and to soften his realism in general—to the ultimate detriment of Wister's art—is the subject of Don D. Walker's "Wister, Roosevelt and James: A Note on the Western," *American Quarterly* 12 (1960): 358–66.

9. Roosevelt, *Letters* 5: 179.

10. Matthews, *These Many Years*, 250–51. The story that Matthews and Bunner sent to Zola—"The Documents in the Case"—is, as Matthews admits, a highly contrived and artificial fiction, hardly the kind of "human-documents" realism that Zola was seeking to promote.

11. Matthews, "Émile Zola and the Present Tendencies of French Drama," in *French Dramatists of the 19th Century*, 264–84; "Of a Novel of M. Zola's," in *Americanisms and Briticisms*, 161–68; "Cervantes, Zola, Kipling & Co.," in *Aspects of Fiction*, 178–81.

12. Matthews, *The Philosophy of the Short-story* (1901; rpt. Folcroft, Pa.: Folcroft Library Editions, 1971), 33. Matthews's claim that this study represents the first attempt to formulate a detailed philosophy of the short story is accepted by many contemporary scholars of the genre (see, for example, Judie Newman, "Kate Chopin: Short Fiction and the Arts of Subversion," in *The Nineteenth-Century American Short Story*, ed. A. Robert Lee [Totowa, N.J.: Barnes & Noble, 1985], 150, and Susan Lohafer's introduction to *Short Story Theory at a Crossroads*, ed. Lohafer and Jo Ellyn Clarey [Baton Rouge: Louisiana State Univ. Press, 1989], 6).

13. Matthews, *Aspects of Fiction*, 48. In his discussion of Zola in this volume, Matthews repeats his charge that Zola has no sense of humor, but he cites the "surprisingly clean" *La Debâcle* as evidence that the French writer's mind has grown to be less sordid and "dirty" (161).

14. Matthews, *French Dramatists of the 19th Century*, 276–77, 300.

15. The "meliorist" vision of American realist novelists is discussed in Carter, *Howells and the Age of Realism*, 155.

16. Matthews, "Mr. Charles Dudley Warner as a Writer of Fiction," in *Aspects of Fiction*, 206–23.
17. Matthews, "Two Studies of the South," in *Aspects of Fiction*, 25–39.
18. Qtd. in John W. Crowley, *George Cabot Lodge* (Boston: Twayne, 1976), 34.
19. Carter, *Howells and the Age of Realism*, 95.
20. Matthews, "The Study of Fiction," in *The Historical Novel*, 100.
21. Matthews, *Aspects of Fiction*, 3, 164, 225–26; *The Historical Novel*, 86 ff.
22. As literary advisor to Longman's, Green & Co., Matthews recommended publication of De Forest's *A Lover's Revolt*, drawing expressions of appreciation from Howells as well as De Forest. See Howells, *Selected Letters* 4: 184.
23. Bliss Perry, "Recollections of the Saturday Club," in *The Saturday Club: A Century Completed 1920–1956*, ed. Edward W. Forbes and John H. Finley, Jr. (Boston: Houghton Mifflin, 1958), 5.
24. Edwin H. Cady briefly discusses Matthews's support of Howells during the Realism War (*The Realist at War: The Mature Years 1885–1920* [Syracuse, N.Y.: Syracuse Univ. Press, 1958], 51–52, 210–11), but none of Howells's other biographers makes more than passing reference to Matthews.
25. Howells, *Selected Letters* 4: 181–82.
26. Matthews, *These Many Years*, 160, 167.
27. Garland to Matthews, 29 Dec. 1889, Matthews Papers. Garland's admiration for Matthews is evident in his many letters to Matthews held at Columbia as well as in his autobiographical works. See, for example, *Companions on the Trail* (New York: Macmillan, 1931), 252–53, and *My Friendly Contemporaries* (New York: Macmillan, 1932), 272–73.
28. Howells, "The Editor's Study," *Harper's Monthly* 79 (July 1889): 314–15.
29. Matthews, "Recent Essays in Criticism," *Cosmopolitan* 12 (Nov. 1891): 124–26; rpt. in *Critical Essays on W. D. Howells*,

1866–1920, ed. Edwin H. and Norma W. Cady (Boston: G. K. Hall, 1983), 114–16.

30. Howells, *Selected Letters of W. D. Howells*, ed. Robert C. Leitz III et al. (Boston: Twayne, 1980), vol. 3: 323.

31. Matthews, "Text-Books of Fiction," in *Aspects of Fiction*, 224–34. In "Mr. Henry James's Later Work," Howells refers approvingly to Matthews's definition of realism as the depiction of the "inevitable" (*North American Review*, Jan. 1903; rpt. in *W. D. Howells as Critic*, ed. Edwin H. Cady [London: Routledge & Kegan Paul, 1973], 443–45).

32. Roosevelt, *Letters* 1: 410.

33. Matthews to Trent, 9 May 1898, Matthews Papers; Howells to Matthews, 23 June 1898, Matthews Papers.

34. Matthews, "Romance against Romanticism," in *The Historical Novel*, 31–46; Louis J. Budd, "W. D. Howells's Defense of the Romance," *PMLA* 67 (Mar. 1952): 32–42.

35. Matthews, "Mr. Howells as a Critic," *Forum* (Jan. 1902); rpt. in *Howells: A Century of Criticism*, ed. Kenneth E. Eble (Dallas: Southern Methodist Univ. Press, 1962), 65–67.

36. "Your praise," Howells wrote Matthews in response to the review, "seems the more reasonable because your blame is so just. I know I have those faults which you hint, and if I were not nearly sixty-five years old I should, under inspiration of your censure, set about correcting them. But as it is I shall have work enough cultivating the merits which you recognize so charmingly that I should love them almost as if they were some one else's. . . . Now it shall never matter to me whatever meaner critics say—Matthews has forever secured me from their harm" (*Selected Letters* 4: 278–79).

37. Howells, *Selected Letters of W. D. Howells*, ed. William C. Fischer and Christoph K. Lohmann (Boston: Twayne, 1983), vol. 5: 230.

38. Matthews, "Ibsen the Playwright," *The Bookman* 22–23 (Feb.–Mar., 1906); rpt. in Matthews, *Inquiries and Opinions* (New York: Scribner's, 1907), 229–79.

39. Matthews, "How Shakspere Learnt His Trade," *North American Review* 177 (Sept. 1903): 424–33.

40. Matthews, *Shakspere as a Playwright* (New York: Scribner's, 1913), 374–80. Like most scientific-minded progressivists, Matthews was a firm believer in Darwin's theory, and he in fact edited Thomas Henry Huxley's *Autobiography and Essays* (1919; rpt. New York: Kraus, 1969). His introduction to that volume explicitly draws the connection between scientific and realist writing: citing Huxley's comment that "science and literature are not two things but two sides of the same thing," Matthews proceeds to emphasize Huxley's precision of style, fierce commitment to the truth, and moral integrity. That science and literature—realist literature, that is—were two sides of the same coin in Matthews's mind is suggested by the fact that whole passages from the Huxley essay could be transplanted to Matthews's writings on Shakespeare, Howells, or Twain without causing a hitch.

41. Howells, *Selected Letters* 5: 62.

42. Howells, "Henrik Ibsen," *North American Review* 183 (July 1906); rpt. in *W. D. Howells as Critic*, ed. Cady, 443–45. There is a bit of a literary mystery here: reading Matthews's and Howells's essays on Ibsen back-to-back, one cannot help inferring that the latter was a response to the former; yet we know that Howells drafted his Ibsen piece in 1903, three years before Matthews's appeared (see *Selected Letters of W. D. Howells* 5: 181–82). It is possible, of course, that Matthews had expressed his opinions on Ibsen to Howells prior to 1903.

43. Howells, "The Editor's Easy Chair," *Harper's Monthly* (Sept. 1905); rpt. in *W. D. Howells as Critic*, ed. Cady, 427–32.

44. Howells, "An Appreciation," *New York Times Review of Books*, 21 Oct. 1917, 405.

45. "Birthday Tributes to Wm. D. Howells," *New York Times*, 25 Mar. 1917, sec. 1, p. 9.

46. Matthews, "Memories of Mark Twain," in *The Tocsin of Revolt and Other Essays* (New York: Scribner's, 1922), 253–94.

47. Matthews, unsigned review of *Huckleberry Finn, Saturday Review* (London), 59 (31 Jan. 1885): 153–54.
48. Matthews, "Memories of Mark Twain," 255.
49. Twain to Matthews, 26 July 1898, Matthews Papers.
50. After poking fun at Matthews's name ("B-r-r-RANder M-m-ATHews! You can curse a man's head off with that name if you know how and where to put the emphasis"), Twain closed his humorous speech by expressing his high regard for the professor: "To have overcome by the persuasive graces, sincerities and felicities of his literature the disaster of a name like that and reconciled men to the sound of it, is a fine and high achievement; and this, the owner of it has done. To have gone further and made it a welcome sound and changed its discords to music, is a still finer and higher achievement; and this he has also done. And so, let him have full credit. When he got his name it was only good to curse with. Now it is good to conjure with" (*Mark Twain Speaking*, ed. Fatout, 269–70).
51. Matthews, "The Penalty of Humor," in *Aspects of Fiction*, 43–56.
52. See *Mark Twain's Correspondence with Henry Huttleston Rogers*, ed. Lewis Leary (Berkeley: Univ. of California Press, 1969), 377n.
53. Matthews, "Biographical Criticism," introd. to *The Writings of Mark Twain* (Hartford, Conn.: American, 1899), vol. 1: v–xxxiii.
54. Twain and Roosevelt are quoted in Gibson, *Theodore Roosevelt Among the Humorists*, 26, 29. Gibson covers the two men's relationship in detail.
55. See *Mark Twain Speaking*, 182–85, 267.
56. Matthews to Joseph Hopkins Twichell, 6 Oct. 1898, Mark Twain Papers, Bancroft Library, Univ. of California at Berkeley; subsequently referred to as "Twain Papers."
57. Twain to Bliss Perry, n.d., Matthews Papers; Howells, "Mark Twain: An Inquiry," *W. D. Howells as Critic*, ed. Cady, 338.

58. Sacvan Bercovitch, "Afterword," *Ideology and Classic American Literature*, ed. Bercovitch and Myra Jehlen (Cambridge, Eng.: Cambridge Univ. Press, 1986), 419–20.

59. *The Historical Novel* bears the dedication: "To Mark Twain, in testimony of my regard for the man and of my respect for the literary artist"; "Biographical Criticism" is reprinted in *Inquiries and Opinions* under the title "Mark Twain" (139–66).

60. Matthews, *An Introduction to the Study of American Literature* (1896; rev. ed., New York: American, 1918), 215–26.

61. Matthews, "Mark Twain and the Theater," in *Playwrights on Playmaking and Other Studies of the Stage* (1923; rpt. Freeport, N.Y.: Books for Libraries Press, 1967), 159–82.

62. Matthews, *These Many Years*, 224.

63. Matthews, "An American Critic," *Library Table* 4 (30 Mar. 1878): 197–98.

64. Matthews, "More American Stories," *Cosmopolitan* 13 (Sept. 1892): 630. Where he awards Twain an entire chapter in the 1918 edition of *An Introduction to the Study of American Literature*, Matthews devotes only a paragraph to James in the chapter on minor writers. James, he asserts here, is an "acute critic," but his later fictions suffer from an opaque and "curiously involved and hesitating" style (245).

65. *Henry James Letters*, ed. Leon Edel (Cambridge, Mass.: Harvard Univ. Press, 1984), vol. 4: 716–18. The two men exchanged letters again in 1915, when Matthews sought James's approval to print a revised version of James's 1887 essay on Coquelin as the introduction to the eminent French actor's *Art of the Actor* (trans. Abby Langdon Alger [New York: Publications of the Dramatic Museum of Columbia Univ., 1915], 1–36; the volume is part of a twenty-six-book series published by the Brander Matthews Dramatic Museum at Columbia between 1914 and 1926). In granting Matthews's request, James closed his letter by exclaiming: "What a very kindly and faithful memory you have of that other younger accident [the first version of the essay, apparently]. . . . How devotedly—to your

general subject—you have *noticed*, and how appreciatively I am yours forever" (letter to Matthews, 21 Apr. 1915, Matthews Papers). A second letter from James to Matthews on the same subject is included in *Henry James Letters* 4: 744–45.

66. Matthews, "Henry James and the Theater," in *Playwrights on Playmaking*, 187–204.

67. Roosevelt, *Letters* 1: 390.

68. Matthews, *These Many Years*, 288–89.

69. See Oliver, "Brander Matthews's Re-visioning of Crane's *Maggie*," *American Literature* 60 (1988): 654–58.

Chapter 4

1. Garland to Matthews, 29 Dec. 1899, Matthews Papers.

2. See Benjamin T. Spencer, *The Quest for Nationality: An American Literary Campaign* (Syracuse, N.Y.: Syracuse Univ. Press, 1957), esp. 290–339.

3. Roosevelt, *Letters* 1: 389–90.

4. Roosevelt, "What Americanism Means," *Forum* 18 (Apr. 1894): 199.

5. The feud between the nationalists and internationalists in late nineteenth-century America is explored by Marc Pachter, "American Cosmopolitanism, 1870–1910," in *Impressions of a Gilded Age: The American Fin de Siecle*, ed. Marc Chenetier and Rob Kroes (Amsterdam: Amerika Instituut, Universiteit van Amsterdam, 1983), 21–42. James's remark is cited in this essay.

6. Matthews, *These Many Years*, 203.

7. David A. Hollinger, *In the American Province: Studies in the History and Historiography of Ideas* (Bloomington: Indiana Univ. Press, 1985), 58 ff.

8. Bourne, "Trans-National America," in *The History of a Literary Radical and Other Papers by Randolph Bourne*, ed. Van Wyck Brooks (New York: Russell, 1956), 260–84.

9. Matthews, "More American Stories," 626–30.

10. Matthews to Laurence Hutton, 12 July 1896, Hutton Correspondence.

11. Matthews, "American Literature," 3–22.

12. Matthews, "Literature in the New Century," *North American Review* 179 (Oct. 1904); rpt. in *Inquiries and Opinions*, 1–25. In a later essay, "What Is American Literature?" Matthews merely rehashed the central arguments of "American Literature" and "Literature in the New Century" (*The Tocsin of Revolt*, 65–78).

13. "Birthday Tributes to Wm. D. Howells," *New York Times*, 25 Mar. 1917, sec. 1, p.9.

14. Roosevelt to Matthews, 8 Dec. 1891, 18 Dec. 1893, Matthews Papers.

15. Matthews to unidentified correspondent, 19 Apr. 1918, Matthews Papers.

16. Roosevelt, *Letters* 1: 376.

17. Matthews to Trent, 2 Mar. 1896, Matthews Papers.

18. See Elsa Nettels, *Language, Race, and Social Class in Howells's America* (Lexington: Univ. Press of Kentucky, 1988), 41–61.

19. Matthews, *Americanisms and Briticisms*, 7, 11. Subsequent references to essays in this volume will appear parenthetically within the text.

20. Roosevelt, *Works* 12: 294.

21. Slotkin, "Nostalgia and Progress," 608–37.

22. Though Matthews and Lang frequently sparred over the merits of American language and literature, they had a mutual respect and affection for one another. In *These Many Years*, Matthews honors Lang as the "most versatile, the most fecund, and the most learned" of his intimate friends (263).

23. George Stewart Stokes, *Agnes Repplier: Lady of Letters* (Philadelphia: Univ. of Pennsylvania Press, 1949), 168.

24. Roosevelt to Matthews, 2 Jan. 1891, Matthews Papers; *Letters* 1: 351.

25. Roosevelt, *Letters* 1: 142, 288; Roosevelt to Matthews, 25 Feb. 1892, Matthews Papers.

26. Roosevelt, *Works* 12: 300–316. Initially, Roosevelt disdained Kipling because of his criticisms of American culture. However, Matthews, who was, as earlier noted, an intimate friend of the British novelist, eventually succeeded in reversing Roosevelt's opinion; in 1895 Roosevelt informed Matthews that he had "come round to your way of looking at Kipling," adding that what he most liked about Kipling was that "he seems almost as fond of you as I am" (*Letters* 1: 439).

27. Roosevelt, *Letters* 1: 370.

28. Agnes Repplier, *Counter-Currents* (Boston: Houghton Mifflin, 1916).

29. See Dennis E. Barron, *Grammar and Good Taste: Reforming the American Language* (New Haven: Yale Univ. Press, 1982), 68–98.

30. Andrew Carnegie to Matthews, 20 Mar. 1911, Matthews Papers; Matthews, *These Many Years*, 441–47.

31. Matthews, "Simplified Spelling and 'Fonetic Reform,'" in *The American of the Future*, 219–31.

32. Matthews to Roosevelt, 22 Sept. 1906, Roosevelt Papers; Matthews, *These Many Years*, 442.

33. Roosevelt to Matthews, 17 May 1906, Matthews Papers.

34. Roosevelt's secretary to Matthews, 27 Aug. 1906, Matthews Papers. See Roosevelt, *Letters* 5: 389–90.

35. Roosevelt, *Letters* 5: 527; Carnegie to Matthews, 16 Jan. 1915, Matthews Papers. In *These Many Years*, Matthews expresses confidence that the next generation of Americans will be receptive to spelling reforms "far more radical than any we dare to urge to-day [1917]" (447).

36. The Platt-Simmonds Act was in fact a series of amendments to the existing copyright law of 1870. By extending copyright protection to foreign authors who published in the United States, the act gained similar protection for American writers who published abroad. The long political battle leading up to the passage of the act is detailed in Aubert J. Clark, *The Movement for International Copyright in Nineteenth Century America*

(Washington, D.C.: Catholic Univ. of America Press, 1960), 149–81.

37. Wrote Cooper: "The fact, that an American publisher can get an English work without money, must, . . . (unless legislative protection shall be extended to their own authors), have a tendency to repress a national literature. No man will pay a writer for an epic, a tragedy, a sonnet, a history, or a romance, when he can get a work of equal merit for nothing (*Notions of the Americans: Picked Up by a Travelling Bachelor* [1828; rpt. New York: Ungar, 1963], vol. 2: 106–7).

38. Platt and Lodge are quoted in "American Copyright League Celebration of the Passage of the Bill," *Publishers Weekly*, 11 Apr. 1892, 567–68.

39. Matthews, *These Many Years*, 224–31. Matthews notes that Henry James was the first person to arrive at his home for the meeting, the two men making each other's acquaintance for the first time at that moment.

40. Matthews, "American Authors and British Pirates," *New Princeton Review* 4 (1887): 201–12.

41. Matthews to Twain, 6 Nov. 1887, Twain Papers.

42. "American Authors and British Pirates," *New Princeton Review* 5 (1888): 47–65. This piece was merged with the earlier one to form the pamphlet *American Authors and British Pirates* (New York: American Copyright League, 1889). Since Twain's "letter" and Matthews's rejoinder appear under the single title, some scholars have mistakenly assumed that the two men coauthored an essay on copyright reform, but that was hardly the case.

43. Matthews, "Memories of Mark Twain," 258.

44. Ibid., 259–60.

45. Roosevelt, *Letters* 1: 213, 216.

46. Matthews, "The Evolution of Copyright," in *Books and Play-Books: Essays on Literature and Drama* (1895; rpt. Freeport, N.Y.: Books for Libraries Press, 1972), 1–32.

47. Roosevelt, *Letters* 1: 213.

48. Matthews, *These Many Years*, 228.

49. Wilson, *The Labor of Words*, 63–91.

50. Roosevelt to Matthews, 27 Sept. 1897, Matthews Papers.

51. Roosevelt, *Letters* 1: 288, 307.

52. Page references to *An Introduction to the Study of American Literature* (1896 ed.) will appear parenthetically within the text.

53. Roosevelt, *Letters* 1: 436.

54. See Kermit Vanderbilt, *American Literature and the Academy: The Roots, Growth, and Maturity of a Profession* (Philadelphia: Univ. of Pennsylvania Press, 1986), 105.

55. Matthews, *These Many Years*, 404.

56. Roosevelt, *Works* 12: 292–95. In a letter to Matthews dated 11 Nov. 1895 (Matthews Papers), Roosevelt stated that both the *Forum* and *Atlantic* magazines had rejected his proposition to review *An Introduction to the Study of American Literature*, adding "I am rather at a loss to know what to do." Matthews, it seems, then made arrangements to have Roosevelt publish the review in *The Bookman*, for on 6 Dec. 1895 Roosevelt wrote his friend: "Of course I will gladly review your *Introduction of* [sic] *the Study of American Literature* in the February number. I suppose they will write me about it. I will have to get them to send me a stenographer" (*Letters* 1: 499). Though not mentioned by name in the letter, *The Bookman* did publish the review in its Feb. 1896 number.

57. Howells, "Life and Letters," *Harper's Weekly* 40 (28 Mar. 1896): 294.

58. Vanderbilt, *American Literature and the Academy*, 552n.

59. Matthews to William C. Brownell, 17 Jan. 1899, 5 Feb. 1899, Charles Scribner's Sons Archives; Matthews to Trent, 3 Aug. 1893, 16 Aug. 1893, Matthews Papers. Brownell was literary advisor at Scribner's.

60. Vanderbilt, *American Literature and the Academy*, 7.

61. After reading *Southern Statesmen*, Roosevelt wrote Trent: "I want to tell you . . . how much I admire it, and how much I admire you for having written it. I can say in all sincerity

that the compliment of having such a book dedicated to me is more than almost anything else could be" (*Letters* 1: 600).

62. Trent, "Brander Matthews as a Dramatic Critic," *International Monthly*, 4 (Aug. 1901), 289–93.

63. See Vanderbilt, *American Literature and the Academy*, 7, 21–22. Vanderbilt notes that Trent found the discussion of Holmes in Matthews's "Writers of Familiar Verse" competent but was displeased by the inflation of H. C. Bunner's merits as a poet (167). In 1924, after their personal feud had been running for over a decade, Matthews called for a truce: "We are too old—& just now I feel very aged—not to be ready to let the dead past bury its dead. What has happened has happened, & we [should?] not discuss it" (20 June 1924, Matthews Papers). Whether Trent buried the past is not known.

64. Trent et al., preface to *The Cambridge History of American Literature* (New York: Putnam's, 1917), iii–xi.

65. Eric Cheyfitz, "Matthiessen's *American Renaissance*: Circumscribing the Revolution," *American Quarterly* 41 (1989): 341–61.

Chapter 5

1. Matthews, *These Many Years*, 383.
2. Ibid., 383–84.
3. Ibid., 389.
4. Matthews to Howells, 25 Dec. 1893, William D. Howells Papers, Houghton Library, Harvard Univ. Subsequent references will be to "Howells Papers."
5. Matthews, *Vignettes of Manhattan* (New York: Harper, 1894), 85–97, 13–21.
6. Howells, "The Editor's Study," *Harper's Monthly* (Nov. 1891); rpt. in *W. D. Howells as Critic*, 204.
7. Matthews, *His Father's Son: A Novel of New York* (New York: Harper, 1895, 1896), 17.
8. Howells, "Life and Letters," *Harper's Weekly* 39 (Aug. 3, 1895): 725–26.

9. Matthews to Howells, 3 Sept. 1895, Howells Papers.

10. Anon., "Recent Fiction," *The Nation* 62 (1896): 81.

11. See, for example, Hamlin Garland's review in *The Bookman* 2 (1895–96): 416–20. Garland commends the novel for avoiding the sensational and sentimental, and he maintains that the portrait of Ezra Pierce is as impressively drawn as that of Silas Lapham; but, remarking that the "theme is greater than the treatment," he finds the book in general to be merely "perfectly adequate" within its limits. William Morton Payne's review of the novel in *The Dial* 19 (1895): 384–85, takes a similar position. In *Companions on the Trail*, written after Matthews's death, Garland offered a more frank assessment of his friend's novels: they tended, he said, to be cold and formal, lacking "juice" (252–53).

12. Howells, "Life and Letters," *Harper's Weekly* 39 (26 Oct. 1895): 1012–13.

13. Qtd. in Leo Lowenthal, "Sociology of Literature in Retrospect," trans. Ted R. Weeks, *Critical Inquiry* 14 (Autumn 1987): 5.

14. Matthews to Howells, 27 Oct. 1895, Howells Papers.

15. Matthews, *A Confident To-morrow: A Novel of New York* (New York: Harper, 1899), 6–7. Subsequent page references will appear parenthetically within the text.

16. Howells, *Selected Letters* 3: 323.

17. Ibid., 4: 278.

18. Matthews, "Mr. Howells as a Critic," 77.

19. Roosevelt, *Letters* 5: 795; 1: 412.

20. Harry Thurston Peck, "A Confident To-morrow," *The Bookman* 10 (1899–1900): 328. Though Matthews would later consider Peck an "abscess" in the Columbia English Department, he was on friendly terms with him at this time, as witnessed by his dedication of *The Philosophy of the Short-story* (1901) to him. Peck admired French realist fiction, Balzac's in particular, but he considered Howells's novels to be trivial.

21. Roosevelt, *Letters* 1: 410.

22. See Cady, *The Realist at War*, 209–10.

23. Howells, "An Appreciation," 405.

24. Howells's treatment of marriage in his fiction has been the subject of numerous studies, the most recent and comprehensive of which is Allen F. Stein's *After the Vows Were Spoken: Marriage in American Literary Realism* (Columbus: Ohio State Univ. Press, 1984), 19–53. As Stein argues, for Howells marriage was a vehicle of liberation from the "prison of the self," offering those whose marriage was based on an affectionate partnership rather than passion a "little sphere of civility and order in a world that otherwise is often chaotic and threatening" (20).

25. Matthews, *Americanisms and Briticisms*, 175–76.

26. Matthews, *The Action and the Word: A Novel of New York* (New York: Harper, 1900), 171. Subsequent page references will appear parenthetically within the text.

27. Matthews, *Inquiries and Opinions*, 258.

28. Matthews was an intimate friend of the day's most prominent Creole writer, George Washington Cable, as well as of *Century* editor Richard Watson Gilder, with whom Chopin had an uneasy relationship. Gilder opened the *Century*'s doors to her; but he considered some of her fiction "immoral," and he twice refused to publish short stories of hers unless she softened their self-assertive women characters (see Per Seyersted, *Kate Chopin: A Critical Biography* [Baton Rouge: Louisiana State Univ. Press, 1980], 68–69). Given Matthews's interest in Creole fiction and Gilder's relationship with Chopin, it seems reasonable to assume that the two men discussed her work.

29. Kate Chopin, *The Awakening and Selected Stories*, ed. Nina Baym (New York: Modern Library, 1981), 273.

30. Howells, "American Literary Centres," *Literature and Life* (New York: Harper, 1902), 179.

31. Howells, *Selected Letters* 4: 204, 233.

32. Cady, ed., *W. D. Howells as Critic*, 406; Gail Thain Parker, "William Dean Howells: Realism and Feminism," in *Uses of Literature*, ed. Monroe Engel, Harvard English Studies 4 (Cambridge, Mass.: Harvard Univ. Press, 1973), 133–61. Occupying the middle ground between Cady's and Parker's positions

is John W. Crowley's "W. D. Howells: The Ever-Womanly," in *American Novelists Revisited: Essays in Feminist Criticism*, ed. Fritz Fleischmann (Boston: G. K. Hall, 1982), 171–88.

33. Seyersted, *Kate Chopin*, 54.
34. Howells, *Selected Letters* 4: 233n.
35. Matthews to Trent, 9 Sept. 1900, Matthews Papers.
36. Howells, "Novel-Writing and Novel-Reading," in *The Norton Anthology of American Literature*, ed. Nina Baym et al., 2d ed. (New York: Norton, 1985), 284, 300.
37. Matthews, *These Many Years*, 388–89.

Chapter 6

1. Matthews, *These Many Years*, 462.
2. Randolph Bourne to Elsie Clews Parsons, in Eric J. Sandeen, "Bourne Again: The Correspondence Between Randolph Bourne and Elsie Clews Parsons," *American Literary History* 1 (1989): 502.
3. Anon., "The Literary Spotlight, XX: Brander Matthews," *The Bookman* 57 (1923): 432–36.
4. Writing in 1916, thirteen years before Matthews's death, Garland described him as being so feeble that he could "scarcely hobble" (*My Friendly Contemporaries*, 108).
5. Matthews to Stuart Pratt Sherman, 30 Nov. 1922, Stuart Sherman Papers, Univ. of Illinois Archives. Subsequently referred to as "Sherman Papers."
6. Matthews, "The Tocsin of Revolt," *Art World* 3 (Mar. 1918): 467–70; rpt. in *The Tocsin of Revolt*, 3–20. Subsequent references will appear parenthetically within the text.
7. Matthews, "Roosevelt as a Practical Politician," *Outlook*, 16 July 1919, 433–35; "Theodore Roosevelt," in *Commemorative Tributes of the American Academy of Arts and Letters 1905–1941* (1942; rpt. Freeport, N.Y.: Books for Libraries Press, 1968), 110–15.
8. Matthews, "Theodore Roosevelt as a Man of Letters," in Roosevelt, *Works* 12: ix–xx.

9. Mencken, *Prejudices: Second Series* (New York: Knopf, 1920), 102–35. Subsequent references to this collection of essays will appear parenthetically within the text. On Mencken's disdain for progressivism, see Douglas C. Stenerson, *H. L. Mencken*, 172.

10. Matthews, *The Tocsin of Revolt*, 65–78. See also his "Literary Colonialism," *New York Times Book Review*, 5 Mar. 1922, 2.

11. Mencken, *The American Language* (New York: Knopf, 1919), 6, 162, 178–79, 255, 259, 265, and 333. See also Mencken's earlier article "The Two Englishes" (*Baltimore Evening Sun*, 10 Oct. 1910, 6), in which he speaks approvingly of an unidentified work by Matthews on Americanisms and Briticisms; his reference to Matthews in this piece as "that learned man" seems to be sincere, not sarcastic.

12. Matthews, *Essays on English* (1921; rpt. Freeport, N.Y.: Books for Libraries Press, 1971), 3–30.

13. Matthews, "Developing the American from the English Language," *New York Times Book Review*, 30 Mar. 1919, 157, 164, 170. Though an advocate of simplified spelling, Mencken criticized the Simplified Spelling Board, over which Matthews presided, for the impolitic manner in which it pursued its objective; he was especially critical of Roosevelt's directive that the Government Printing Office adopt the board-endorsed spellings, claiming that Roosevelt's "buffoonery" during the incident severely undermined the cause (*The American Language*, 261–64).

14. Mencken, *The New Mencken Letters*, ed. Carl Bode (New York: Dial, 1977), 98.

15. Sherman, *Points of View* (New York: Scribner's, 1924), 258. Subsequent references to this volume of essays will appear parenthetically within the text.

16. Matthews to More, 19 Sept. 1921, More Papers. Matthews informed More (letter dated 9 June 1922, More Papers) that he had a "high regard" for Babbitt's work and would be happy to support his nomination to the Academy of Arts

and Letters. In an earlier letter to Trent (1 Aug. 1909, Matthews Papers) he had expressed hope that Columbia could lure Babbitt from Harvard. Sherman's change of attitude toward the New Humanists is discussed in Vanderbilt, *American Literature and the Academy*, 246–47.

17. Matthews to Sherman, 29 Oct. 1922, Sherman Papers.

18. Sherman, "The Naturalism of Mr. Dreiser," *The Nation*, 2 Dec. 1915, 648–50; "Mr. Mencken, the Jeune Fille, and the New Spirit in Letters," in Sherman, *Americans* (New York: Scribner's, 1923), 1–12. Sherman's well-known feud with Mencken is summarized in Stenerson, *H. L. Mencken*, 185–86.

19. Matthews to Ernest Bernbaum, 20 Mar. 1923, Sherman Papers.

20. For an account of *The "Genius"* affair, see Stenerson, *H. L. Mencken*, 186–89.

21. *Dreiser-Mencken Letters*, ed. Thomas P. Riggio (Philadelphia: Univ. of Pennsylvania Press, 1986), vol. 1: 258.

22. Mencken to Matthews, 9 Dec. 1916, Matthews Papers.

23. Matthews, *The American of the Future*, 328.

24. Mencken to Matthews, 14 Dec. 1916, Matthews Papers. F. O. Matthiessen states that some people suspected that the suppression of Dreiser's novel was a "piece of very shrewd advertising" (*Theodore Dreiser* [New York: Sloane, 1951], 168).

25. See Mencken's comments in *Prejudices: Second Series*, 90.

26. Winston Churchill to Matthews, 25 Feb. 1916, Matthews Papers.

27. Matthews to Julian Street, 29 June 1916, Julian Street Papers, Princeton Univ. Library; subsequently referred to as "Street Papers."

28. Matthews to Street, 2 Aug. 1916, 31 Aug. 1922, Street Papers.

29. Street to Matthews, 27 Aug. 1922, Street Papers.

30. Garland to Matthews, 25 July [1916], Matthews Papers.

31. Like Roosevelt's and Matthews's, Garland's enthusiasm for assimilating immigrants into the great "melting pot" was

tempered by his fear of Others. In *My Friendly Contemporaries*, for instance, he states that, though he feels sympathy for the immigrants of New York's Lower East Side, giving them political power would "unchain strange beasts" (365). Elsewhere he bemoans the devastation of once-fashionable Chicago neighborhoods by "these Africans, with the soil of the Southern plantations still on their shoes" (*Companions on the Trail*, 513). Street makes the "Yiddish" comment in a letter to Matthews, 2 Apr. 1925, Street Papers.

32. Matthews to Leonidas Westervelt, 19 July 1925, Matthews Papers.
33. Matthews to Street, 3 July 1916, 25 Aug. 1916, Street Papers.
34. Matthews to Street, 15 July 1916, Street Papers.
35. Matthews to Street, 2 Aug. 1916, Street Papers.
36. Matthews to Street, 31 July 1916, Street Papers. Matthews suggested that Roosevelt's "shrewd, sensible letter" be held in reserve until the meeting with the Executive Council, when it could be sprung as a "surprise." I have not been able to locate the letter in question. Putnam, it might be noted, supported the protest but never signed the petition because he objected to an unspecified passage in it.
37. Matthews to Street, 27 July 1916, Street Papers.
38. Street to Matthews, 16 Oct. [1916], Street Papers.
39. Garland, *My Friendly Contemporaries*, 382.
40. Garland, *Companions on the Trail*, 507.
41. Matthews to Roosevelt, 16 Feb. 1913, 19 Feb. 1913, Roosevelt Papers.
42. Roosevelt, *Works* 12: 325–36.
43. Garland, *My Friendly Contemporaries*, 130.
44. Anon., "Women as 'Immortals' Favored by Matthews," unidentified newspaper clipping dated 1913 in Archives of the American Academy and Institute of Arts and Letters.
45. Matthews to Robert Underwood Johnson, 6 Jan. 1918, American Academy and Institute of Arts and Letters; Gar-

land to Matthews, letters dated Jan. 27, Jan. 29., and May 22, n.y., Matthews Papers. Garland does not name the women writers who were turned down for membership. He does note in a diary entry that he and Matthews voted to award the academy's Gold Medal to Wharton in 1923 but were outvoted by other members on the committee charged with selecting the winner (*Hamlin Garland's Diaries*, ed. Donald Pizer [San Marino: Huntington Library, 1968], 224).

46. See William Summerscales, *Affirmation and Dissent: Columbia's Response to the Crisis of World War I* (New York: Teachers College Press, Columbia Univ., 1970), xi, 69, et passim.

47. Qtd. in Gene R. Hawes, "The Men from Morningside," 249.

48. For a full account of the episode, see Summerscales, *Affirmation and Dissent*, 72–102.

49. Matthews, *These Many Years*, 412.

50. Nicholas Murray Butler to Matthews, 14 Dec. 1914, Matthews Papers; Butler, "Brander Matthews," in *Commemorative Tributes of the American Academy of Arts and Letters*, 234–38.

51. Matthews, "Are We Americans a Warlike People?" *New York Times Magazine*, 29 Apr. 1917, 4–5.

52. Matthews to Roosevelt, 20 July 1918, Roosevelt Papers.

53. John Milton Cooper, Jr., *The Warrior and the Priest: Woodrow Wilson and Theodore Roosevelt* (Cambridge, Mass.: Harvard Univ. Press, 1983), 328–29.

54. Matthews, "The Duty of Intellectuals," *Educational Review* 56 (Oct. 1918); rpt. in *The Tocsin of Revolt*, 21–39.

55. Matthews, rev. of *Straight Deal*, by Wister, *New York Times Book Review*, 9 May 1920, 235, 249; "An Observant American in France," *Literary Digest International Book Review* 1 (Jan. 1923): 12–13, 63.

56. Mencken's uncritical attitude toward Hitler and Fascist Germany during the 1930s is discussed by Riggio, *Dreiser-Mencken Letters* 2: 558, 561n. References to Hitler in Mencken's recently published diary merely confirm Riggio's conclusions (*The Diary of H. L. Mencken*, ed. Fecher).

57. Matthews to [?] Tyson, 19 Apr. 1918, Matthews Papers; Cooper, *The Warrior and the Priest*, 329.
58. Van Wyck Brooks, introd. to Bourne, *The History of a Literary Radical*, 3.
59. Bourne, "The Experimental Life," in *Youth and Life* (1913; rpt. Freeport, N.Y.: Books for Libraries Press, 1967), 245. Bourne's attitude toward progressivism is analyzed by Edward Abrahams, *The Lyrical Left* (Charlottesville: Univ. Press of Virginia, 1986), 35 ff.
60. Matthews to Bourne, 22 Nov. 1911, Matthews Papers.
61. Bourne, rev. of Boas, *The Mind of Primitive Man*, *Columbia Monthly* 9 (Nov. 1911): 27–28; "Bigoted indeed," wrote Bourne in his review, "must be the reader whose whole troop of racial and nationalistic prejudices are not in full retreat, if not already annihilated, long before he has come to the end of the book."
62. Bourne, *The Letters of Randolph Bourne*, ed. Eric J. Sandeen (Troy, N.Y.: Whitson, 1981), 147.
63. Bourne, *The History of a Literary Radical*, 62. Subsequent references to essays in this collection will appear parenthetically within the text.
64. Writing his friend Alyse Gregory in 1916, Bourne stated that Roosevelt had become a "madman" and that Eastern genteels were doing the loudest ranting for war (*Letters of Randolph Bourne*, 363).
65. Bourne, "A Vanishing World of Gentility," *The Dial* 64 (Mar. 1918): 234–35.
66. Harold Stearns, *America and the Young Intellectual* (New York: Doran, 1921), 9–23. The chapter "A Dilapidated Scarecrow" disparages Wister's *A Straight Deal*, a book that Matthews effusively praised.
67. Matthews, "America and the Juvenile Highbrows," *New York Times Book Review*, 29 Jan. 1922, 8.
68. Matthews to Sherman, 14 Jan. 1922, Sherman Papers.
69. Stearns, preface to *Civilization in the United States* (1922; rpt.

Westport, Conn.: Greenwood, 1971), iii–viii; Matthews, "Inquest on American Civilization," *New York Times Book Review*, 12 Feb. 1922, 18.

70. See Sandeen, "Bourne Again," 493 ff.
71. Brooks, *Letters and Leadership* (New York: Huebsch, 1918), xvi.
72. Brooks, *America's Coming-of-Age* (1915; rpt. New York: Octagon, 1975), 3–35.
73. See James Hoopes, *Van Wyck Brooks: In Search of American Culture* (Amherst: Univ. of Massachusetts Press, 1977), 52.
74. Brooks, *Letters and Leadership*, 10–11.
75. Matthews, "Concerning a Cosmopolitan Critic," *New York Times Book Review*, 10 July 1921, 9.
76. Brooks, *The Wine of the Puritans: A Study of Present-Day America* (1908; rpt. Folcroft, Pa.: Folcroft Library Editions, 1974), 121. Hoopes notes the influence of Arnold and Taine on Brooks's criticism (*Van Wyck Brooks*, 42, 62–67, 88, et passim).
77. Matthews, "A Study of the Temporary," *New York Times Book Review*, 19 Mar. 1922, 2.
78. Ezra Pound to Matthews, 22 Mar. 1922, Matthews Papers.
79. Anon., "Brander Matthews, Educator, Is Dead," *New York Times*, 1 Apr. 1929, 1, 10.
80. Anon., "Hoover Eulogizes Brander Matthews," *New York Times*, 2 Apr. 1929, 31.

Epilogue

1. Ludwig Lewisohn, *Expression in America* (New York: Harper, 1932), 58. Lewisohn and Matthews seem to have been on good terms from 1903, the year in which Lewisohn took his M.A. in English from Columbia, until at least 1913. When Lewisohn was not able to pay his tuition in 1903, Matthews

joined colleagues William P. Trent and George Carpenter in lending him money (Lewisohn to Carpenter, 18 Nov. 1903, Matthews Papers). Matthews was equally generous in 1909, when Lewisohn was again struggling financially because of his failure to find a teaching position—a failure which Matthews believed was due not to anti-Semitism, as Lewisohn charged, but to Lewisohn's deficiency of character (Matthews to Trent, 26 May 1909, Matthews Papers). Perhaps as a sign of his appreciation for the assistance, Lewisohn in 1909 presented Matthews with a signed copy of his dramatic poem *A Night in Alexandria*; in 1913, Lewisohn (then teaching at Ohio State University) gave him a signed copy of his edition of the dramatic works of Gerhart Hauptmann (both in the Matthews collection at Columbia). The breach that developed between the two men during the years that followed may have been due to their opposing views on World War I (Lewisohn was sympathetic toward Germany), or to Lewisohn's discovery of Matthews's low opinion of his character (an opinion that may have been influenced by anti-Semitism), or to a combination of both. In any case, by the time Lewisohn's autobiography *Up Stream* appeared in 1922, Matthews was making no secret of his animosity toward him (Matthews to Stuart Sherman, 21 May 1922, Sherman Papers).

2. Lewisohn, *Expression in America*, 314. Similar sneers occur on 44, 85–86, and 418.

3. Santayana, *The Genteel Tradition*, 38–64.

4. Santayana, "Marginal Notes on Civilization in the United States," *The Dial* 72 (June 1922): 553–68. Matthews's review appeared in February of the same year (see chap. 6, note 69). Santayana's rather contemptuous attitude toward Brooks and the Young Intellectuals is the subject of Wilfred M. McClay's excellent essay "Two Versions of the Genteel Tradition: Santayana and Brooks," *New England Quarterly* 55 (1982): 368–91. As McClay notes, the coiner of the phrase "genteel tradition" was himself "impeccably genteel" in his person (381).

5. Falk, *The Victorian Mode*, 4–5.
6. Ibid., 15.
7. Clayton Hamilton, "Brander," *Scribner's Magazine* 86 (July–Dec. 1929): 83.
8. May, *The End of American Innocence*, 63.
9. Lears, *No Place of Grace*, 320.
10. Gerald Graff, *Professing Literature: An Institutional History* (Chicago: Univ. of Chicago Press, 1987), 81–82.
11. Allan Bloom, *The Closing of the American Mind: How Higher Education Has Failed Democracy and Impoverished the Souls of Today's Students* (New York: Simon and Schuster, 1987).
12. Nicholas Murray Butler, "Brander Matthews," *Commemorative Tributes of the American Academy of Arts and Letters*, 238.

Selected Bibliography

Collections of Unpublished Materials

William D. Howells Papers. Houghton Library, Harvard Univ.

Laurence Hutton Correspondence. Princeton Univ. Library.

James Weldon Johnson Collection. Collection of American Literature, Beinecke Rare Book and Manuscript Library, Yale Univ.

Brander Matthews Papers. Rare Book and Manuscript Library, Columbia Univ.

Paul E. More Papers. Princeton Univ. Library.

Theodore Roosevelt Papers. Microfilm. Library of Congress.

Charles Scribner's Sons Archives. Princeton Univ. Library.

Stuart Sherman Papers. Record Series 15/7/21. Univ. of Illinois Archives.

Julian Street Papers. Princeton Univ. Library.

Mark Twain Papers. Bancroft Library, Univ. of California, Berkeley.

Books and Articles

Abrahams, Edward. *The Lyrical Left: Randolph Bourne, Alfred Stieglitz, and the Origins of Cultural Radicalism in America.* Charlottesville: Univ. Press of Virginia, 1986.

Armstrong, William M. *E. L. Godkin: A Biography.* Albany: State Univ. of New York Press, 1978.

Arnold, Matthew. *Matthew Arnold's Essays in Criticism, First Series.* Ed. Sister Thomas Marion Hoctor. Chicago: Univ. of Chicago Press, 1968.

Barrineau, Nancy Warner. "Brander Matthews." In *Dictionary of Literary Biography,* ed. John W. Rathbun and Monica M. Grecu. Vol. 71. Detroit: Gale, 1988. 153–62.

Bender, Thomas. *New York Intellect: A History of Intellectual Life in New York City, from 1750 to the Beginnings of Our Own Time.* New York: Knopf, 1987.

Bercovitch, Sacvan. "The Problem of Ideology in American Literary History." *Critical Inquiry* 12 (Summer 1986): 631–53.

Berthoff, Warner. *The Ferment of Realism: American Literature, 1884–1919.* 1965. Rpt. Cambridge, Eng.: Cambridge Univ. Press, 1981.

Boas, Franz. *The Mind of Primitive Man*. New York: Macmillan, 1911.

———. *The Shaping of American Anthropology 1883–1911: A Franz Boas Reader*. Ed. George W. Stocking, Jr. New York: Basic Books, 1974.

Bourne, Randolph. *The History of a Literary Radical and Other Papers by Randolph Bourne*. Ed. Van Wyck Brooks. New York: Russell, 1956.

———. *The Letters of Randolph Bourne*. Ed. Eric J. Sandeen. Troy, N.Y.: Whitson, 1981.

———. "A Vanishing World of Gentility." *The Dial* 64 (Mar. 1918): 234–35.

———. *Youth and Life*. 1913. Rpt. Freeport, N.Y.: Books for Libraries Press, 1967.

Bowen, Howard R., and Jack H. Schuster. *American Professors*. New York: Oxford Univ. Press, 1986.

"Brander Matthews, Educator, Is Dead." *New York Times*, 1 Apr. 1919, 1, 10.

Brooks, Van Wyck. *America's Coming-of-Age*. 1915. Rpt. New York: Octagon, 1975.

———. *Letters and Leadership*. New York: Huebsch, 1918.

———. *The Wine of the Puritans: A Study of Present-Day America*. 1908. Rpt. Folcroft, Pa.: Folcroft Library Editions, 1974.

Burgess, John W. "Germany, Great Britain, and the United States." *Political Science Quarterly* 19 (1904): 1–19.

Butler, Nicholas Murray. "Brander Matthews." In *Commemorative Tributes of the American Academy of Arts and Letters, 1905–1941*. 1942. Rpt. Freeport, N.Y.: Books for Libraries Press, 1968. 234–38.

Campbell, Oscar Joseph. "The Department of English and Comparative Literature." In *A History of the Faculty of Philosophy, Columbia University*, ed. Jacques Barzun. New York: Columbia Univ. Press, 1957. 58–101.

Carter, Everett. *Howells and the Age of Realism*. New York: Lippincott, 1954.

Cheyfitz, Eric. "Matthiessen's *American Renaissance*: Circumscribing the Revolution." *American Quarterly* 41 (1989): 341–61.

Conn, Peter. *The Divided Mind: Ideology and Imagination in America, 1898–1917*. Cambridge, Eng.: Cambridge Univ. Press, 1983.

Cooper, John Milton, Jr. *The Warrior and the Priest: Woodrow Wilson and Theodore Roosevelt*. Cambridge, Mass.: Harvard Univ. Press, 1983.

Crunden, Robert M. *Ministers of Reform: The Progressives' Achievement in American Civilization, 1889–1920*. New York: Basic Books, 1982.

Dreiser, Theodore, and H. L. Mencken. *Dreiser-Mencken Letters*. Ed. Thomas P. Riggio. 2 vols. Philadelphia: Univ. of Pennsylvania Press, 1986.

Dyer, Thomas G. *Theodore Roosevelt and the Idea of Race*. Baton Rouge: Louisiana State Univ. Press, 1980.

Eble, Kenneth E., ed. *Howells: A Century of Criticism*. Dallas: Southern Methodist Univ. Press, 1962.

Falk, Robert. *The Victorian Mode in American Fiction 1865–1885*. East Lansing: Michigan State Univ. Press, 1965.

Fenton, Charles A. "The Academy of Arts and Letters vs. All Comers." *South Atlantic Quarterly* 58 (1959): 572–86.

———. "The Founding of the National Institute of Arts and Letters in 1898." *New England Quarterly* 32 (1959): 435–54.

Fleming, Robert E. *James Weldon Johnson*. Boston: Twayne, 1987.

Garland, Hamlin. *Companions on the Trail: A Literary Chronicle*. New York: Macmillan, 1931.

———. *My Friendly Contemporaries: A Literary Log*. New York: Macmillan, 1932.

Gibson, William M. *Theodore Roosevelt Among the Humorists*. Knoxville: Univ. of Tennessee Press, 1980.

Giddings, Franklin H. "The American People." *International Quarterly* 7 (June 1903): 281–99.

Gossett, Thomas F. *Race: The History of an Idea in America*. Dallas: Southern Methodist Univ. Press, 1963.

Graff, Gerald. *Professing Literature: An Institutional History*. Chicago: Univ. of Chicago Press, 1987.

Hamilton, Clayton. "Brander." *Scribner's Magazine* 86 (July–Dec. 1929): 82–87.

Hawes, Gene R. "The Men from Morningside." In *A History of Columbia College on Morningside*. New York: Columbia Univ. Press, 1954. 232–66.

Hollinger, David A. *In the American Province: Studies in the History and Historiography of Ideas*. Bloomington: Indiana Univ. Press, 1985.

Hoopes, James. *Van Wyck Brooks: In Search of American Culture*. Amherst: Univ. of Massachusetts Press, 1977.

"Hoover Eulogizes Brander Matthews." *New York Times*, 2 Apr. 1919, 31.

Howells, William Dean. "An Appreciation." *New York Times Review of Books*, 21 Oct. 1917, 405.

———. *Literature and Life*. New York: Harper, 1902.

———. "The Modern American Mood." *Harper's Monthly* 95 (July 1897): 199–204.

———. "Recent Literature." *Atlantic Monthly* 29 (Feb. 1872): 236–44.

—————. *Selected Letters of W. D. Howells*. General eds., George Arms, Richard H. Ballinger, and Christoph K. Lohman. 6 vols. Boston: Twayne, 1979–83.

—————. *W. D. Howells as Critic*. Ed. Edwin H. Cady. Boston: Routledge & Kegan Paul, 1973.

Johnson, James Weldon. *Along This Way: The Autobiography of James Weldon Johnson*. New York: Viking, 1933.

—————. *The Autobiography of an Ex-Coloured Man*. 1912. Rpt. New York: Hill and Wang, 1960.

—————. *Fifty Years & Other Poems*. 1917. Rpt. New York: AMS Press, 1975.

Lears, T. J. Jackson. *No Place of Grace: Antimodernism and the Transformation of American Culture 1880–1920*. New York: Pantheon, 1981.

Lentricchia, Frank. *Criticism and Social Change*. Chicago: Univ. of Chicago Press, 1983.

Levy, Eugene. *James Weldon Johnson: Black Leader, Black Voice*. Chicago: Univ. of Chicago Press, 1973.

Lewisohn, Ludwig. *Expression in America*. New York: Harper, 1932.

"The Literary Spotlight XX: Brander Matthews." *The Bookman* 57 (1923): 432–36.

Matthews, Brander. *The Action and the Word: A Novel of New York*. New York: Harper, 1900.

—————. "America and the Juvenile Highbrows." *New York Times Book Review*, 29 Jan. 1922, 8.

—————. *American Authors and British Pirates*. New York: American Copyright League, 1889.

—————. "American Character in American Fiction." *Munsey's Magazine* 49 (Aug. 1913): 794–98.

—————. "An American Critic." *Library Table* 4 (30 Mar. 1878): 197–98.

—————. *The American of the Future and Other Essays*. 1909. Rpt. Freeport, N.Y.: Books for Libraries Press, 1968.

—————. "Americanism." *Harper's Round Table*, 6 July 1897, 873–74.

—————. *Americanisms and Briticisms: With Other Essays on Other Isms*. New York: Harper, 1892.

—————. "Are We Americans a Warlike People?" *New York Times Magazine*, 29 Apr. 1917, 4–5.

—————. *Aspects of Fiction and Other Ventures in Criticism*. New York: Harper, 1896.

—————. "Biographical Criticism." Introd. to *The Writings of Mark Twain*. Hartford, Conn.: American, 1899. Vol. 1: v–xxxiii.

—————. *A Book about the Theater*. New York: Scribner's, 1916.

—————. *Books and Play-Books: Essays on Literature and Drama*. 1895. Rpt. Freeport, N.Y.: Books for Libraries Press, 1972.

———. "Concerning a Cosmopolitan Critic." *New York Times Book Review*, 10 July 1921, 9.

———. *A Confident To-morrow: A Novel of New York*. New York: Harper, 1899.

———. "Developing the American from the English Language." *New York Times Book Review*, 30 Mar. 1919, 157, 164, 170.

———. *The Development of the Drama*. New York: Scribner's, 1903.

———. *Essays on English*. New York: Scribner's, 1921. Rpt. Freeport, N.Y.: Books for Libraries Press, 1971.

———. *French Dramatists of the 19th Century*. 1881. 5th ed. Rev. New York: Scribner's, 1914.

———. "The Future Literary Capital of the United States." *Lippincott's Magazine* 37 (Jan.–June 1886): 104–9.

———. *Gateways to Literature and Other Essays*. 1912. Rpt. Freeport, N.Y.: Books for Libraries Press, 1971.

———. *His Father's Son: A Novel of New York*. New York: Harper, 1895, 1896.

———. *The Historical Novel and Other Essays*. 1901. Rpt. Freeport, N.Y.: Books for Libraries Press, 1968.

———. "Inquest on American Civilization." *New York Times Book Review*, 12 Feb. 1922, 18.

———. *Inquiries and Opinions*. New York: Scribner's, 1907.

———. "Introduction." *Autobiography and Essays*, by Thomas Henry Huxley. Ed. Matthews. 1919. Rpt. New York: Kraus Reprint Co., 1969. 9–22.

———. "Introduction." *Fifty Years and Other Poems*. By James Weldon Johnson. Boston: Cornhill, 1917. xi–xiv.

———. *An Introduction to the Study of American Literature*. New York: American, 1896.

———. "Literary Colonialism." *New York Times Book Review*, 5 Mar. 1922, 2.

———. "Matthew Arnold and the Drama." *The Bookman* 44 (Sept. 1916): 1–8.

———. "Memories." *Scribner's Magazine*, 6 Aug. 1889, 168–75.

———. *Molière, His Life and His Works*. New York: Scribner's, 1910.

———. "More American Stories." *Cosmopolitan* 13 (Sept. 1892): 626–30.

———. "Mugwumps." *Saturday Review* (London), 58 (24 Nov. 1884): 658–59.

———. "An Observant American in France." *Literary Digest International Book Review* 1 (Jan. 1923): 12–13, 63.

———. *Outlines in Local Color*. 1897. Rpt. Freeport, N.Y.: Books for Libraries Press, 1969.

———. *Parts of Speech: Essays on English*. 1901. Rpt. New York: Scribner's, 1916.

———. *The Philosophy of the Short-story.* 1901. Rpt. Folcroft, Pa.: Folcroft Library Editions, 1971.

———. *Playwrights on Playmaking and Other Studies of the Stage.* 1923. Rpt. Freeport, N.Y.: Books for Libraries Press, 1967.

———. "Recent Essays in Criticism." *Cosmopolitan* 12 (Nov. 1891): 124–26.

———. *Rip Van Winkle Goes to the Play and Other Essays on Plays and Players.* 1926. Rpt. Port Washington, N.Y.: Kennikat, 1967.

———. "Roosevelt as a Practical Politician." *Outlook,* 16 July 1919, 433–35.

———. *Shakspere As a Playwright.* New York: Scribner's, 1913.

———. "A Study of the Temporary." *New York Times Book Review,* 19 Mar. 1922, 2.

———. "Suggestions for Teachers of American Literature." *Educational Review* 21 (Jan. 1901): 12–14.

———. *The Theatres of Paris.* New York: Scribner's, 1880.

———. "Theodore Roosevelt as a Man of Letters." In *The Works of Theodore Roosevelt: National Edition,* ed. Hermann Hagedorn. New York: Scribner's. 12: ix–xx.

———. *These Many Years: Recollections of a New Yorker.* New York: Scribner's, 1917.

———. *The Tocsin of Revolt and Other Essays.* New York: Scribner's, 1922.

———. *Vignettes of Manhattan.* New York: Harper, 1894.

May, Henry F. *The End of American Innocence: A Study of the First Years of Our Own Time, 1912–1917.* New York: Knopf, 1959.

McClay, Wilfred M. "Two Versions of the Genteel Tradition: Santayana and Brooks." *New England Quarterly* 55 (1982): 368–91.

McFarland, Gerald W., ed. *Moralists or Pragmatists? The Mugwumps, 1884–1900.* New York: Simon and Schuster, 1975.

Mencken, H. L. *The American Language.* New York: Knopf, 1919.

———. *The Diary of H. L. Mencken.* Ed. Charles A. Fecher. New York: Knopf, 1989.

———. *The New Mencken Letters.* Ed. Carl Bode. New York: Dial, 1977.

———. *Prejudices: First Series.* New York: Knopf, 1919.

———. *Prejudices: Second Series.* New York: Knopf, 1920.

———. "The Two Englishes." *Baltimore Evening Sun,* 10 Oct. 1910, 6.

Morris, Edmund. *The Rise of Theodore Roosevelt.* New York: Coward, McCann & Geoghegan, 1979.

Murphy, Brenda. *American Realism and American Drama, 1880–1940.* Cambridge, Eng.: Cambridge Univ. Press, 1987.

Nettels, Elsa. *Language, Race, and Social Class in Howells's America.* Lexington: Univ. Press of Kentucky, 1988.

Norton, Charles Eliot. *Letters of Charles Eliot Norton*. Ed. Sara Norton and M. A. DeWolfe Howe. New York: Houghton Mifflin, 1913.

Oliver, Lawrence J. "Brander Matthews and the Dean." *American Literary Realism* 21 (Spring 1989): 25–40.

———. "Theodore Roosevelt, Brander Matthews, and the Campaign for Literary Americanism." *American Quarterly* 41 (1989): 93–111.

Pachter, Marc. "American Cosmopolitanism, 1870–1910." In *Impressions of a Gilded Age: The American Fin de Siecle*, ed. Marc Chenetier and Rob Kroes. Amsterdam: Amerika Instituut, Universiteit Van Amsterdam, 1983. 21–42.

Raleigh, John Henry. *Matthew Arnold and American Culture*. Berkeley: Univ. of California Press, 1961.

Randall, John Herman, Jr. "The Department of Philosophy." In *A History of the Faculty of Philosophy, Columbia University*, ed. Jacques Barzun. New York: Columbia Univ. Press, 1957. 102–45.

Rathbun, John W., and Harry H. Clark. *American Literary Criticism, 1860–1905*. Boston: Twayne, 1979.

Rodgers, Daniel T. "In Search of Progressivism." *Reviews in American History* 10 (Dec. 1982): 113–32.

Roosevelt, Theodore. *The Letters of Theodore Roosevelt*. Ed. Elting E. Morison. 8 vols. Cambridge, Mass.: Harvard Univ. Press, 1951–54.

———. *The Works of Theodore Roosevelt: National Edition*. Ed. Hermann Hagedorn. 20 vols. New York: Scribner's, 1926.

Sandeen, Eric J. "Bourne Again: The Correspondence Between Randolph Bourne and Elsie Clews Parsons." *American Literary History* 1 (1989): 489–509.

Santayana, George. *The Genteel Tradition: Nine Essays by George Santayana*. Ed. Douglas L. Wilson. Cambridge, Mass.: Harvard Univ. Press, 1967.

Sherman, Stuart P. *Americans*. New York: Scribner's, 1923.

———. *Points of View*. New York: Scribner's, 1924.

Slotkin, Richard. "Nostalgia and Progress: Theodore Roosevelt's Myth of the Frontier." *American Quarterly* 33 (1981): 608–37.

Spencer, Benjamin T. *The Quest for Nationality: An American Literary Campaign*. Syracuse, N.Y.: Syracuse Univ. Press, 1957.

Sproat, John G. *"The Best Men": Liberal Reformers in the Gilded Age*. New York: Oxford Univ. Press, 1968.

Stearns, Harold. *America and the Young Intellectual*. New York: Doran, 1921.

———, ed. *Civilization in the United States*. 1922. Rpt. Westport, Conn.: Greenwood, 1971.

Summerscales, William. *Affirmation and Dissent: Columbia's Response to the Crisis of World War I*. New York: Teachers College Press, Columbia Univ., 1970.

Taine, Hippolyte. *History of English Literature*. Trans. H. Van Laun. New York: William L. Allison, 1895.

Trent, William P. "Brander Matthews as a Dramatic Critic." *International Monthly* 4 (Aug. 1901): 289–93.

Trilling, Lionel. "The Van Amringe and Keppel Eras." In *A History of Columbia College on Morningside*. New York: Columbia Univ. Press, 1954. 14–47.

Twain, Mark. *Mark Twain Speaking*. Ed. Paul Fatout. Iowa City: Univ. of Iowa Press, 1976.

———. *The Writings of Mark Twain*. Ed. Albert Bigelow Paine. 37 vols. New York: Gabriel Wells, 1923–25.

Vanderbilt, Kermit. *American Literature and the Academy: The Roots, Growth, and Maturity of a Profession*. Philadelphia: Univ. of Pennsylvania Press, 1986.

———. *Charles Eliot Norton: Apostle of Culture in a Democracy*. Cambridge, Mass.: Harvard Univ. Press, 1959.

Weinstein, Leo. *Hippolyte Taine*. New York: Twayne, 1972.

Wellek, René. *A History of Modern Criticism: 1750–1950*. Vol. 4. New Haven: Yale Univ. Press, 1965.

White, Hayden. *Metahistory: The Historical Imagination in Nineteenth-Century Europe*. Baltimore: Johns Hopkins Univ. Press, 1973.

Wilson, Christopher P. *The Labor of Words: Literary Professionalism in the Progressive Era*. Athens: Univ. of Georgia Press, 1985.

Wister, Owen. *Roosevelt: The Story of a Friendship, 1880–1919*. New York: Macmillan, 1930.

Ziff, Larzer. *The American 1890s: Life and Times of a Lost Generation*. New York: Viking, 1966.

Index

Holmes, Oliver Wendell, 137, 139, 142-43
Holt, Henry, 23, 125
Hoover, Herbert, 195
Howe, Julia Ward, 179
Howells, William Dean, xi, 12, 15, 16, 18, 20, 23, 54, 59, 82, 84, 90-102, 107, 109, 112, 114, 117-18, 121-22, 135, 140-41, 143, 174, 194-95; anti-imperialism of, 65, 67, 92; influence on and responses to Matthews's fiction, 146-63 passim; on Matthews's criticism, 94-95, 101, 151, 217-18n; portrayed in *A Confident To-morrow*, 150-57; and the theater, 92; and Woman Question, 157, 161-62, 228n
—Works: *Criticism and Fiction*, 94-95, 97-98; *Hazard of New Fortunes, A*, 96, 147, 151, 155; *Literature and Life*, 160; "Modern American Mood, The," 65-66; *Out of the Question*, 92; *Parlor Car, The*, 92; *Rise of Silas Lapham, The*, 93; *Story of a Play, The*, 96
Hugo, Victor, 17, 19-21, 28, 166
Huneker, James Gibbon, xii
Hutton, Laurence, 102

Ibsen, Henrik, xiv, 98-100, 110, 153, 159-60
Imperialism, xvii, 63, 66-69, 72-73; *see also* Americanism; jingoism; Spanish-American War

James, Henry, Jr., xiv, 11, 16, 76-77, 85, 91-92, 95, 101, 105, 108-10, 113-14, 116, 145, 161, 185, 197, 220n
James, Henry, Sr., 16
James, William, 16, 87, 125, 197
Jefferson, Thomas, 167
Jessop, George H., 14
Jingoism, 8, 65-66, 140-41; *see also* Americanism; imperialism; nationalism; Spanish-American War

Johnson, James Weldon, xii, 47-62, 64, 73, 81, 116, 210n; admiration for Matthews, 52; and Roosevelt, 49, 51, 53, 58, 209n
Johnson, Robert Underwood, 23, 179
Johnson, Rosamond, 48-49, 51, 53

Kazin, Alfred, xv
Kipling, Rudyard, xii, 33, 55, 58, 123, 195, 223n
Kitchener, Horatio H., 63

Lang, Andrew, xii, 121-22, 223n
Lears, T. J. Jackson, xv, 199
Lemaître, Jules, 8
Lentricchia, Frank, xvii, 29-30
Lewis, Sinclair, xiv, 196
Lewisohn, Ludwig, xiii-xiv, 196-98, 236-37
Lincoln, Abraham, 33, 68, 167
Literary realism, xi, xvii, 18, 82-111 passim, 112, 145-63 passim
Lodge, George Cabot, 33, 89
Lodge, Henry Cabot, xii-xiii, 22, 120-22, 129, 136, 138
Longfellow, Henry Wadsworth, 137, 181, 196
Lorimer, George Horace, 74
Lounsbury, Thomas R., 16, 125, 141
Lowell, James Russell, 5, 7-8, 11, 14, 16, 20, 24-25, 64, 66, 74, 108, 134, 137, 139, 142-43, 184
Lynching, 40-42, 50-51, 56

McFarland, Gerald, 23
Manly, John Matthews, 194
Marx, Karl, 30, 206n
Matthews, Ada Smith (wife), 13
Matthews, Brander: on American Indians, 64; and Americanism, 105-7, 112-44 passim, 156, 176; and Anglophilism (also "colonialism"), xiv, 69, 88, 94, 96, 102, 117, 119, 121-22, 140, 169; anti-Semitism of, 176, 197, 208n; on Aristotle, 5, 74; and Matthew Arnold, xiv, 5-8, 14, 19-20; and capitalism, 72-73, 87, 150, 156; champions

Matthews, Brander (*cont.*)
the Study of American Literature, An, xi, 64, 108, 136-41, 143; *Molière, His Life and Works*, xi, 188; *Philosophy of the Shortstory, The*, xi, 86; *Playwrights on Playmaking*, 108-110; *Poems of American Patriotism*, 60, 138; *Shakspere As a Playwright*, xi, 100, 188; *Theatres of Paris*, 17, 83; *These Many Years*, 1-3, 5, 7, 12, 14, 16, 25-26, 40, 85, 93, 101, 110, 157, 164, 182, 188; *Tocsin of Revolt, The*, 165-66, 169, 183

—Essays and reviews: "America and the Juvenile Highbrows," 189-90; "American Authors and British Pirates," 130-33; "American Character in American Fiction," 54-55; "American Literature," 116-17, 140, 144, 178; "American of the Future, The," 70-72; "Americanism," 64-66; "Americanisms and Briticisms," 54, 120; "As to 'American Spelling,'" 125, 128; "Biographical Criticism," 104-7, 118; "Dramatic Outlook in America, The," 93-94; "Duty of Intellectuals, The," 183-84, 187; "Economic Interpretation of Literary History, The," 30-32; "Evolution of Copyright, The," 133-35; "Henry James and the Theater," 109; "How Shakspere Learnt His Trade," 99-100; "Ibsen the Playwright," 98-99; "Is the English Language Degenerating?" 170; "Literary Independence of the United States," 121-22; "Literature in the New Century," 117-18, 140, 144; "Mark Twain and the Theater," 108; "Memories of Mark Twain," 102, 107, 132-33, 166; "More American Stories," 115-16; "Mr. Howells as a Critic," 97-98, 152, 156; "Of Women's Novels," 77-78, 158;

"Penalty of Humor, The," 104-5; "Reform and Reformers," 73-76, 99; "Romance against Romanticism," 97; "Roosevelt as a Practical Politician," 167; "Scream of the Spread-Eagle, The," 73; "Study of Fiction, The," 89-91, 156; "Study of the Temporary, A," 194; "Text-Books of Fiction," 95-96; "Theodore Roosevelt as a Man of Letters," 166-67; "Those Literary Fellows," 28-29, 122, 174, 179; "Tocsin of Revolt, The," 166; "Two Studies of the South," 88-89, 141; "What Is American Literature?" 169; "Women Dramatists," 78-79, 108

—Fiction and plays: *Action and the Word, The*, 146, 157-63; "Before the Break of Day," 146-47; *Confident To-morrow, A*, 146, 150-57, 175; *Frank Wylde*, 13; *Gold Mine, A*, 14-15; *His Father's Son*, 146-50, 161; "Memories," 35-36, 41, 146; *On Probation*, 14; *Outlines in Local Color*, 146; *Vignettes of Manhattan*, 146

Matthews, Edward (father), 1-5, 12-14, 147

Matthews, Virginia Brander (mother), 1-2, 14

Matthiessen, F. O., 143-44

May, Henry F., xv, 198-99

Melville, Herman, 7, 137, 143

Mencken, Henry L., xiv, 62, 144, 164, 177, 180, 183-84, 187, 196, 212n; and Matthews, 168-74, 185, 190, 192, 231n; and Roosevelt, 167-68

Modern Language Association, xii, 7, 30-31, 143

Molière, Jean Baptiste, 18, 79, 93, 109

Mommsen, Theodor, 38

Moore, Fred, 59, 61

More, Paul E., 168, 172, 192, 195

Mugwumps, 21-26, 68-69, 74, 82, 106, 199, 204n

Murphy, Brenda, xv

Brander Matthews